LUCKY DOG LESSONS

LUCKY DOG LESSONS

TRAIN YOUR DOG IN 7 DAYS

Brandon McMillan

HarperOne

An Imprint of HarperCollinsPublishers

HarperOne

Photographs © Litton Entertainment. *Lucky Dog* and Litton Entertainment are trademarks of Litton Syndications, Inc.

All photographs by Craig T. Mathew/Mathew Imaging wth the exception of the following: © Brandon McMillan: p. 31 (Chloe), p. 57 (Apollo), p. 96 (Ari), p. 250 (Ernie). Courtesy of Litton Syndications, Inc.: p. 24 (Randy), p. 41 (Skye), p. 53 (Luke), p. 69 (Kobe), p. 87 (Glory), p. 114 (Darby), p. 128 (Poppi), p. 138 (Jemma), p. 152 (Leah), p. 164 (Sandy), p. 198 (Chance), p. 213 (Lolita), p. 232 (Flash), p. 246 (Daisy), p. 272 (Tweety), p. 289 (Grover).

Shake & Break is a trademark of Animal Expert LLC.

The techniques presented in this book are for informational purposes only. As each individual situation is unique, you should use proper discretion, in consultation with a professional dog expert, before utilizing the information contained in this book. The author and publisher expressly disclaim responsibility for any adverse effects that may result from the use or application of the information contained in this book.

FIRST HARPERCOLLINS PAPERBACK EDITION PUBLISHED IN 2018

Designed by Terry McGrath

Library of Congress Cataloging-in-Publication Data is available upon request.

ISBN 978-0-06-247902-0

18 19 20 21 22   LSC   10 9 8 7 6 5 4 3 2

To the millions of shelter dogs who never made it out.

CONTENTS

INTRODUCTION

I was in a pub a few years ago and told the bartender what I do for a living—and then he asked me to leave because he thought I was drunk. The funny thing is, I hadn't had a single sip of alcohol. I shouldn't have been surprised, because when I tell people about my background, they often think I'm lying. I guess training lions and tigers, working with grizzly bears, tagging crocodiles, catching venomous snakes for antivenin, and diving with eighteen-foot great whites for research isn't a standard answer to "What do you do?" But it's always been my reality.

My childhood was unlike that of any other kid I've ever met (except for my siblings), and I wouldn't have it any other way. It is because I grew up in the constant presence of animals that I learned to be in tune with their feelings and needs. That unusual connection is what brought me to the career and the personal mission that define my life today.

My parents were wild-animal trainers, and I grew up training elephants, tigers, bears, primates, and other animals for the circus, television, movies, commercials, and even magic shows. I can't remember a time in my life when working with animals wasn't a big part of who I was and what I was doing. Remember the tiger in

The Hangover? I raised her from birth and trained her. Same with the animals in *The Jungle Book*, *We Bought a Zoo*, *I Am Sam*, *Jackass*, *24*, *Mike & Molly*, a few other TV shows, and a hundred or so commercials and music videos. I've trained tigers to do fake attacks, trained dogs for Super Bowl commercials, and even trained cockroaches for a Nine Inch Nails video (yes, even cockroaches can be trained). In my career so far, I've worked on more than three hundred Hollywood productions in more than thirty countries. I've continued to study animal training everyplace I go, learning something new from every country and culture.

And did I mention that over the years I've trained thousands of dogs of all different breeds and sizes? After I earned a solid reputation on film sets, some of the talent on productions even started asking me to work with the pets in their homes. I've trained dogs for hundreds of private clients, including Ellen DeGeneres, Andy Cohen, Rod Stewart, James Caan, Chris Hardwick, Wolfgang Puck, Hugh Hefner, Don Cheadle, Snoop Dogg, Eddie Murphy, Jaime Pressly, and Ronda Rousey.

Knowing I could train a dog to do just about anything, I wanted to utilize my ability for something I felt was bigger than any Hollywood production. After having the powerful and unforgettable experience of training a mobility-assistance dog for a wounded warrior who lost both legs to an improvised explosive device (IED) in Afghanistan, I started the Argus Service Dog Foundation. Watching this heroic marine and his dog bonding and helping each other inspired me to want to do more. Through the foundation, I'm able to train dogs to perform complex tasks like retrieving objects, supporting handlers with balance problems, opening doors, turning on light switches, and even coping with post-traumatic stress disorder—and then I have the honor of providing those dogs to disabled veterans.

But let me back up a little bit to how dogs in particular became such an important part of my life. When I was twenty-two, I had a life-changing experience: I read the statistics on shelter dogs in America and learned that every year in the United States alone, over 1,000,000 dogs are euthanized because they can't find homes. That's one *million*. That's a *lot* of dogs. And they're not dying in some far-off place we've never heard of; it's happening right here in our own cities and suburbs. I couldn't stand the thought of it, and ever since I caught on to that statistic, I've dedicated more and more of my life to rescuing unwanted dogs who stood no chance of finding homes and to proving they're just as trainable, if not more so, than breeder-bought dogs.

Back then, I was working for a Hollywood company that trained animals for film and television. We were a successful old-school company, and my boss had always worked mainly with breeder-bought dogs with known bloodlines. He believed that knowing everything about the dogs from birth made them better dogs to train. But my view was a little different. At the time, I lived in an apartment where I could see the yard of a local animal shelter. Every day after working with my company's stable of purebred dogs, I'd go home and look out my window and see some of the same breeds—German shepherds, rottweilers, Chihuahuas, pit bulls, and others—at the shelter. At first I was annoyed by the never-ending barking, but after reading the stats on shelter dog deaths, I came to the sickening realization that those dogs were living on borrowed time. Many were destined to end up among the million. The knowledge ate at me and inspired me to take action. My plan was simple, even if it was a little ambitious. I'd rescue dogs who stood no chance of finding a home and turn them into movie stars. I went to my boss and asked if I could rescue one dog to train for the business. After a debate, which turned into an argument, he agreed on one condition: my job was on the line if I failed.

The next day I went to a shelter in LA that had one of the highest mortality rates in the Southwest. This was the Shawshank of shelters, a cold and outdated facility that had seen its funding stripped away by city budget cuts. It was bursting at the seams with dogs, and animals there had a greater chance of getting euthanized than of finding homes.

As I made my way down the row of kennels, I spotted a young rottweiler named Raven. She seemed sweet, had a good attention span, and was more interested in me than in all the distractions around her. I adopted her out of the shelter that day and took her home.

Raven had a few issues to work out, but after a couple of months of intensive training, she went on her first job, a music video for OutKast. Raven knocked it out of the park. The director told me my dog performed better than the humans did that day. After that, Raven went on to become the most-booked dog in the company. I didn't just get to keep my job; I got a green light to grow the company's pack with more shelter dogs.

Like Raven, my new rescues also went on to become obedience scholars, proving that shelter dogs aren't damaged goods. They are hidden treasures with an ocean of untapped intelligence and loyalty. From then on, everything changed for me. I advocated for rescue dogs for every job, and I also started helping people find shelter dogs who would be good matches for their families, then training the dogs specifically to meet the needs of their new homes.

In 2011, I opened a boarding and training ranch just outside Los Angeles. I used the facility to train dogs for my service dog foundation, for movies and commercials, and for private clients. In addition, I kept a small pack of dogs I called my death-row dogs, animals I had rescued from shelters and brought home to rehabilitate, train, and place in homes. It was a labor of love, and I had a network of thousands of people on social media who were helping me with placement.

That small, private rescue operation caught the attention of a Hollywood production company. They were looking for an animal-themed show to round out a new CBS Saturday-morning lineup, and because some of the producers were rescue advocates themselves, they were fans of the work I was doing and wanted to see it firsthand.

I invited the producers out to visit the ranch for a few hours, and their stay extended to a few days and then a few weeks. The team decided to go with me to a city shelter to save a dog's life and document the process that followed. We all knew we might be able to do a lot of good with a program based on a rescue as it happened. That first dog's name was Bruno, and he was a wildly out-of-control terrier mix. I brought him to the ranch and started out by cleaning him up, evaluating his knowledge, and realizing he'd had no previous training at all. The production group observed Bruno's basic obedience lessons, and after a week, this dog had mastered the 7 Common Commands—plus an extra one.

Bruno was such an energetic, charismatic dog that I also taught him to dance. He'd stand up on his hind legs and spin in circles on command. The producers couldn't believe it. This dog who'd been close to execution, who didn't even know what *SIT* meant when we met him, took to the *DANCE* command with so much joy they laughed until their stomachs hurt.

A few days after his training was complete, Bruno went to his forever home with a middle-aged couple in West LA—a home where he's still living his happily-ever-after today. For me, it was a continuation of my mission. But it was a bittersweet ending to Bruno's story for the producers who'd witnessed the process. One of them commented, "That dog's future was hopeless. You saved his life and found him a home."

My response was, "That's my mission . . . one dog at a time."

Little did we know we'd just created a tagline we'd be using for years to come: *From hopeless to a home, that's my mission . . . one dog at a time.* The next day, the production team called to tell me they wanted to share the stories of my rescued and rehabilitated dogs on a new television series. They wanted to call it *Lucky Dog™*. Every episode would be the story of a second chance and a reminder of a very basic premise we all believed in: no dog is a lost cause; each one deserves a chance.

My biggest limitation in accomplishing my mission of saving shelter dogs comes down to simple math: I can train only so many of them at once. At the end of every *Lucky Dog* episode, I wish I could say "a thousand dogs at a time." I hope this book will be the next step in making that happen—that it will enable and empower other people to train rescued dogs.

So many books make dog training seem harder than it needs to be—as though you need a degree to teach a dog to *SIT*. But here's the truth: if you just spend a few fifteen-minute sessions a day, in seven days your dog can go from a blank slate—or even one with a few flaws—to a *Lucky Dog* graduate.

My methods are easy because I know what works and what doesn't. I've had a lot of years to figure out the quickest way from point A to point B. After training with some of the best dog trainers in the world and teaching thousands of dogs—from pampered pooches to death-row rescues—I want to share what I've learned. I'll start with the basics: trust and bonding, focus and control. Then I'll tackle obedience with my 7 Common Commands. Over the years, I've found that these few commands (*SIT, STAY, DOWN, COME, OFF, HEEL,* and *NO*) are the essentials—the ABCs of obedience.

Once you've got basic obedience under control, I'll turn your attention to behavior problems. Does your dog have an issue that needs to be dealt with? If so, you can choose to live with that problem or to fix it. If your dog has a bad habit like jumping up on your guests, barking all the time, darting through doors, digging holes in the yard, or marking in the house, I'll teach you how to quickly and efficiently bring that behavior to an end.

Any book of mine wouldn't be complete if it was just about training. The chapters that follow are full of the stories of dogs

I've rescued. Dogs like Grover, who'd been taken to shelters so many times he was terrified of being left alone; Randy, who'd been abused to the point that he screamed if you just touched him; and Kobe, a pint-size but hugely out-of-control dog who'd been labeled untrainable by the owner who abandoned him. People had given up on each of these special dogs, and each one of them went on to become a *Lucky Dog* alum. I've also included a few behind-the-scenes outtakes from my own learning experiences, including stories of a few dogs who pushed me to the furthest limits of my training ability.

Shelters are bursting at the seams with dogs whose owners didn't take the time or have the knowledge to properly train them. Many blame the dog, even when all it would have taken was a few fifteen-minute sessions a day—each quicker than the ride to a shelter—to solve the problem. It falls to me, to you, and to everyone else with the compassion and optimism to recognize the vast potential in these abandoned, vulnerable dogs to save them—one dog at a time.

—*Brandon*

PART ONE

GETTING TO KNOW YOUR DOG

1

WHAT MAKES YOUR DOG DIFFERENT?

Here's your word of the day: *variables*. These are the aspects of your dog that you need to assess to become a confident handler and an effective trainer. For our purposes, variables are your dog's breed, age, life experiences, and distinct personality. Your dog is also the product of his training, and that's where you come in. Even though the same basic principles work for all dogs, knowing what makes your pet different will help determine your approach to training. Let's break this down by category.

Variable 1: Breed

Breed is a massive factor in your dog's appearance, temperament, intelligence, energy level, and health. In essence, it's the "nature" side of what makes your dog different. But remember that when it comes to dogs, *nature* doesn't necessarily mean natural evolution; it's genetic design by people who've manipulated canine DNA to

BREED GROUPS

Long before it was possible to use a computer to order any product or service imaginable and have it at your door in a matter of days (if not hours), dogs were one of the most adaptable tools at man's disposal. For thousands of years, if a job needed to be done, a breeder would set about designing a dog to do it. Those jobs have ranged from tracker to herder to warrior to companion, and each new "prototype" was followed by more fine-tuned and increasingly specialized breeds, until a small army of dogs of differing size, appearance, and temperament existed to perform the same kind of job.

A collection of breeds created for a specific kind of task is known as a group in the dog world. There are seven recognized groups; five are defined by what the dog was initially bred to do, and two are catchall categories. Here's a short summary of each:

1. *Herding Dogs.* These are highly intelligent, independent, energetic dogs originally bred to control livestock. This group includes shepherds, sheepdogs, corgis, collies, and cattle dogs—each bred as one kind of herding specialist or another.

2. *Hounds.* All hounds were originally bred as hunting dogs, with most considered either sight hounds, with excellent vision, speed, and stamina; or scent hounds, with a powerful sense of smell and tracking ability. This group includes a wide range of breeds, including sight hounds like greyhounds, wolfhounds, and borzois; and scent specialists like basset hounds, bloodhounds, and dachshunds.

3. *Sporting Dogs.* Dogs in this category aren't hunters in their own right, but they've been bred to be hunters' helpers by pointing, retrieving, or flushing game. They're usually deeply loyal and highly trainable. Dogs in this group include retrievers, setters, and spaniels.

4. Terriers. In Latin, *terrier* means "of the earth," and that neatly sums up the work environment of these typically tenacious and independent dogs. They were originally bred to dig, burrow, and chase pests and prey like rats, badgers, and otters on and below ground. They were the world's original exterminators, and their group includes the Staffordshire terrier, Scottie, Jack Russell, schnauzer, Westie, and bull terrier.

5. Working Dogs. This group includes many of the most powerful dog breeds, including boxers, Akitas, rottweilers, mastiffs, and Saint Bernards. Traditionally, they've performed important and respected jobs like guarding, drafting, or working with police or military personnel. Many still do these jobs today.

6. Nonsporting Dogs. What do the shar-pei, bulldog, Boston terrier, dalmatian, Lhasa apso, and poodle all have in common? To be honest, not very much. But each falls under the catchall nonsporting classification because the jobs they were once bred to do no longer exist.

7. Toy Breeds. The toy category is also a catchall group but with a twist. Dogs in this group have just one thing—size—in common across the board. Many of these dogs, like the Italian greyhound and the Yorkshire terrier, have their roots in other dog groups. Others, like the Pekingese, Maltese, and Havanese, were bred first and foremost to be pint-size companions.

build a better dog. What defines *better* depends on the breeder. Some want big, intimidating guard dogs; others are after quiet, loyal retrievers. Some want dogs who can run down rabbits, rats, or deer. Others want breeds to herd cattle, sheep, or even fish.

I don't know about you, but I don't need my dog to do any of those things. She doesn't have to chase, dig, herd, or fight. Like most modern-day dog owners, I just need my dog to be a good companion with enough sense and training to be able to live peaceably in the house.

The thing is, just because we don't need our dogs to do the jobs they were bred for over centuries doesn't mean we can turn those instincts off—and in many cases we wouldn't want to. Genetic traits don't just drive work instincts and their associated behavior problems. They also help determine some of the things we love about our dogs: the way they want to be close to us, the way they play, and even quirky traits like the way some dogs love water or learning a new trick or watching over the kids. A lot of behaviors are hardwired in a dog's DNA, so as owners and trainers, we're always trying to find some kind of balance between genetic drive and our modern lives.

Of course, the best time to consider how breed impacts a dog's behavior and needs is *before* bringing that dog home. I see the tragic results of ill-fated breed choices every day at animal shelters—dogs who are abandoned because they needed too much exercise, were slow to housebreak, barked nonstop, or had a hard time getting along with a family's other pets.

There's a genetic component to all those problems, so pet owners have to learn to either live with a DNA-driven problem or commit the serious time and energy it takes to teach a more acceptable behavior. You know which road I take. Part of my role as a rescuer is making absolutely sure each family I place a dog with is ready, willing, and eager to take on the challenges that might come with a particular breed. I take that matchmaking part of my program very seriously because the dogs on *Lucky Dog* have all been abandoned before, and I won't let them go through that again.

Why Breed Matters in Training

Whenever I consult with a new client about training, the first thing I do is haul out my old, dog-eared encyclopedia of breed histories and make a copy of the pages that represent his or her dog's breed or the breeds we believe the dog to be. That's the starting point for any conversation about what the dog's been up to, what kind of training will be effective, and how to change unwanted behaviors.

Often, this is an eye-opening conversation because both the behaviors owners love about their dogs and the ones they're struggling with are right there in black and white. Sometimes the behaviors are obvious, as they are with a rat terrier. That dog's job is right in its name, and so it shouldn't come as a surprise when he goes tearing after every chipmunk, squirrel, rabbit (or rat) that crosses his path. But there are several other breeds—like the miniature schnauzer, the German pinscher, and the West Highland terrier—that got their start doing the same kind of work even though their reputations for crittering aren't as well known.

Do you know what job your dog's breed was created to do and when? What was the world like back then? And how have conditions and expectations changed since that time? These questions are all key to understanding your pet. Consider a couple of examples.

English bulldog. Although there's debate about exact dates, the original Old English bulldogs were bred sometime between the 1400s and 1600s, many of them for the sole purpose of being used in the barbaric sport of bull baiting. To bait a bull, a dog needed to be fearless enough to attack an angry beast thirty times its size and tenacious enough to hang on until it either forced the bull off its feet or died trying. The dog needed to be powerfully built, low to the ground, and stubbornly aggressive.

I think it's fair to say a dog with these personality traits probably would not make an ideal family pet . . . unless you're trying to get rid of a bull in your backyard.

In 1835, bull baiting was outlawed, but as of this writing—181 years later—many of the Old English bulldog's personality traits live on. Breeders have made significant changes, like breeding more for protectiveness than aggression. Today's English bulldog has also been genetically selected for companionship, which makes it a great family pet. But evolution—even the human-made kind—takes a very long time, and today's version of this once-ferocious fighter still has characteristics that hark back to the old days. English bulldogs are still physically low and broad and powerful. Most are still courageous and often stubborn. And these dogs are well known for tugging on toys, hanging on with a powerful grip, and being prone to excessive chewing. That need for them to grip and pull is hardwired into their DNA—a leftover genetic impulse from their days as champion bull baiters.

Beagle. Excessive barking is the number one reason beagles are abandoned at shelters. I bet there's not a dog trainer in the country who hasn't had a beagle owner call to ask, "What is *wrong* with this dog? He barks all the time."

From a genetic standpoint, there's nothing wrong with a barking beagle at all. These dogs, like all hounds, were bred over hundreds of years to chase foxes, rabbits, and other small game, running ahead of their handlers and maintaining a steady stream of barks and bays their owners could follow. Generation after generation, dogs were selected for, among other things, their good, reliable communication skills. So barking and baying—it's kind of what they're meant to do.

Maltese. For thousands of years, these little dogs were bred for the job of pampered pet. They were the canine equivalent of a panic alarm—a dog that would stay near, not take up too much space, and make a heck of a lot of noise if a stranger got too close. They sat on very important laps in civilizations from ancient Rome and Egypt to Renaissance England and France, serving as a combination guard dog and companion. They weren't going to take anyone down, but they'd get very territorial, barking and even biting to protect their owners.

What's the behavioral legacy of a dog bred to be babied? Maltese make devoted family pets, but they need someone around to keep them company or they can get depressed, anxious, or destructive. And did I mention that these dogs were engineered over centuries to bark? As a result, they're a very yappy breed, and trying to stop them from barking—loudly, enthusiastically, and often—is about as easy as trying to train them not to eat or sleep or breathe.

So here's the question: Once you know a little about your pet's breed, how does this variable factor into training your dog to be a Lucky Dog? There are two things I hope you'll keep in mind. First, things will go better for everyone if you don't expect your dog to act like something he's not. I get a lot of calls from frustrated dog owners dealing with a terrier's digging, a herder's nipping, a water dog who won't stay out of the sprinklers, a husky's pulling, or a retriever who keeps grabbing at their hands. Each of those behaviors is hardwired into that particular dog.

I'm not saying you can't teach your dog to manage a behavior. You can. I've trained thousands of dogs and have seen firsthand that almost anything can be learned. But there's a big difference between training a dog to do something that's new or unfamiliar, and training a dog to do something that goes against an innate behavior. A good rule of thumb is that any behavior your dog has learned can be unlearned. But a behavior your dog was born with will be more difficult to manage. For example, most dogs are born with an instinct to bark. I can train a dog to *stop barking* on command, but training the dog to *not bark* at all is a whole different kind of challenge—one that is nearly impossible. Going against genetics is always an uphill battle, and Mother Nature tends to put up a heck of a fight.

The second thing to remember about this variable is that the more you understand the specifics of your dog's breed, the more in tune you'll be with his thought process, which will make you a better equipped and more effective trainer. You'll know which practical methods and tactics to use. You'll be able to find the perfect motivation to keep your dog focused. You'll be able to anticipate behavior problems and figure out how to correct them. You'll even be able to help your dog find acceptable outlets for the activities he instinctively loves.

Meet Lulu. *My dog's name is Lulu, and she's a brat. I tell you this in the interest of full disclosure and because I don't think a pet has to be a perfect dog to be a great one. I train hundreds of dogs each year to do everything from SIT and STAY to much more complex commands, but* my dog *barely listens to a word I say. She has a mean streak and (sometimes) a bad attitude, but I love her anyway. I met Lulu at a local animal shelter. Her kennel was right up front, so each time I went, she was the first dog I passed on the way in and the last one I saw on the way out. She was there for months—long enough that I started saying hello to her and asking the shelter staff about her. I was told she didn't show well, which happens a lot with Chihuahuas. They are one of the breeds most*

commonly found in shelters, and they're small and not always eager to win visitors over. Some can be prone to housebreaking issues and barking. For all these reasons, they often go unadopted. But someone on staff had a soft spot for Lulu because they kept her around for months. And then one morning they told me she was scheduled to be euthanized in the afternoon.

I felt like I already knew this dog, and even though I didn't have an owner in mind for her, I took her home. Lulu was scared and edgy, and she was hard to place. Once she mastered her 7 Common Commands, I placed her with a family. They called the next day and basically said, "Come and get this beast." Lulu had bitten one of their children. So I made a note: no kids.

I placed her again, this time in a household with no children, but that family called on the second day, too. Lulu had gone after their other dog. I added to my note: no kids, no dogs.

That was pretty much how things went with Lulu for a long time. I'd place her in a home, she'd act like a she-devil, and I'd go back and get her again. After a few months, I looked at this Chihuahua, who'd managed to get rejected by family after family but who had become fiercely devoted to me, and I realized she must be *my* dog.

Lulu has a unique and challenging combination of all the variables we'll talk about in this chapter—a combination that might not endear her to some potential owners. But even with all her quirks and attitude, she was able to master the Common Commands and her big behavior problems to become *my Lucky Dog*. Believe me when I tell you that if Lulu can do it, then your dog can, too.

Special for Mixed Breeds

Many shelter dogs are mixed breeds, but even if your dog appears to be a mutt of untraceable origin, chances are you'll soon detect the behavioral leanings of a certain breed. Is he chasing your kids and nipping at their heels to keep them in line? That's classic herding behavior, and he'll probably show a preference for thinking independently and taking charge. Does your dog come alive at the sight of a tennis ball or throw toy? Maybe tries to turn his water bowl into a swimming hole on hot days? There's a lot of retriever in a dog who behaves that way, and yours will likely be sensitive to your criticism and eager to bond. He may also have an obsessive mouth—one that can't seem to resist chewing on forbidden objects.

The good news about mixed breeds is that some common behavioral issues and health problems found in individual breeds are less likely to occur in mixed breeds. One large-scale study found that ten common health woes were more prevalent in purebred dogs than in mixed breeds, whereas only one condition was more common in mixes. A Heinz 57 dog can be just as even-tempered and trainable —or even more so—because of his mixed-breed DNA than his purebred peers.

Variable 2: Age

Age is just a number, but it's a number that can make a difference in how your dog responds to training. Training a puppy and working with an adolescent dog, for example, require tweaks in your approach to find success. This variable is obviously always changing, but it's important to acknowledge your dog's development and maturity level when you're training.

Puppies

Just like a child's mind, a puppy's brain is an efficient, eager learning tool, soaking up a world of information and processing it all the time. You can picture it like a sponge, ready to soak up everything the dog sees, hears, smells, tastes, and feels. If you're setting out to train a puppy, you have the chance to shape his young mind before anyone else can influence him the wrong way. But that means you have to be extra careful you don't mess him up, either. You'll need to know, for instance, how to socialize him, when to house-train, and just what you can expect of him.

The age of your puppy will determine where you start training. Until a pup is about six weeks old, most of his training comes courtesy of his mother and littermates. But after that, it's time for you to take a serious role. The second and third months of a puppy's life are a time when you should make every effort to expose him to new people, places, and things, all the while offering encouragement and rewards to make them good experiences. Be sure your pup is up-to-date on his shots, then take your dog to noisy places and quiet places, places with new and different smells, and places full of new people and unfamiliar sights so he can start discovering the world.

One of the saddest things I encounter when I rescue shelter dogs are animals who've never been socialized. I've met dogs who've never worn a collar, never been around cars or bicycles, never put their feet in the water, or never learned to tolerate other dogs or loud noises or even being touched by human hands. For a dog who misses out on socialization at an early age, every one of these things can become a fear factor, and some fears take a long time to get over later in life.

You can begin house-training your puppy as early as ten weeks. You'll find an entire chapter on how to go about this process later in the book.

As you begin to introduce basic obedience lessons into your puppy's life, you may find getting and keeping his focus is a challenge. In Chapter 3, we'll talk about strategies for holding a dog's attention. As you work your way through my 7 Common Commands with your puppy, remember that his spongy little brain is taking in a *lot* of information at once, and he may take a little more time and regular repetition to become reliable with his responses than a mature dog.

Adolescent Dogs

Did you know that nearly half of all dogs coming into animal shelters are between the ages of five months and three years? It's no coincidence that those ages bracket a dog's adolescence. Typically, large dogs hit this phase of development first (at around nine to twelve months), then medium-size dogs (around ten to fourteen months), and finally small dogs (around twelve to sixteen months). The difference in the onset of adolescence is related to the wide range of canine life spans, with large dogs expected to live the fewest years and small dogs the most.

If you've ever raised a dog through this period, you might be able to appreciate why this age group is overrepresented among dogs who've been given up by their owners. Just like human teenagers tend to be a handful as they move past childhood and try to find their places in the adult world, teenaged dogs are often a little wild, a little naughty, and prone to testing their limits.

But that doesn't mean you should give up on them! The adolescent period is tricky—especially with bigger breeds—because these dogs are at about 90 percent of their mature size, but their minds are still very puppylike. Picture a twelve- or thirteen-year-old kid in your life—preferably one with great big feet, long and skinny legs, and a smart mouth. This kid gets tangled up in his own limbs when he walks, forgets he's too old for the free cookies at the grocery store, is sure he's already learned everything he needs to know in this life, and seems to be deaf to parents, teachers, and other authority figures. Your adolescent dog is basically that kid with four legs and fur. And like all adolescents, he's constantly pushing the limits to see what he might be able to get away with. If you say

SIT, this dog may shake it off. If you tell him to *STAY*, he may run the other way. He's an energetic upstart, and most people who lose the obedience battle lose it during this time.

But it doesn't have to be that way. An oversize puppy who's full of himself needs firm and frequent reminders of what the rules are and what's expected. That means extra training sessions and overtime when it comes to conditioning. He also needs plenty of exercise—just like that spooled-up teenager, he can't think straight when he's full of pent-up energy. This might be the main reason why adolescence is the most common age for dogs who are turned in to shelters.

Everyone wants a puppy, but when that puppy hits this short but sometimes troublesome age, far too many pet owners give up rather than step up training and digging deep for a little more patience and consistency. As you meet some of the dogs I've rescued over the years in the coming pages, note how many fall into this critical age range. They all turned out to be amazing pets, but they needed love, training, security, consistency—and sometimes a dose of discipline—to reach their potential.

Mature Adults

Adulthood is the longest stage of your dog's life, comprising about 80 percent of his years. At this point, your dog is most likely calming down from the destructive, high-energy puppy and adolescent stages. At one-and-a-half years, you have a full-size animal with a puppylike brain, but by two to three years, his body stops growing and the brain finally catches up, bringing everything into sync. This stage—especially in the early years—is the easiest time to fix any bad habits your dog might have acquired while growing up. His brain is still relatively spongy and his behaviors aren't set in stone yet. With each passing year, those behaviors get a little more rooted and become a little tougher to change.

During the adult years, your dog has a fully formed personality that should remain pretty consistent until the slowing down of old age begins to set in. This is an opportune time to train.

Meet Randy. *Randy was a medium-size white poodle mix found roaming the streets of Los Angeles, starving and covered in grease. He must have had an owner once, but nobody claimed him. He was a mature six-year-old dog with a heartbreaking response to being touched: if you tried to put your hands on him, he'd squeal. It was no surprise he wasn't getting adopted—no one is looking for a dog with issues that run that deep.*

When I first saw Randy, he was minutes away from being put down. Even when he was being saved, he was afraid to be touched. At first, I thought it might be a medical issue. I occasionally meet dogs in a shelter who have old, painful injuries or neglected conditions. Randy checked out okay at his veterinary visit, but each time I reached out to him or put a leash on him, he started yelping again. It didn't take long to figure out that at some point Randy had been hit with a leash. It was the object of his greatest fear, and when I held it above him, he'd recoil and try to get away. If Randy was ever going to let an owner give him any form of physical affection, first he'd have to learn to trust. There was no point in my starting a training program with him until I could help him get comfortable with human contact. To accomplish this, I used a gradual program of contact conditioning to get him used to being touched without fear of being abused.

Working with a dog who was a few years old took more patience and time than it might have with an adolescent, but eventually Randy started to feel at ease with me. After that, he was able to learn his 7 Common Commands like a pro and show he was ready to go to his new forever home.

Senior Dogs

You know the old saying "You can't teach an old dog new tricks." I completely disagree. Of course you can teach an old dog; you just can't teach him as fast as some at-the-top-of-his-game youngster. Just as a dog's body ages, so does his brain. That's a normal part of getting older for every creature, you and me included. If we picture a puppy's brain as a big, empty sponge, capable of soaking up vast amounts of information, then we can use that same analogy to consider an older dog's brain. An older brain is more saturated with information and connections and impressions. As a result, it is more challenging to teach a senior dog than it is to teach one in the earlier years of adulthood. But it is by no means impossible. I've taught eleven-, twelve-, and even thirteen-year-old dogs full obedience starting from *SIT*, and they've been up to the task.

The keys to teaching older dogs are really no secret: patience and repetition. Approach it the same way you'd tackle teaching your grandfather to use a computer. You know that this person is long past the developmental stages, where acquisition of new information comes naturally, so you start with small-scale, short lessons of easy material. Repeat each one multiple times. Move forward slowly, and if you hit a snag, back up and review. Keep in mind that just like Grandpa, your senior dog may be a little stuck in his ways, so you have to be patient.

Variable 3: Life Experiences

Everyone has a story, and those stories are full of the people we've met, the places we've been, and the things that have happened to us. In just the same way, every dog has a past. We have to acknowledge and accept that to get anywhere together. Your dog's life experiences are the "nurture" side of the equation that defines who he is. Everything that's happened since birth—and everything the dog learns from those experiences—impacts what he thinks and feels and how he learns.

Has your dog always been sheltered and well fed? Has he experienced neglect? Has he been exposed to lots of people, places, animals, sounds, and smells? Has he had much training? Has he developed habits that make him difficult to live with? All those things come down to life experiences.

The good news here is that anything that's been learned can be unlearned and it's possible to teach any dog the 7 Common Commands as the foundation of a healthy owner-dog relationship. The bad news is some life experiences leave a deep impression that may take a real effort to undo—and the longer they've been going on, the harder you're going to have to work to unravel them.

If you've adopted a dog later in his life, you may never know many of the experiences that helped shape his personality or create behavior problems. And it doesn't do any good to spend much of your time dredging up the past or letting history dominate the present. Instead, know that when you bring a dog into your home, he becomes your responsibility to work out any issues that came with him. The longer you let a problem fester, the more likely it'll manifest into something bigger and harder to correct. So the minute you realize a bad habit is happening, that's the time to deal with it.

I'll give you a perfect example. I worked with the owner of a schipperke with a bad barking problem. At first, the owner thought it was cute because the dog was barking as a way of protecting her. After a while, though, the issue got out of control, with this dog barking incessantly and loudly, not willing to settle down for any command.

Now this owner got her dog when he was about a year old and finally sought help seven years later. The dog had been an adolescent with a preexisting problem in the beginning, but by the time we met, he was the canine equivalent of a fifty-year-old man with a very deep-seated bad habit. When was the last time you met a fifty-year-old man whose behavioral issues were an easy fix? I was able to help resolve that dog's barking problem, but it took a whole lot more time and effort than it would have if I'd been able to deal with it years earlier.

The Blank-Board Theory

Here's a helpful way to put your dog's experiences into perspective as you turn your attention to training: Think of your dog's past life as marks on a dry-erase board. In order to start a new training program, you want to get that board nice and clean. You're not likely to start with a clean slate, but you want to help your dog deal with any big issues that might impact trust and training going forward. If your dog has made a habit of burning pent-up energy by barking or chewing or digging holes in the yard, start by making sure a long walk is part of the daily routine. If your dog has been abandoned or had to get by on the streets, be steady and consistent and positive in all your interactions, proving each day that you are a reliable and safe person to be around.

Do what you can to clear away the past problems that may mar your dog's experience board, but know that sometimes life marks us with permanent ink, and even after we scrub as hard as we can, a completely clean slate may not be possible. There may always be

---

THE 7 COMMON COMMANDS

There are hundreds of commands you can teach your dog—everything from *SIT* and *STAY* to *CRAWL, DANCE,* and *GIMME A HIGH FIVE*. In my years of training, I've met dogs who crave more and greater obedience challenges and dogs who only grudgingly learn the basics, but every single dog I train has to learn my 7 Common Commands to be considered ready for a forever home. If you've watched my show *Lucky Dog,* you've seen how consistently I teach these and emphasize them. Here are the 7 Common Commands:

SIT	*DOWN*	*OFF*	*NO*
STAY	*COME*	*HEEL*	

Why just seven? To quote the great Bruce Lee: "I fear not the man who has practiced ten thousand kicks once, but I fear the man who has practiced one kick ten thousand times." The same philosophy applies with dog training. It's always better for a dog to be 100 percent reliable on a small number of key commands than hit-or-miss on a dozen or more. These 7 Common Commands are the ones we use most with our dogs on a daily

some ghostly residue of your dog's past on his board, and that's okay. It's part of what makes your dog special, and over time you'll learn how to train around those dark patches to help him add a wealth of healthy, trusting interactions to his life experiences. Sometimes that means making adjustments to accommodate your dog's needs.

The best example I can give you is my little one, Lulu. She'd obviously been physically abused when I got her. I believe she was

---

basis, and they eliminate many commands that are basically the same. For example, *NO* and *LEAVE IT* are redundant, but many people teach their dogs both. Why ask your dog to learn another command when you don't need to? Same with *STAY* and *WAIT*. Now I'm not saying your dog isn't smart enough to learn them both, but the more behaviors you teach, whether obedience commands or tricks, the more diluted your dog's reliability will be. Obedience is necessary. Tricks are for kids.

One of the first lessons of Dog Training 101 is that obedience is not about the number of commands your dog knows, but about whether you've practiced, conditioning your dog to the point of perfection. Some of the best-trained dogs I know have only a few commands, but they're perfect and quick with each.

If your dog is an achiever, that's great; there's always more to teach. But not every dog is meant to be an obedience champ, and not every owner has the time or energy to invest in extensive training. If this sounds like your dog or you, don't sweat it. The 7 Common Commands are really all you need for your dog to be polite, controlled, and safe.

kicked, because when I first adopted her I used to try petting her with my foot if she was lying on the floor. When I made even the slightest contact, she'd cry out as if she were fighting for her life. She wasn't so bad when I pet her with my hands. For months I worked on this issue and eventually hit a plateau—a place that was much better than where she had been before. I realized that might be all the progress Lulu could make, and it was my turn to make adjustments to accommodate her needs. I started talking to her in a reassuring voice before touching her with my foot to let her know everything was okay. To this day, she still has a residue of fear from her past, but her training and my adjustments have made the circumstances fine for both of us. When training alone isn't enough to overcome your dog's past experiences, this kind of compromise is a completely acceptable solution.

A Word About Where Your Dog Comes From

It's possible to get a great dog from a breeder or a shelter. You know which one I feel strongly about. Your chances may be a tiny bit better of getting a well-socialized dog from a good breeder, but we don't always have that choice, or even want it. Many of us would rather save a life than marginally increase our odds of bringing home an easy-to-train dog. There are times, though, when a rescue may come with some extra baggage—like abandonment issues, a history of abuse, or even the condition sometimes known as kennel stress, which I refer to as shelter shock. Shelter shock is PTSD for dogs, and every case is different. The way one dog copes with a bad experience may be completely different from that of another dog. One dog may live its first years in a warm, loving household, wind up in a cold shelter with time running out, and eventually walk out unscarred, as though nothing happened. Another may be so traumatized by the experience that it changes his personality forever.

Meet Chloe. *I had a client about ten years ago who called me to train an Aussie shepherd. At the time, Chloe was about five months old, a perfect age to begin training. In the years that followed, I continued to work with her and watched her grow up to be a well-mannered, well-trained, beautiful dog. Later, the family fell on sudden and dramatic hard times. Without informing me, they turned Chloe over to a shelter. I just happened to be at that facility one day and stumbled across her. I knew Chloe right away. I knew this dog like the back of my hand—the look, the markings, and most importantly her unmistakable personality.*

But there was something off about Chloe in the shelter. She'd always been calm, cool, and collected; she'd been stable and secure in her previous life. In the shelter, she was spinning in circles, biting her own tail, and panting so heavily it looked like she might have a heart attack. It seemed as if she knew her life was on the line. Her survival instincts had kicked in, but there was nothing she could do.

The day Chloe became available, I rushed to the shelter to adopt her. I already had a great family lined up. But when I got their daily reports on how she was doing, they described a dog much different from how I remembered Chloe to be. They said she was really rambunctious, stressed, and panting constantly. Weeks went by with little change, even though the normal stress a dog experiences in a new home typically subsides in a week or two.

Chloe was a classic example of a dog who was very susceptible to the harsh effects of the shelter, and she was going through shelter shock. Its effects had taken hold of her personality and changed it.

Chloe is much better and more comfortable today than she was then, but as the person who trained this dog from a puppy, I see that she's not—and never will be—the same dog she once was. Her shelter experience left her with a permanent emotional scar.

Variable 4: Personality

Your dog's personality is what makes him one of a kind. Even when you take two dogs of the same age, same breed, and similar life experiences, they won't have the same personalities. Just like people, no two dogs are alike. They're much too complex for that. Some are fun, and some serious; some are tense and some are always at ease. Some will do anything—absolutely anything—for a treat or a few minutes of your time. Some bond best to other dogs, and others are drawn more to people. Dogs can be blessed by or afflicted with many of the same personality quirks as you and me: hope, love, worry, jealousy, fear—they feel all of them.

I could write a whole book about the funny, clever, charming, and amazing canine personalities I've encountered, but for our purposes here, the main thing that matters is how personality can impact training. Getting to know your dog and what makes him tick will help you become an effective trainer.

So how do you make this assessment? There's really no personality test your dog can take to give you a step-by-step method for teaching him. (Those puppy prediction tests don't work, by the way.) And a shelter is about the worst place to get an idea of personality, since it brings out the worst in a lot of dogs. Even when your dog comes home with you, it's going to take him a while to settle in and start showing you his cards.

That said, there are a couple of general rules of thumb about dog personality that can help you figure out how difficult (or easy) the road to being well trained might be for your dog:

Rule #1. The easiest dogs to train are those with a strong food or prey drive (the instinctive inclination of a predator to find, pursue, and capture prey) and the ability to focus. A dog who can be mesmerized by the treat in your hand or the tennis ball under your arm or that squeaky mouse toy that causes him to nearly hold his breath with excitement is going to be more open to learning whatever you're teaching than one who is less interested. Dogs who are a little more cool to food and play rewards are a tougher crowd and will require more time and ingenuity from you.

Rule #2. Just because a dog is difficult to train does not mean that dog is not intelligent. There's a saying I love that's sometimes attributed to Albert Einstein, though nobody ever seems to be able to pinpoint where or when he might have said it: "Everybody is a genius. But if you judge a fish by its ability to climb a tree, it will live its whole life believing that it is stupid."

I often see this quote in the context of education, but I've found it's just as well suited to describing dogs as it is kids. It's pretty common to meet clients who think they've somehow acquired a stupid dog. People talk about certain breeds as though they're slower or less capable of learning than the next. Here's what I hope you'll remember as you train: Your dog is a genius at something. Maybe it's not at learning commands or speedily picking up housebreaking or understanding that he's going to get scratched every single time he tangles with the cat. But there is something. Don't judge his intelligence on his speed of mastering a command or his ability to perform tricks.

If you really want to see the litmus test for canine intelligence, ask your dog to do the job he was bred for. The beagle is a perfect example. These dogs always get the short shrift when we talk about dog smarts. Yes, they can be challenging to house-train. And, yes, they can easily fall into the habit of barking at all hours. But these dogs were bred to track, and their noses are incredibly powerful. When you put them in their element—when you see a trained beagle out tracking in the woods—you're seeing a whole different dog, a dog with an awesome and unique intelligence.

A dog who isn't inclined to *SIT* and *STAY* on command may require more of your time and energy to train, but I hope you'll keep in mind that even though learning the 7 Common Commands is a necessary step in training *any* Lucky Dog, how eager or willing your dog is to learn those commands does not define what he is capable of.

Common Personality Traits

There's no way to capture every dog personality trait here, but there are a few trends that I've found can have a big impact on what kind of training works, so let's talk about those.

Outgoing or Shy. Will your dog go to any friendly stranger? Happily sleep over at a neighbor's house? Race through the door into an unfamiliar place? A dog with the kind of outgoing attitude that allows for any of those possibilities may be a little easier to train than a shy dog. Outgoing dogs are usually more easily convinced than their shy counterparts of just about anything—up to and including the idea that they should follow your commands such as *STAY, COME,* and *DOWN.*

Dogs who go through life a little more carefully and those who have shy natures may take more time to train. My dog Lulu is one of these. She's guarded and careful—but she's also devoted in a way

only a dog you couldn't coax into a stranger's house with a fresh fi-
let mignon can be. The extra time it takes to train a shy dog usually
pays its own kind of return—once that dog finally opens up enough
to commit to a command, he's not likely to ever forget or disregard
it because something more appealing or interesting is going on.

High or Low Energy. Some dogs are energetic and always eager
to engage—remember Astro from *The Jetsons*? Their bodies and
minds are always in the On position, and it may require an extra effort to gain their focus before you can begin training. Once
you've got them started, though, high-energy dogs can be great at
learning both the basic commands and tricks. In fact, channeling
some of that excess energy into training can help cut down on behavior problems that stem from a dog having too little stimulation
to keep up with his energy level.

On the other hand, some dogs are more like Huckleberry
Hound—mellow, sleepy, and not especially excitable about anything. A low-energy dog may be slow to engage in training—and
quick to call it a day. This doesn't have to be a problem as long as
you consistently find the small windows of opportunity during
which they're up for the work. In my experience, once they've
learned their 7 Common Commands, some low-energy dogs who
are good students are actually ideal candidates to work as service
dogs. Such a big part of that job is being able to stay still and quiet
and *wait* for the handler, and the combination of well trained and
low-key is perfect for it.

Both breed and age play into any dog's energy level, but this is
also a very individual factor. I've worked with some golden retrievers, for example, who'd rather spend their days fat and happy on a
soft bed than anywhere else in the world, and others who'd trade
their kibble for a hike in the hills. Maybe you know two dogs who
look alike but have nothing in common when it comes to this personality factor, too.

Silly or Serious. One common misconception about dog training is that treats are the only way to get the work done. This couldn't be further from the truth. Some dogs do respond best to food—in fact, some dogs will practically walk on water for it. But others dogs need toys and play. If your pet is the kind who can't take his eyes off a tennis ball or a lure toy or a rope pull, you may get more focus and better results by using toys for training than by using treats. This is common in dogs who have a heavy prey drive.

And then there are the dogs who just do what you ask out of pure love. You'd be surprised how many fall into this category.

As you assess your dog's personality, give some thought to whether he finds the most satisfaction in a silly romp on the floor, a trade of work for food, or some other compromise between silliness and seriousness. That knowledge will serve you well when you choose your training tools.

Stubborn or Willing. Most of us have somebody in our family who can't get behind any idea unless he or she came up with it. You know the type: the person who needs to choose what's for dinner or where you're going on vacation or which house rules apply in any game. It's a control thing, and most interactions have room for a little of it, but not too much. Some dogs are like that, too. They're stubborn, and they like to come to new things in their own way and in their own time. Dogs of any breed can have this personality trait, but many bully breeds are known for their stubbornness. It's not uncommon in toy breeds that were bred to be lapdogs, either, so don't be surprised if your pint-size pup is less eager to dive into training than many bigger, sportier dogs.

Training dogs with stubborn personalities requires some extra effort to establish control at the beginning of the process. In Chapter 3, I'll tell you just how to go about doing this as you work with eager—or headstrong—dogs.

THE BOTTOM LINE

In a nutshell, getting to know your dog involves looking at four main variables. Understanding each of them will help you become your dog's ideal trainer.

1. Breed. Breed is pure genetics: the traits your dog was born with. In general, an effective training program will recognize—and even incorporate—these traits rather than fighting them all the time. Even difficult genetic traits can be managed, but you don't want to spend all your time fighting a losing battle against Mother Nature.

2. Age. Any dog can be trained, but it'll be easier to work with yours if you keep in mind that puppies, adolescents, mature dogs, and senior dogs respond best to a varying pace of learning and methods.

3. Life Experiences. If breed is the nature part of your dog, then life experience is the nurture. Your dog's experiences are everything that's happened to him and everything he's learned since birth. Remember: DNA is hardwired, but anything learned can be unlearned.

4. Personality. This is the secret ingredient that makes your dog one of a kind. Whether your dog is an Energizer bunny or a couch potato, playful or serious, highly motivated or not-that-into-obedience, there's a way to customize training to match his traits.

2

TRUST IS
THE FOUNDATION

To be trusted is a greater compliment than to be loved.
—George MacDonald

Your dog's first lesson is . . . actually not a lesson at all. The first step in the training process has very little to do with you commanding or your dog obeying. The first step is all about trust. Without this essential element in your relationship with your dog, you cannot be an effective trainer.

The assumption that trust and bonding are critical keys to training is at the heart of everything I believe about working with dogs. So many approaches to training are based primarily on dominance, but that philosophy doesn't work for me—and it especially doesn't work for the dogs I rescue from shelters. At best, these animals have been lost, neglected, or locked up for reasons they can't begin to understand. At worst, they've been abandoned or physically abused. One way or another, they've all been given good reasons to be suspicious and guarded with their trust. The last thing they need is another person in their lives who can't be relied on to be predictable, patient, and kind. I begin every relationship with a new dog by making sure it's clear I can be counted on to be all those things.

I often get asked if this approach undermines me as a leader in the dogs' eyes—and the simple answer is, *absolutely not*. There's no rule that says you have to dominate to lead. In all honesty, there's a time and place for dominance in training, and that's when you're working with an aggressive dog. But we're not training aggressive or dominant animals here, so we're not going to be aggressive and dominant ourselves. Our goal is to build a bond and teach basic obedience. And we want our dogs to do those things out of love, not fear.

There's a good comparison here to the way people look for leadership. Think about the ways you relate and respond to people in leadership roles in your own life—whether they're family, mentors, bosses, colleagues, or teachers. I'd be willing to bet that the best of those relationships are built on trust and get regularly reinforced through bonding.

Let's look at it this way: at its essence, training is teaching—only our pupils are animals instead of children. What kind of teacher is the most effective? It's not a teacher you're afraid of or a teacher you dislike or one you wish you could walk away from or dominate. There's always a hard line between ineffective instructors and their pupils—and dogs are wary of teachers like that, too. The most effective teacher is the one who's knowledgeable, fair, and engaged—someone who inspires respect and cooperation rather than demands it. That teacher cares about the students, and the students know it.

I firmly believe that same logic applies to a dog's relationship with a trainer. A dog needs to be able to trust you and feel close to you to be truly trainable. Otherwise, you'll spend a lot of your time trying to compel your dog to do what you want instead of working with a willing partner. Compulsion training only works when you're dealing with highly dominant or aggressive dogs. Using compulsion while training obedience isn't recommended because you're replacing your dog's eagerness to want to do what you ask with the notion that he must do it. Why bother forcing something that doesn't require any pressure? It's like the difference between being a warden and being a teacher. Either way, you can get results, but why would you want to be the warden if you don't have to?

If you have a puppy or a newly adopted dog, establishing trust before you start training is absolutely essential. If your dog is shy or lacks confidence, working on trust will help with that, too. But even if you've had your dog for years and feel ready to start training, the tips in this chapter can help you deepen and strengthen your relationship. You'll be rewarded when your dog answers your efforts by giving 100 percent and then some during training.

Meet Skye. *I don't meet very many dogs who actually try to run away from me at the animal shelter, but Skye was one of that small minority. She's a beautiful white shepherd—shy, sensitive, and dignified—and when I met her, she was about eighteen months old, behind the bars of a city shelter, and terrified of the world. When I walked into her kennel, this dog was so alarmed she*

made a break for it, trying to go up the wall and out the window. I needed to defuse the situation, so I backed up, spoke in a quiet, reassuring voice, and sat down next to the kennel door with my eyes turned away from her. And then I waited. It took about twenty minutes of inching closer to Skye at a painstakingly slow pace, but by the time we were side by side, she'd decided she wasn't afraid of me anymore. Abused animals do math in their heads very quickly. They understand how to spot threats because they've dealt with so many of them in the past. Skye wasn't threatened for the first twenty minutes we were together, so she let down the first of many walls. But just because she didn't feel an immediate threat from me didn't mean she fully trusted me. Not even close. It just meant she'd allow me to get a few inches closer. That was more than enough for me. She let me put a leash on her and walk her to my truck. Stage 1 complete, but we'd barely scratched the surface.

Back at the ranch, Skye was a little better but still so skittish she was incapable of relaxing or focusing while she was wearing a leash. Any sudden movement or sound sent her running for cover. This was her past showing its ugly face, and it was impacting her personality. Doing an assessment at that point would have been a total waste of time. And if I tried to start training when she was still so on edge, it would have been easy for Skye to perceive me as her enemy. That was the worst thing that could happen.

So the game plan was simple: build trust. I told Skye we'd train when she was ready, and for the next week, I honored that promise, spending hours getting down to her level, sitting with her, feeding her, petting her, and giving her affection and attention without asking for anything in return. After a few days, she had a breakthrough. Skye came up to me, kissed my face, and looked right at me, steady and ready. She might not have had 100 percent trust in me yet, but she'd let her guard down, and I had the green light to start her training.

———————

Earning Your Dog's Trust

Building trust with your dog can take anywhere from a few days to a few months or more. Most dogs get there pretty quickly, but if you have a rescue dog whose life experience has made him guarded, it could take longer. My dog Lulu was one of these. Whatever abuse she'd endured before she came to me, she had created a hard shell to keep people and even other animals out. She didn't trust me one bit at first, and even after she'd let down her guard enough to train, she stayed careful, as if she was waiting for me to disappoint her. It took a year before she started to truly relax and have a little faith that I would never hurt her or fail her. The bond we have today was definitely worth the wait.

However long it takes to establish a trusting relationship with your dog, be sure you do it with the genuine intentions to build a bond. This can't be rushed, and it definitely can't be faked. Unlike some people, dogs can spot a phony from a mile away. Later in this chapter I'll give you some suggestions for bonding activities you

Getting down to Lulu's level helped reduce her fear of me.

can do with your dog. But right now, let's talk about what it takes to establish trust. These six behavioral approaches will put you on the right path:

1. Be Calm. Being loud or taking an aggressive stance is the quickest way to send a shy or fearful dog running for the hills. Everything about you needs to be steady and understated while your dog is learning to trust you. As you get to know each other, you can show your louder, wilder, and sillier sides, but they can be overwhelming for a dog who doesn't know you yet. If you have a rescue, keep in mind that an abused dog has typically been victimized by an aggressive, possibly loud person, so taking the opposite stance is recommended.

Part of presenting a calm face to any dog is not overwhelming him with your body language. This is an especially critical issue with rescues. If you've ever watched me interact with a fearful dog in a kennel on *Lucky Dog*, you may have noticed that I make a point of avoiding direct eye contact if I know that dog has fear issues, and I almost always sit down on the floor to give the dog a chance to come to me. This body language is intentional. Many dogs who are timid or fearful don't like eye contact. They can perceive it as a challenge or a threat from a stranger, and I don't want to convey either of those things. Getting down on the floor is also my standard way of meeting a shelter dog—especially one who may have been abused. The reason I sit is simple; I'm a big guy, and to most dogs, size equals intimidation. Getting down on their level eliminates a huge portion of the initial threat of me coming into their environment as a stranger. To emphasize the fact that I'm not some alpha coming into the cage to dominate, I often let shelter dogs crawl right up on me. I want them to know I'm there to become a friend. Later, when they can trust in that, I can become a leader.

One other body language tip for connecting with a fearful or shy dog is not to approach them head-on, another move that can be perceived as aggressive and domineering. I practiced this with Skye for days after I brought her back to the ranch. I knew that a dog with her level of fear and worry would take any direct approach from me as an onslaught. So I sat a short distance away, not directly facing her, and let her get used to the idea that my presence wasn't a danger in any way.

2. Be Patient. Establishing trust and a true bond with any animal takes time. Before you can begin to teach commands or solve issues, you have to learn the art of patience. That's the first rule every animal trainer has to learn. It's also one of the most difficult things to do because we have no control over how long an animal is going to take to accept us or to learn. An impatient trainer can actually take an animal *back* a few steps in his training, so as difficult as it may be, part of this getting-to-know-you period is letting the dog come to you. Some new rescues come straight to

A shy dog may see you as a threat. Avoiding eye contact can defuse a tense situation and start the process of building trust.

me and climb on my lap or lean against my legs like we've known each other forever. But others need to think about it for a while. If I go to them, I'm missing the opportunity for the dogs to decide I'm okay on their own. Once a dog does that, we're on our way to building a good relationship.

As a bonus, waiting for a dog to come to you is a very subtle way of getting him to begin to see you as a leader. Think about who does the chasing and approaching in a litter of puppies, in a family with multiple dogs, or in a pack. Puppies go to their mom; younger and less dominant dogs go to the ones who are older and more secure; and you'll never see the leader of a dog pack chasing members of the canine family around for their attention. When the dog does come to you, make sure you show the kind of leader you're going to be by speaking in a soft, reassuring voice and giving lots of treats. As time goes on, you can gradually build your voice back up to its normal level.

During this getting-to-know-you period, you can reinforce the impression of being patient by giving your dog a place he can think of as his own—like a bed or an open crate. When your dog goes there, give him some quiet time alone.

3. Be Understanding. You know the famous line from *To Kill a Mockingbird*, "You never really know a person . . . until you climb into his skin and walk around in it"? That's a great metaphor for what it takes to really understand other people—and for what it takes to understand dogs and other animals, too. One skill any good trainer must have is the ability to get inside the mind of the animal. In fact, there's an unspoken rule in the wild-animal world that when you train, you don't just have to think like the animal, you have to feel like you've become the animal. It's that elemental connection that keeps us from making dangerous mistakes when we're up close and personal. Your own instincts can get you into trouble; anticipating the animal's instincts can keep you safe.

A perfect example is what I've learned over the years while swimming with great white sharks. When you find yourself next to a fish that's eighteen feet long and weighs as much as five thousand pounds, your first human instinct is to swim away fast. But the shark's first instinct, every time, is to chase whatever's swimming away. Sharks are used to being near and even in among schools of fish. And in those schools, if one creature breaks away, prey instinct causes all the others to immediately hone in on it. They're looking to see what the fish that changed the pattern is up to, what it sees, if it's hurt, if there's danger or if there's food. It took me a while to really understand that the safest way to share the water with these giant predators is to become a "big fish" yourself. You want to swim next to them, to be a part of their environment, to move when they move—basically to blend in. As soon as you start doing anything abruptly—including trying to get away—you're prey.

When we're dealing with dogs, we need to acknowledge their species' instincts: they want to be part of a pack, they need to know where they stand in the family, they have strong drives for food and for whatever specific jobs they were bred to do. We also want to know them well enough to recognize their fully developed, unique personalities and preferences. You learn some of these right off the bat when you bring a new dog home, and some of this information comes later as the dog begins to trust you and show his cards.

The more you get to know your dog, the easier it'll be to understand how he thinks and where he's coming from. Ask yourself what motivates your dog? What scares him? Does he have a limit to how much togetherness he can take before he needs to be alone and quiet? Is he so energetic he can hardly see straight when he needs to be still? Take the time to observe your dog and think about his likes, dislikes, and needs. There are lots of areas where he'll be able to meet you halfway—or even learn to do things your way—in the long run. But if you're able to look at the world through your dog's eyes and imagine what he sees and how he feels, you will find it much easier to gain his trust—and ultimately it will be much easier to be his trainer.

4. Be Consistent. From time to time I consult with clients and quickly find that the root of the problems they're having with their dogs is a lack of consistency. The owner is sending mixed signals, and the dog just can't decode them quickly or well enough to keep up. Some examples are owners who use multiple commands for the same behavior, owners who reprimand their dog long after he's forgotten what he did wrong, and owners who are unintentionally reinforcing bad behavior. When you're building trust with a puppy, a rescue, or a shy or fearful dog, one of the most important things you can do is continually demonstrate that you are a consistent, predictable person.

To start this process, establish a routine for your dog that gives him an idea of what to expect day to day. The most important piece of that routine should be the dog getting fed at the same times and places each morning and evening. For rescues, it's amazing how just learning that food will be pinging into a dish twice a day can start to put them at ease. Other predictable elements of a schedule— like a walk time and regular opportunities to get outside for a few minutes—will all help your dog feel he knows what to expect.

5. Be Reassuring. Somewhere along the line, a big myth got turned loose on the dog world that says owners shouldn't comfort dogs when they're afraid—that this might reinforce their fears. I can only say that after decades of working not only with dogs but also with wild animals, I've found this to just not be true. If your dog is afraid of something, show him you care and reassure him in a calm, low tone. As you start training, you may be able to gradually ease his fears through distant exposure in a safe environment.

During the trust period, though, don't force your dog to confront his fears if you can help it—and don't worry that your reassurance will somehow make him worse. There will be time later to help him learn to face his issues, to show him he can get past them on his own and reassure him through the process.

6. Be a Friend. Spend time with your dog. Give treats. Pet and praise. All of these things reinforce the idea that you are someone your dog can count on in good times and in bad. They show you can be trusted. A three-month-old puppy may think everyone is his friend because he has no experience with the world. But as a dog gets older—especially a shelter dog and most especially an abused shelter dog—he meets a lot of people. Some are friends; others foes. Over the course of their lives, dogs gather data to understand which is which. They learn that one of the main elements that can help them survive is friendship. A true bond with someone betters their chances of consistently eating, drinking water, being tended to when they're sick or cold or lonely, and, most importantly, being loved. I know it sounds way too simple, but dogs are just that: simple animals.

Bonding

Bonding is an important part of building trust, but it's also an aspect of dog ownership we can all use and benefit from. Whether you've had your dog for a week or a decade, your relationship will benefit if you take a little time to focus on strengthening the bond between you. Activities that build bonds are easy to incorporate into even the busiest routine. Here are a few examples to get you started:

Exercise. This one's a win-win. Exercising with your dog is an easy way to build the bond between you. If walking is your thing,

SPECIAL FOR SHY DOGS

To some extent, dogs come by shyness naturally. Just as a person might have a genetic predisposition toward a certain height or intelligence or temper, a dog inherits physical and behavioral traits, too. Thanks to fairy tales and Hollywood projections, you may associate the word *wolf* with *big* and *bad*, but as a trainer with decades of experience working with real wolves, I can attest to the fact that they are actually one of the shyest species on the earth. Simply by virtue of being descended from a profoundly shy creature, your dog may have been born with this trait.

The German shepherd is a perfect example. Genetically, these intelligent and devoted dogs are among the closest breeds to wolves that exist today. Early German shepherds were actually bred with wolf in them, and so it's not surprising that many of these imposing-looking dogs are actually pretty shy, at least until they develop confidence through training.

However, in many cases there's more at issue than just genetics. Any dog can revert to the elemental roots of fear when the chips are down or when he's intimidated. And something as simple as a lack of experience and exposure to unfamiliar surroundings can cause a dog to lock into an instinctive retreat mode.

Taking steps to build trust with your dog is the first component in helping him overcome shyness. Time spent bonding will help with this, too. Later, when you start training, your dog will have regular opportunities to build confidence—and confidence is the key to helping a shy, fearful dog start to see that this world is not such a mean and intimidating place, after all.

that's great for both of you. Make it more interesting by chang-ing your route or your pace. Exploring new places (and smells) together is a great way to help your dog feel more connected with you.

Play. There are hundreds of different ways to play with a dog, so take a little time to find out which ones suit yours best. I've seen some dogs who live and breathe for the next toss of a tennis ball, and others who get more excited at the idea of finding a hidden ob-ject or going for a run or tugging on a pull toy. What matters here is that if you take the time to play, your dog will quickly learn to associate time spent with you with the joyful feeling of a favorite

Playing with Lulu.

toy or game. In the long run, that association will make training infinitely easier on both of you.

Socialize. As your dog begins to show trust in you, take the opportunity to introduce him to some of the experiences of the wider world. At the Lucky Dog Ranch, I get to introduce each new dog to the pack in the play yard. For many of the dogs who spend time at the ranch, this is a highlight experience. Some of them have never had the chance to just play to their heart's content in a safe environment before, and they act like they can't believe their luck. You can create a great social experience for your dog by arranging a puppy play date, visiting a dog park, or having a friend visit and bring treats. It doesn't have to be a big interaction—just an opportunity to try something new in the world with you there to look out for him and cheer him on.

Take It Easy. Nobody ever said bonding time always has to require high energy. Sometimes just getting down on the floor to pet your dog, sitting on the porch together, or taking a nap together on the couch is exactly the kind of quiet bonding experience that really lets your dog know you are worthy of trust and love.

Feed. No list of bonding activities could possibly be complete without a recommendation to give your dog treats. Most dogs love nothing more. Offering a variety of dog-safe goodies as both surprises and rewards will help bond your dog to you and create a dedicated training partner.

Give Affection. To a dog, nothing is better than a good massage. Petting your dog is a simple way to build a bond, especially after a long day of all the activities listed above. This is a no-brainer and a great way to form a tighter friendship between you and your pet. Unfortunately for you, the favor can't be returned.

Meet Luke. *Some dogs come with more issues than others. As far as I'm concerned, that just makes it all the more rewarding when I help them overcome their problems and find their forever homes. Luke was one of those challenging dogs. At just eight months old, he had seen way too much of how negative the world can be. He'd spent his life on the run, dodging people, scavenging food, and hiding out. Luke didn't trust the ground he walked on. When I met him in the shelter, the last thing this skinny, scared shepherd-Lab mix wanted was for me to put a leash on him—and I knew better than to force the issue. I was going to have to draw this dog out and earn his trust if I was ever going to be able to show him a different side of the world.*

That first day, I had to wait for Luke to come to me, for his natural curiosity to bring him close enough to touch. When he was comfortable accepting a collar, I took him home to the ranch. But we had our work cut out for us. Each time I closed a gate, Luke flinched at the sound. When I gave him a command with any volume or emphasis in my voice, he responded as if I'd yelled at him, lowering his head and raising the muscles above his eyes toward me in a "What did I do wrong?" expression. It seemed like everything was a punishment for this dog, and his constant instinct was to run away. The mom waiting for Luke was a therapist who wanted a dog who could help shy kids come out of their shells, and I was beginning to wonder if he would be capable of filling that role. Based on my observations of his behavior and his reactions, I was sure Luke had been physically abused.

Luke's past was his Achilles' heel, and until he was able to build a little trust in me, there wasn't much point in pursuing his 7 Common Commands. Instead of diving into training, I spent time with him. I sat beside him, petted him, gave him treats, spoke in a reassuring voice, and let him get to know me. In response, he took more interest in me, daring to come close, to let me touch him, and to relax a little bit. At the end of three days, Luke was finally ready to start training. Luke learned faster than most abused dogs to trust me, maybe because of his resilient personality. Whatever the reason, he broke through.

Once Luke decided to put a little faith in me, he was able to master his 7 Common Commands. And by the time he was finally able to go to his new home, Luke was able to put his fears behind him, and, fittingly, to become a reassuring companion for the special-needs students his new mom worked with every day in her home office.

The End Game

Ultimately, if you put in the time and energy to build trust and bond with your dog, you'll be able to participate in the biggest bonding exercise of all: training. Without complete trust in you, your dog might only ever reach half of his potential in training. But when a dog completely trusts you, there's no limit to the lengths he'll go to please you and learn from you.

3

TRAINING BASICS

Every well-trained dog had to start somewhere, and of all the
dogs I've trained, the one who was probably the deepest in the
hole on day one was a gigantic Doberman named Apollo. Apollo
was nine months old when I met him. He was a beautiful dog,
and unlike most of the animals you'll read about in this book,
he came to me not from an animal shelter but from a prestigious
kennel. He'd been sold and then returned because he was difficult
to handle. The breeder knew his dog had potential, so he donated
him to a wounded veteran to become a service dog. I volunteered
to train him.

I flew across the country to get Apollo, renting a car in Philadel-
phia and driving out through the Pennsylvania countryside to the
breeder's ranch. When I got there, I talked with the owner for a
while, and then he went to get my new trainee. He came back with
the huge, powerfully built Doberman, and I said, "Hi, boy!" to get
Apollo's attention. I got it. The hundred-pound dog came barrel-
ing at me at full speed, leaped into the air as he got close, landed

both front paws on my chest, and body-slammed me all the way to the nearest wall. Once he had me pinned, Apollo didn't stick around to make friends. Leaving me against the wall, he took off at a gallop—around the room, over the coffee table, onto the desk—moving so fast I couldn't even get a hand on his leash. I thought, *Okay, there's a lot of work to do with this dog.* I couldn't get him back to my ranch soon enough to get started.

My first thought was to crate Apollo, but this boy needed a crate big enough for a lion, so the backseat would have to do. It was no easy task loading him into my rental car, but that turned out to be the least stressful part of the trip. As we drove away, Apollo started chewing on the back of my seat. By the time we hit the highway, he was working on the bench in back. I stopped and put a leash on him so I could correct him from the front, but somewhere between the ranch and the airport, he gnawed the inside of one of the doors until the hand rest and cup holder came completely off. I was just starting to take a mental tally of the damage when Apollo lifted his leg and peed like a racehorse on the backseat for about forty-five seconds. I was ill, flying down the highway at sixty-five miles an hour, thinking we may have just reached the point where it would cost less to buy a new car than to pay for the damages to the one I was driving.

Just when it seemed there was nothing else Apollo could do to make things worse, he found one more way to raise the bar. The leash I'd put on him was my lucky leash. I'd had it for about fifteen years and trained thousands of dogs with it. It was leather, softened and worn in all the right places from years of work. It was one of my proudest possessions, and I was counting on it to help me tame the giant in the backseat. When I heard Apollo chewing again, I gave the leash a quick tug to stop him—and half of it came flying up and hit the windshield. The other half was still hanging from Apollo's collar.

That was my breaking point. I stopped the car—and started

Apollo, from leash-wrecking troublemaker to star service dog.

Apollo's training right there on the side of the highway. It couldn't wait a minute longer.

I want you to know about Apollo because he may have been the most out-of-control dog I ever began a training program with—the combination of his size, strength, and complete lack of discipline was pretty incredible. It would have been easy to decide that he didn't have it in him to be trained, let alone to become a companion for a wounded veteran who deserved an impeccably trained dog at his side. But Apollo *was* trainable. In fact, if you go to the website for my Argus Service Dog Foundation, you'll see him right there on the front page with his owner, Tyler. That crazy, jumping, car-chewing, backseat-peeing, leash-wrecking dog literally became a poster dog and the prototype for every service dog I've trained since. If you saw him today, you'd never know Apollo was once so wild I could barely get him to the airport. He didn't learn just his 7 Common Commands. He learned to brace himself so Tyler can lean on him to go up and down steps. He learned to pull the wheelchair when it arrives at an incline. He learned to pick up almost anything Tyler drops or asks for by name. He learned the difference between left and right so he could steer the wheelchair on command. He learned to be patient and ready at all times. In the end, Apollo didn't just train; he matured into a dog who is as dignified, intelligent, devoted, and capable as any animal I've ever met.

I still have the broken pieces of my lucky leash. I hung them on my wall as a souvenir. They're a reminder that every dog can be trained, no matter how challenging things may look at the kickoff. In the process of training your own dog, I hope you won't have to pay for damages to any rental cars or peel yourself off any walls after getting crushed, but whatever unique challenges come with the experience, try to think of them in terms of the stories you'll have to tell later—*after* you've succeeded in revealing the well-trained animal within.

6 Key Training Components

There are a few basic guidelines I rely on in every training program—whether I'm working with an untrained puppy, helping a dog brush up on a few basic skills, or dealing with a behavior problem. In this chapter, we'll look at each of these critical components. As a group, they're a kind of Lucky Dog 101—everything you need to know to get started. These are the six aspects of training that'll help make the time you invest with your dog efficient and effective:

1. Mental preparation

2. Control

3. Focus

4. Technique

5. Tools

6. Conditioning

Mental Preparation

It's easy to perceive dog training as something that's mostly physical; we teach a technique, then repeat it until the desired response becomes muscle memory for the dog. Along the way, a few things will probably become part of your muscle memory, too—like the way you hold your hand to give the *STAY* signal, or the leash correction that reminds your dog to *HEEL* at your side. More subtle physical cues—many of which we'll discuss in the coming chapters—will also become second nature to you. But when you really examine what factors contribute to effective dog training, the one that's too often overlooked is the mental element of making it work. It's your mental game that will set the tone for how your dog-training time is going to flow; it's your mental strength that will get you through the moments when it seems like nothing you're teaching is sinking in.

There's a philosophy I learned from one of the mentors who taught me about training when I was a teenager, and it has been a mantra for me ever since: "The face you show your dog is the face that's shown back to you."

So what face do you want to show your dog? You want to show the face of a boss, not an employee; a teacher, not a student. This is not an angry or aggressive face. Instead, it's one that doesn't show frustration or doubt or hesitation. Think about someone you know who's a great teacher or coach. That person is confidently in charge, positive in the way he or she teaches, and eager to share knowledge. That's someone who has nothing to prove and everything to offer. Think of Bill Gates giving a computer class or Warren Buffett explaining investment basics. That's the kind of face I want you to show your dog during training. It doesn't matter if you've trained one hundred dogs before or not a single one. Nobody knows your dog better than you do, and nobody understands the training you want to accomplish better than you do. You are the expert during training time, and that's the attitude you need to bring. At other times, you can show your dog the face of a playmate or a pal, but during training, position yourself as the wise teacher.

There's a simple reason why this really matters. Animals are always looking for leadership, waiting on you for cues to tell them what to do. If you don't deliver, they look somewhere else—or assume a leadership role themselves. In most cases, this is not about dominance—it's about an animal with a deep-seated, inborn drive to be part of a hierarchical pack wanting someone to look up to. The same rules apply when I train large predators. The only way I can get a four-hundred-pound Siberian tiger to do what I ask is to mentally run the training experience. Physically, I can't even compete—and anyone who thinks they can force a tiger to do their bidding through physical force is both deluded and creating a very dangerous situation. They're basically asking for a Darwin Award. My game face is where I always find success, and it's the training difference between getting one of nature's great predators to calmly do exactly what I ask and having him decide I haven't earned that kind of respect and doing whatever the heck he wants instead.

As you delve into the training techniques in this book, remember that you need to be a confident, secure, and understanding leader for your dog. That's the mental game, because I can promise that you will not *feel* confident or secure or understanding all the time—and I'd be a total liar if I told you I never get flustered or frustrated during training myself. I feel it the same as anyone else, especially when I'm looking at an unfamiliar, untrained animal at the end of a leash and knowing I've got just a week or two to teach him some manners, obedience, or even tricks.

The secret, as they say in the deodorant commercials, is to "never let 'em see you sweat." Tamping down frustration, fear, or worry is a mental exercise every good animal trainer has to master. If you show your dog frustration or anxiety or that you don't know how to handle a situation, you might as well walk away.

Your dog will read it in your face. Instead, always approach training with determination and calm. No matter how you feel inside, your face should say, "We're doing this. I'm not quitting, and I don't want you to quit, either."

When you do get frustrated, keep in mind that your partner in this endeavor is "just a dog." I don't mean that in a disparaging way. What I mean is that a dog has less capacity than you do to learn and process language, and a dog has to learn at his own pace. Take your time, start with the easy stuff, and be patient. Remember that you're the one who has thumbs and walks upright, so you're the leader in this relationship. Your dog will slowly, steadily learn everything he needs to know.

Control

My most basic summary of what it takes to train a dog has always been "control, train, treat." Anyone who's ever worked with me has heard that phrase—probably more than once. It's a rule I live by. Whether you're starting on your first day of training with a puppy who never stops moving, or working with an older dog who doesn't want to get off the sunny end of the couch, these are the steps that will allow you to successfully train. This process should be your blueprint for approaching everything that's covered in this book. If you find yourself training your dog and not seeing results in a timely manner, I want you to stop, remember those three words, and ask yourself if you are following them in order.

In dog training, everything starts with control. Why is this one issue so important? Think about it like this: a teacher has twenty kindergartners and is responsible for teaching all of them to recognize, pronounce, and write their ABCs. What are the first steps that teacher will take to get twenty small children under control? Take them into a classroom, have them sit in chairs, turn those chairs toward one focal point, and occupy that space. That's a pretty good system for taking a chaotic situation and gaining some control.

Your dog is like your twenty kindergartners (dog training is starting to sound easier than teaching, isn't it?). He is a creature with a brain not nearly as developed as yours, interests entirely different from yours, and a world full of sights, smells, animals, people, and distractions of every kind. Before you can even think of teaching this animal, you have to establish some kind of control. I know this seems almost too simple to explain, but I see people every day trying to train dogs when they haven't taken this step yet. I bet you see them, too—being dragged down the street by a dog on a leash; chasing a runaway pet at the dog park; saying, "sit, Sit, SIT, **SIT**" over and over to a dog who isn't even listening. We've all seen it, and we've probably all done it at some point, too—and we know it's not effective.

That's why the very first step in starting any training session is going to be establishing control.

Fortunately, this step is an easy one. A room or other space that's free of distractions gives you a little control. Getting your dog up off the floor—especially if you have a small breed—gives you more. A leash is probably the simplest way to gain control, because once your dog is clipped in, running away is no longer an option. And here's a training trade secret: two leashes give you twice as much control.

Over the years, one of the training staples I've come to rely on is a technique I call the Double Leash Lock-Off. If you watch *Lucky Dog*, you've seen me use this time and again. I swear by it because it works so well, helping me to establish control on easily 95 percent of the dogs I use it on.

Remember as you move forward with your training program that control is always the cornerstone. I've shared this simple method of gaining control with dog owners all over the world, and in response I get e-mails every day from people who want to send their thanks and say those two words I love to hear: "It worked."

THE DOUBLE LEASH LOCK-OFF

The best part of the Double Leash Lock-Off (besides the fact that it works) is that it's easy to use. You don't have to be an experienced dog handler to master this one or use it effectively, but the results are very high level anyway. To use this technique, you'll need:

- Two six-foot leashes
- A harness
- A flat collar
- A bag of treats

The Double Leash Lock-Off

Start by harnessing your dog, then loop the handle end of the first leash—the anchor leash—around the leg of a couch, heavy table, or other stationary object. In the training barn, I use mounted O-rings for this purpose, and you can easily install one in your garage or backyard if you want to have a permanent training station. Once the leash is anchored, clip the other end of it to your dog's harness. Next, attach the second leash to your dog's collar—this is your guide leash.

Hold the end of the guide leash in your hand and pull it

toward you gently, there's no need for force with this technique because the leashes do the work. As you pull, the tension between the two leashes will automatically straighten your dog's body and limit his movement left, right, forward, or back. And just like that, you are in control of the situation.

A close-up of the Double-Leash Lock-Off

Your dog may not like it at first, and that's okay. You're not causing any harm or pain with this method. Hold a treat up in the air a foot or so away from his snout. Your dog may lunge or dive for it, but that won't work in the lock-off position, so just wait for him to stop struggling. If your dog refuses to settle down, simply pull the leash toward you to maintain control. You'll notice that when you pull, this technique will straighten out your dog's body. You can give him a *CALM DOWN* or *EASY* command as you work to help him understand where you're going with all this. Keep in mind that if you choose to use a command here, you'll want to be consistent with it from that point on. It will be a useful command in the future if you train it right. Most dogs settle down after just a few seconds; some take a little longer. As soon as your dog is completely still, silently count to three. When you get there, if your dog is still calm, praise him and reward him with a treat. Reward your dog only while he is still and calm—you don't want to create any confusion by rewarding lunging or pulling.

Like most obedience exercises, this takes some practice to sink into your dog's brain. Repeat the exercise ten times. The next time you do it, add one second to your count-off (four whole seconds of calm!), and repeat ten times again. Gradually work up to ten seconds or more. Once your dog hits the ten-second mark and reliably stays calm, you can start using the command and the treats without the help of the anchor leash, and then you can remove the guide leash. If your dog loses control during that ten-second count, simply start over and try again to make it to the same goal. Each time your dog makes the association between being calm and receiving a reward, he becomes a little more trainable. Without the immobilizing factor of the leashes, it could take weeks—if not months—for a dog to figure out that simply being calm and quiet earns rewards. Once your dog has become comfortable with the Double Leash Lock-Off technique, you'll have it in your arsenal whenever you need to exercise a little extra control during training. Try to keep up the practice of this exercise throughout the training process because the more you do it, the better control you'll have, and the easier training will be.

Focus

In order to effectively train, you need more than just control—you need your dog's undivided attention. When you're working with a puppy or an adolescent, this can be a lot tougher than it sounds. The best way to get the focus you need is to offer something your dog just can't ignore. Remember in Chapter 1 when we talked about breed and motivation? This is where that comes into play. Most dogs like treats, others respond to toys, and some just love to be loved. If you can find out what your dog responds to best, before long you'll have him doing backflips all over the house for you.

If your dog has a strong food drive (as a majority of dogs do), then almost any treat will do. If your dog has a less-pronounced food drive, you'll have to up the ante. The way to approach this is to keep in mind that food is like money to a dog—and like money, it comes in different denominations. Think about the foods your dog really loves—things that go way beyond the kibble in the bowl. Let's say a piece of your dog's regular food is a one-dollar bill. Then a biscuit might be a five-dollar bill. A liver treat might be a ten- or twenty-dollar bill. And a bit of steak might be the emergency hundred-dollar bill in the back of your wallet. When you set out to train, be ready with a variety of rewards so you can command your dog's attention and keep his interest from start to finish during the session. Don't be in any hurry to give up the big bucks too soon. They're what will keep your dog focused from beginning to end and will reward his absolute best efforts. There's a good chance he'll be able to smell them in your pocket or bait bag the whole time.

One important thing to remember about using food to gain focus is that it works way better on a hungry dog. Don't bother trying to get your dog's attention with treats right after a meal. Instead, try training thirty to sixty minutes *before* mealtime, when your dog is already starting to think about food and is likely to hone in on any treats you use. If you have a dog who follows you around like a hawk near dinnertime, that's because his internal clock is telling him mealtime is right around the corner. Those moments when your dog is already mentally bellying up to the bowl provide a perfect opportunity to capitalize on his food-oriented focus by working in a training session before the meal.

Some dogs are more easily motivated by play or toys than by food. If you've ever seen a retriever with a cherished tennis ball or a bully breed working over a rope or tug toy, you know what I mean. That was the case with Murphy, a very energetic, very powerful, and very ornery one-year-old, eighty-pound Lab I rescued.

Murphy was the combination of all the things that can make a dog too much for a new owner to handle: size, strength, an adolescent's stubborn attitude, a complete lack of focus, and enough horsepower to challenge even the most seasoned trainer. This was

**Treats aren't the only way to gain your dog's focus.
Sometimes a favorite toy is more effective.**

a dog who put me through my paces right up until I decided to put his fascination with all the dog toys I had around the ranch to work for me. I gave Murphy a big pile of toys and let him choose his favorite. After trying (and failing) to fit *all* of them in his mouth, he finally settled on a Chuckit! ball—he couldn't take his eyes off it. Instead of me blindly choosing a toy he *kinda* wanted, I let Murphy pick something he *really* wanted to motivate him through training. This made him more eager to work and learn. Once that ball was in play and I took control of it, I had Murphy's complete and total focus. As I trained his commands, I held that ball in my hand, and each time the big, goofy, wildly exuberant dog did something right, I'd throw it for him and give him a few seconds to play. It worked like magic, providing far better results than I'd been able to wrangle from him with treats alone. So if your dog loves nothing more than a particular toy, don't hesitate to incorporate it into training, using it first to gain focus, and then as part of a reward.

Another factor in the equation is your dog's energy level. When it's too high, focus is hard to come by. Let's go back to that analogy that a dog trainer is like a teacher. If you ask any teacher worth his or her salt how to handle a classroom full of energetic three- or five- or seven-year-olds, you're going to find all their answers have something in common. Those kids need a physical outlet for their energy. Without it, they can be impossible to teach. If you have a high-energy dog, take a walk before training to take the edge off. Be sure to wait a good twenty minutes after the walk to let your dog's adrenaline ease up a bit. Otherwise, he'll still be in exercise mode.

Remember that control and focus go hand in hand, so if you're having trouble getting and keeping your dog's attention for training, use the Double Leash Lock-Off to limit his mobility and with it the options for his focus. Think of that technique as your go-to move when things aren't going as planned.

Meet Kobe. *One thing I've learned over the years is that when it comes to control, size doesn't matter. I've worked with plenty of small dogs who were capable of bringing just as much chaos and distraction to training as the most difficult giants. Kobe was one of those dogs, and when I met him he'd already paid a high price for his lack of focus. His owner surrendered this terrier mix to a shelter after having him for just one month, saying the nine-pound, year-old dog could not be trained. Being labeled* untrainable *can be a death sentence for a shelter dog, but the staff believed Kobe might have been mislabeled, so they called me.*

In the training yard at the ranch, Kobe showed he was outgoing and fearless—racing up to dogs of all shapes and sizes, jumping up and down to say hello. But when it came time to train, he showed me a different side of his personality. This was much more than the case of a dog who didn't know anything. Yes, it was obvious he didn't have any commands, but I've trained lots of dogs who came in the door with their experience at zero. The bigger issue with Kobe was that his lack of focus was so profound; even if he did know his commands, he still might not tune in long enough to show me. His attention was all over the place—the grass, the pedestal, the treats, the toys, the wall, my hand, my shirt, my shoes— it was like every single thing was competing for his attention every second of the day. If Kobe were a kid, he'd be the kind who never stops moving or who provides a running monologue of his experience. I could almost hear the thoughts racing through Kobe's head: "Hey, a hand! Two hands! Did I see a treat? Look—a toy! And it squeaks! Whoa, a bird! A squirrel! A fly! A leaf! Dude, get outta my way with that leash. I'm busy!" And then he'd blow by me and on to the next distraction. This dog was incorrigible, and I could almost see how an inexperienced owner might think he could not be trained.

Lucky for Kobe, I had no intention of giving up. What this dog needed was control and focus, and as our hours training together added up, I started sensing a pattern that told me what else he needed. Kobe was undisciplined, for sure, but he was also headstrong and smart. People often think that because a dog is stubborn, he's not intelligent, but the opposite is often true. A smart dog can anticipate what you want and, sometimes, beat you at your own game by figuring out a way to avoid it. That was part of what was going on between Kobe and me. I wanted him to play my game. He wanted to play his own.

In order to succeed with this dog, I was going to have to elevate his training to another level. First, I took control, putting him on a short leash and perching him on a training pedestal. The extra height made eye contact possible between us and helped keep his attention on me. Next, I broke out the treats. One thing about Kobe that did make him a good candidate for training was that he was totally, shamelessly food motivated. It didn't matter much what treat I had—he wanted it.

The last step in turning this training around was something a little less conventional. Kobe needed to be surprised. Whenever my training got too predictable, he tried to turn the tables on me. And so I changed up my methods as I taught him the NO command, using multiple techniques to keep him guessing. That was when we finally reached a breakthrough. Kobe paid enough attention to actually learn the command instead of just fighting against it. Once he'd figured out how to work with me, he was happy to master the command and earn rewards for his accomplishments. Equally important is that learning that command gave him a newfound respect for and interest in me. I'd surprised him, taught him something, and rewarded him for learning. From then on, he looked at me as someone worthy of his respect and not just his ill-behaved antics. The rest of his commands came a lot more easily.

Technique

Every once in a while I encounter a dog trainer who claims to "speak dog," to have some magical insight into how to communicate with animals that the rest of us don't. Who knows? Maybe there's something to that, but I've never seen it. Nor has there ever been any scientific evidence of it. The truly great animal trainers I've met all over the world rely on one thing above all others to get results: technique. And knowing how to apply proper technique requires years of experience. The fact is the best dog trainers in the world are the most experienced at their craft. They've seen the issue they're trying to solve hundreds of times before, so they know the exact technique to apply and the right moment to use it. It comes down to experience, plain and simple. After enough years of practice working effective techniques, these trainers develop instincts to match their skills—and then I guess it might *almost* look like they've pulled a Dr. Doolittle and learned to talk with the animals.

The bottom line is that dog training is a lot like martial arts in that it's all about technique and conditioning. Learn the technique one day. Condition with it for days, weeks, and months. The best martial artists in history didn't "speak" their craft. They became masters of it through a lot of training and practice. Eventually, when you work that steadily at anything, it becomes part of your lifestyle. Training our dogs helps them seamlessly blend into our everyday lives, living by the rules we've set.

This book is full of techniques in almost every chapter—methods like the Double Leash Lock-Off—that simplify and streamline the training process. And just like techniques for anything—karate, cooking, carpentry, *anything*—the more you practice them, the better you'll get at executing them effectively. As you choose techniques in the coming pages to use in your dog's training, keep in mind that they'll probably seem a little awkward at first. It's totally normal to feel that way because, much like your dog, you are learning something new here. I

ALWAYS HAVE A PLAN B

Every dog we meet comes with a combination of DNA and experiences that makes him as unique as a thumbprint. These are living, breathing, feeling beings, so of course no two are alike, and no two behavioral issues are ever exactly the same. So it only makes sense that not every dog responds to every training technique. One of the most important lessons I've learned over my decades of working with animals is that it pays to always have a plan B. That way if I get pushback from a dog with my first approach, I can quickly switch gears and go in another direction. Sometimes it's even a mix of approaches that leads to a breakthrough for a particular dog.

Throughout this book, I've included variations for all but the simplest and most consistently reliable training methods. As you read, and as you train, keep in mind that if you get stuck, you've got good alternatives right there on the page. Think of them as your training insurance. You may never need your plan B, but if you do, you'll be ready.

promise that over time the techniques swill get easier. Nobody walks into that first karate class and does a perfect round kick. Nobody makes a perfect soufflé on the first try. And whatever the first thing is you build with your hands, it'll probably end up in the garage or the basement—not exactly a family heirloom.

The point here is that just because a technique challenges you (or your dog), it doesn't mean you can't do it or that it won't work. The secret to your success will be in applying the proper technique over and over again—not just in a single perfect lesson. I've taught every method included in this book to clients who had never trained dogs before, and most of those clients ended up getting great results. As you conduct regular training sessions, your technique will steadily improve—and so will your dog's obedience.

Tools

Tools go hand in hand with technique. Here are a few that can help you train almost any dog:

The Right Collar and Leash. There are a lot of collar varieties to choose from—everything from a simple flat nylon band to a spiked metal choker. If you've ever watched *Lucky Dog*, you may have noticed that the training collars I prefer are neither of the above. For most training, I recommend and use martingale-style collars.

Martingales aren't named after the person or the company that invented the collar—they're named after a piece of horse tack by the same name that riders use to keep their horses' heads up. Even though the collar is a completely different piece of equipment, when you pull it, it cinches up—*without choking your dog*—and keeps his head high. If it chokes your dog, you're using it wrong and may need someone experienced with this kind of collar to help you understand it. When this collar is used correctly, it utilizes an important concept any experienced dog trainer can confirm: the higher a dog's head is, the more control you've got. If your dog can get his head low, he'll have more freedom to choose to disregard your training. He'll also have more horse-power, if he's the type to push or pull. This is key to remember when working a powerful breed known for pulling like a Lab, a husky, or any bully breed.

The way a martingale works is through a two-loop system. The larger loop is designed to close to the size of your dog's neck and no further. The smaller loop—the one the leash attaches to—has enough slack to allow you to narrow that larger loop or leave it slack. Most of the time, your dog will have *more* room in this kind of collar than in a regular flat collar. When you need more control, you'll be able to apply enough pressure to narrow the large loop without hurting your dog. These collars are easy to understand and to use—a nice tool to have around when you need it.

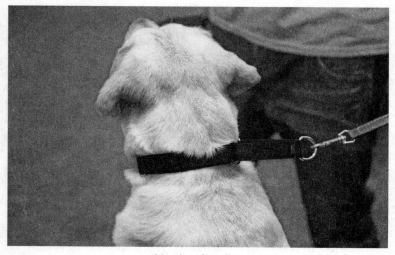

Martingale collar

If your dog is a heavy puller, you may find that neither a flat nor a martingale collar provides enough leverage for you to maintain control. In that case, a halter-style head collar may be your solution.

This collar also borrows a concept from horse tack, incorporating an over-the-nose strap that helps the handler control the dog's movement. There are a few different brands of this kind of collar, and they can all work, but there is a learning curve for both owner and dog when using them. I don't recommend using this kind of collar unless you're willing to watch an instructional video and—if needed—get a little guidance from someone who knows how it works.

Halter-style head collar

Any leash will work for most of the training techniques you'll find in this book, but you'll need at least two of them on hand to utilize some of my methods.

Platform or Pedestal. Not every dog needs to be elevated to be trained, and if you've got a big dog, you probably won't need a pedestal. For small dogs and for any dog with control issues, though, a raised training surface can help you gain some control and focus. On a pedestal, a small dog is closer to your eye level—a better place to communicate than by your ankles (plus it saves your back from breaking). In addition, a pedestal eliminates all kinds of distrac-

**Use a pedestal or other raised surface, such as a couch or chair,
to gain control and focus with a small dog.**

tions. Even though your dog *could* hop off and go investigate those
things, most dogs don't. That one extra measure of distance between them and their environment is usually just enough to keep
them in place. In fact, sometimes even positioning a big dog on a
curb can give you this small extra edge. At the ranch, I have pedestals of different heights and diameters, but a professional training
pedestal may not be a practical accessory for your living room or
yard. You can easily make do with something you have or with a
homemade version. Picnic tables work great as pedestals (although
you'll have to be cautious your dog doesn't pick up the bad habit
of jumping on tables after, so feel this one out before you commit).
For small dogs, try stools or benches. In the house, you can make
a light-duty pedestal by putting a small rubber-backed mat on top
of a sturdy dog crate.

A Penny Bottle or a Shake & Break™. Fair warning: you're
going to be coming across these simple, effective, inexpensive
tools several times in this book. I swear by them and use them

to train a lot of dogs—and from time to time I even try them on my friends. The reason they work is almost too simple: dogs get startled by the sounds they make. The noise literally stops dogs in their tracks when they're behaving badly, giving you a chance to redirect them to more acceptable behaviors.

The penny bottle is the make-it-yourself version of this tool, and it's as easy to own one as tossing a handful of coins in an empty water bottle and putting the cap back on. When you shake the bottle, the unorthodox noise will startle your dog and capture his attention. The Shake & Break is a more adaptable, kicked-up-a-notch version of this simple tool. It's a training bottle I designed with dense hardened plastic on one end and aluminum on the other. That composition makes it possible to get the same kind of sound distraction you'd get with a penny bottle when the metal weights inside are shaken toward the plastic—and to get a sharper,

**The Shake & Break: my versatile, kicked-up-a-notch version
of the humble penny bottle.**

more piercing sound when they're shaken toward the metal. I tested the Shake & Break on hundreds of dogs during its development and found its range of sounds and the option of its intense metal-on-metal tone to be especially effective on stubborn dogs, multiple dogs, and dogs who get so focused on the trouble they're up to that it's sometimes difficult to get their attention.

I've known people who have used everything from air horns to dog whistles to aversive collars to stop their dogs' bad behaviors, but I don't think any of those tools holds a candle to the humble penny bottle or the versatile Shake & Break.

A Clicker. You won't need a clicker to train most of the techniques in this book, but there are few times when you'll find it very helpful. In addition, some dogs respond really well to clicker training. If yours is one, you can easily incorporate the clicker into almost every method in this book.

Teaching your dog to respond to the clicker may be the simplest training technique you'll ever encounter. All you need to get started is a clicker and a handful of treats. With your dog controlled and focused, click and then immediately give him a treat. Repeat. Repeat. Repeat. The point of this exercise is simply to teach your dog to equate the sound of the clicker with a reward. Later, we'll utilize this tool to teach your dog to *COME* when called, but it has applications to any training technique when you might have trouble getting a treat to your dog at the exact moment he does something right. The clicker is a way to tell your dog, "Yes! That's it!" even when you're out of reach. I also find the clicker to be very effective in training shelter dogs who've been abused. Most of these dogs have been yelled at and verbally abused along with any physical mistreatment, and some become fearful when people talk to them. Even hearing "good dog" might scare them. On the other hand, the clicker—which is quick, quiet, and closely associated with rewards—can do no wrong.

Conditioning

There are very few techniques in this book that most dogs can't master in a week. But there's a big difference between teaching a dog to recognize a command and helping that dog to really *know* it. What's the difference? A dog who still has to think about a command is at risk of regressing, or losing it altogether. But a dog who has practiced responding to a command so many times over an extended period that the action has become a matter of muscle memory—that dog likely has the command for life.

While you're involved in a dedicated training program, I recommend working on each skill in a few sessions each day, repeating it ten times or more during each session. In my experience, dogs learn much better in multiple short sessions than in a single long one. If you sense your dog is reaching his limit, wrap up the session on a high note and set aside the skill until the next time. Overtraining is never a good idea. Done right, training can be fun and rewarding for you and your dog, but training too hard will make it stressful and unpleasant, and neither of you will want to stick to it. In addition, if you have a dog who's out of control in a lot of areas, don't start with a difficult training concept. Start with something easy, like *SIT* or *DOWN* so your dog can have early success. Work up to more difficult concepts like *HEEL* or *QUIET* over time. To increase your dog's odds of success, train in a few fifteen-minute sessions spread out over the day. And *always* end each session on a successful, good note.

After a few days of practicing a new skill successfully, the next step is to taper off the rewards, ensuring your dog will still obey when you aren't dangling a treat in front of his nose. To accomplish this, you'll need to adopt what I call a lottery system—a pattern of rewards where the dog doesn't hit the jackpot every single time he plays. The way to go about this is to keep the first and last rewards in play while eliminating a few of the treats that would come in between. Take your time at this, gradually reducing your dog to eight rewards out of ten tries, then six, then four, and then two—first and last. All the while you're cutting back on treats, your dog will still be learning and internalizing the command, getting better at it every day. By the time you get to just two rewards per session, he'll be ready to perform the command out of habit—not just for a prize. After that, you can still give random rewards to keep your dog on his toes, but you should be seeing a consistent response to the command when you're empty-handed.

Once you've taught your dog a command and weaned him off rewards—don't stop there! If you keep up the practice for just a single session every day, after a few weeks your dog will become truly automatic at it. That extended practice is the difference between a kinda trained dog and a well-trained dog. I know which kind I prefer to have.

Outtake

Since the success of *Lucky Dog*, sometimes when I train a new dog in public, I wear a ball cap or sunglasses. Don't worry—I haven't gone Hollywood—I just need to give each dog I work with my full attention at training time. That can be tough to manage if someone recognizes me while I'm on the job, because a chance encounter often ends up with me fielding twenty questions about how to solve their dog's issues. Besides, sometimes when I'm working with a brand-new client, the dog's behavior isn't a very positive reflection on my professional skills. That was the case when I took a five-month-old goldendoodle to an outdoor mall in LA to work on her out-of-control behavior around new people. Her owner told me the problem was terrible, but I needed to test the waters in a public place to see it for myself. The way I actually test a dog is usually to let him go completely out of control and see how bad things get before I even start training. This gives me a foundation to build from. To someone just passing by, I'm sure it sometimes appears my dog-handling skills are a lost cause.

During this particular real-time assessment, it quickly became clear the dog's issues were bad with a capital *B*. As soon as we got out of the car, this big, excitable puppy started going nuts, jumping so high as she approached each new stranger that she was nearly doing backflips. She actually got so excited when someone approached her that she started jumping up and down and peeing all over herself, spraying the stranger in the process.

Of course, it seemed like everyone else in the shopping center was on their best behavior that day—so they all noticed me and my crazy student as she romped around like a maniac. I could feel the eyes on us, with some people openly staring and shaking their heads. I even heard one man mutter, "Poor guy." But I focused on the task at hand—figuring out the first step in breaking this otherwise good dog of her bad behavior. I was so locked in that I barely acknowledged when a woman came up beside me and said, "Excuse me, you look like you're having a little trouble. I know a great dog trainer if you'd maybe like his card?" As she held out the business card, I turned toward her—and then burst out laughing.

The woman was one of *my* clients—and she was offering me my own card. I faced her and tipped my glasses up. "Jessica, it's me!" Glancing at the bouncing dog, I added, "Remember what *your* dog was like on the first day?"

The moral of this story is this: Every tough training case starts with a day like that day in the mall—just me at one end of the leash and a student with a big problem at the other. Dogs don't just look at me and start to behave—no such luck. If that were the case, I wouldn't even be writing this book . . .

PART TWO

THE 7 COMMON COMMANDS

4

SIT

Before we delve into this first command, let's talk a little about what it takes to tackle the 7 Common Commands in seven days. I recommend that you start here, with *SIT*—the simplest command—and then let your dog's variables help dictate your choices as you move through the remaining ABCs of obedience.

Many dogs will already know the *SIT* command, and many others will pick it up almost immediately. They may be ready to move on to *DOWN* before you've even finished your morning coffee on day one. Others, though, will need a little extra time for each command. In general, you can expect to be able to teach your dog the basics of one command each day, and then reinforce those commands throughout the week. That said, let's acknowledge one important fact here: a dog is not a mechanism like a Rubik's Cube that we can simply manipulate a couple of turns in one direction and then a few turns in another to "solve." Your dog is far more complex and unique than that.

So while I recommend teaching one command each day and then practicing those commands a few times each day for a week, I strongly encourage you to pay attention to how your dog seems to learn best and adjust accordingly. Some dogs are eager to learn and may be able to grasp three or more new commands in a single day. Others are slower and steadier, needing a full day—or more—to take in one new command before tackling another. Likewise, some dogs retain training best if you work them for three or four twenty-minute sessions each day. Others do best with twice as many ten-minute sessions instead.

Regardless of your dog's learning style, she is capable of learning all 7 Common Commands. Just follow the steps in these chapters, remember that repetition is the key to success, and focus on positive, confident training. The face you show your dog is the face that'll be shown back to you.

Now let's get started on that *SIT* command.

The *SIT* command serves a vital purpose in obedience and manners for any dog. It's usually the simplest command to teach, and it's one of the most practical as well. A dog with a good *SIT* is not only obedient but also controlled. And a controlled dog is a well-mannered dog.

This command is ideal for a lot of different situations. It's almost the canine equivalent of putting your car in park. It can help settle down a dog if she's running wild. It can also help calm her if she's anxious, or help you gain your dog's focus when you need it. Lastly, it teaches and reinforces respect. A dog who has a well-refined and reliable *SIT* has good manners and knows how to use them.

Besides serving as a baseline for control, the *SIT* command is a prerequisite for just about every one of my other 7 Common Commands. Even though they can be taught in any order, teaching the *SIT* is the logical place to start obedience training. And since this command helps your dog focus, once she has it down, teaching some of the other commands will be easier for both of you.

Here's the best news: even many dogs who seem to have no training at all have a *SIT* inside them somewhere. That's because it's usually the first command any owner or trainer teaches. Most dogs have encountered it at some point in the first months or years of their lives.

There are many ways to teach this command, but the method I'm going to explain here is the easiest by a landslide. It's also a method that dependably works on dogs of almost all breeds, personalities, and ages. The only tools you'll need are a leash and a bag of your dog's favorite treats. Play rewards won't work as well for this one, but you're not likely to need them. If your dog is not especially food motivated, choose something special, like little pieces of cooked chicken or steak or liver treats, to get her attention.

Before we dig in to learn this step-by-step, I'd like to tell you about a rescue dog who was the rare exception to what I just explained about most dogs knowing a *SIT*—or at least having a flicker of memory of learning it. Glory was five years old when I found her, and she'd been so neglected all her life that no one had even bothered to teach her the most basic and simplest command.

Meet Glory. *When I first met Glory in the shelter, she was in sorry shape. This little poodle mix's off-white coat was greasy and stained from her time on the streets. She had sap covering her fur. Her nails were so long it sounded like she was tap-dancing on the floor as she walked—something that's not just uncomfortable for*

a dog, but an obvious sign of neglect. She was going to need some serious grooming just to make her comfortable, let alone adoptable.

Sadly, Glory's issues were more than skin-deep. Neglect is one of the most common types of abuse dogs experience. It takes a physical toll, but it can also do psychological damage. Glory was a poster child for this. What should have been a warm glow in her eyes had been replaced by a milky-gray stare—the look of a dog who had spent too long peering out from behind bars. She was middle-aged and out of shape—probably a good ten pounds over-weight. That may not sound like much to a person, but on a small dog it can easily work out to 25 percent or more of her total body weight. That's like an extra fifty pounds *on an average man—enough baggage to lead to serious health problems. You might wonder how a neglected dog ends up being overweight, and often the answer is an owner who keeps a big bin of pet food around, leaving the dog to feed herself. I'd guess that was the case for Glory, and that both she and the bin resided outside year-round.*

Despite her condition, my first impression of Glory wasn't that she was defeated or neglected, greasy or out of shape. I never look at dogs that way in a shelter. I look at them and see what their potential is, then I try to figure out how I can help them reach it. It was easy to see Glory's potential. She was extremely sweet. She obviously loved attention. She was sensitive and affectionate. She had the personality of a dog who belonged in a warm home with a loving family and a soft bed—even though I doubt she'd ever had any of those things. The moment I sat down on the floor in her kennel, she crawled into my lap and rested her head on my stomach as if to say, "Please get me outta here." I knew then that once she'd had some TLC and training, it would be a no-brainer finding this dog a home.

So I hooked Glory on a leash, walked her outside, and loaded her into my truck. When she hit the backseat, she just collapsed, as if the pressure and anxiety of getting that far had knocked her off

*her feet. Seeing a dog wiped out by the stress of what she's been
through is never pretty. Unfortunately, I see it all too often. I hoped
Glory knew she was one step closer to being in a loving home.
Starting that day, we had a long road of recovery, rehabilitation,
and training ahead of us.*

*It didn't take long to realize it was going to be a little bumpy.
When I got Glory back to the ranch, I started by assessing her
knowledge of the 7 Common Commands. The first thing I do in
any dog's evaluation is ask for a* SIT. *Seems easy enough, right?
And most dogs can do it. But Glory didn't know how. The fact that
she was never taught to* SIT *still blows my mind because even the
most untrained dogs know this one. If they've had even an hour
of training in their lives,* SIT *is what they learned. But this dog was
five years old with zero training, so I was starting her 7 Common
Commands from scratch.*

*Luckily, Glory's personality made her eager to learn and to go
along with the exercise regimen I set up to help her shed some
extra weight. At the end of her time at the ranch, Glory went to her
forever home with a widow who'd written to me saying she wanted
to find a loving companion as she adjusted to her new life. The two
of them—both optimists despite having been through hard times—
ended up being a perfect match.*

Teaching the *SIT*

The *SIT* command is so easy to teach that you almost don't have to
train it. Why so easy? Because dogs sit naturally—all you have to
do is capture the moment.

There are a lot of ways to teach the command, but the way I
taught Glory is one of the most foolproof. Let's call it the basic
SIT. Unlike some commands that have a lot of different techniques

that work for different dogs, this one works for almost everyone.

Start by making sure your dog is on-leash. A short leash is perfect for this technique, since you'll be staying close to your dog. Always remember that the leash is an extension of your arm, which means your arm can prevent things from happening and correct things that are already going on. In this case, you'll use it in one of two slightly different ways, depending on the size of your dog. If your dog is small, put her on an elevated surface (I use a pedestal) and grasp the leash a few inches from her collar so you're ready to limit her mobility. Your big dog can stay on the ground. For big dogs, before you move on to the next step, anchor the leash to the ground with your foot. For small dogs, hold the end of the leash down low to keep your dog from jumping. Either of these positions will give you the control you need to get started. Remember, control is the cornerstone of training!

Now it's time to get to work. Take a treat—a good one that your dog can get excited about—and hold it about six inches in front of her. If your dog hasn't had much training or learned much control yet—like Glory—she'll naturally go lunging toward it. But the leash in your hand or under your foot is going to stop that. This is the key to the technique because most untrained dogs will just go for the food if they're not restricted, and you don't want to reinforce that behavior.

When Glory stopped lunging, I took the treat and once again held it a few inches away from her snout. Do the same with your dog. (If your dog doesn't lunge, by the way, you can jump straight to this part.) Now, move that treat along a forty-five-degree arc up and over your dog's head. This keeps your dog focused on the treat. Her head will follow the treat, lifting farther and farther upward. As you move the treat over your dog's head, say *SIT*. When the treat gets so high your dog can't crane her neck any farther north, she'll do the basic math and figure out that if she sits down, she can once again see it comfortably.

With a big dog, anchor the leash to the ground with your foot
to prevent her from lunging for the treat.

If your small dog starts to lunge for the treat,
use the leash to limit her mobility.

Arc the treat over your dog's head until she sits.

The moment your dog's butt hits the ground, say, "Good *SIT*" and give her a treat. Timing is everything: If you wait too long, your dog won't make the connection between sitting down and getting the reward. Making that association is vital to successfully training this command. Once you've had that first success, walk your dog a few steps to a different spot and repeat the process. Hold the treat six inches from her nose, move it in an angle up over her head while giving the command, and wait for her butt to hit the floor. The moment that happens, reward with praise and food.

As with any command, you want to condition your dog so she knows it and knows it well. Most dogs can understand just about any basic command in a short period of time. But understanding a technique and being properly conditioned are two different things. Think about it this way: I can go take an hour-long karate class and understand how to do a kick or two, but that doesn't mean I'm good at karate, and it definitely doesn't mean I'll be ready to use those kicks when a moment calls for them. If all I'm relying on is a single lesson, I probably can't fight my way out of a paper bag. But if I continuously take lessons every day and train on those same kicks over and over, I'll eventually be a well-trained and well-conditioned fighter who can put the art to practical use. We all remember how Mr. Miyagi trained Daniel in *The Karate Kid*, conditioning him through muscle memory while Daniel didn't even know it was happening. The exact same rule applies here. Our pets have to learn a technique first, but then we have to condition them until that technique is just a matter of muscle memory. If you don't follow through with this step, any kind of distraction or just a lack of focus will interfere with the command, possibly when you need it most. If you do this right, though, your dog won't even have to think about what you're asking her to do. She'll just do it.

That kind of conditioning is exactly what I did with Glory. Every few hours over a week, I spent ten to fifteen minutes conditioning her to *SIT* on command. Every day we worked together, she got quicker and more reliable. By the end of the week, I didn't even need the food reward anymore. Glory just knew that *SIT* means sit, and she had mastered the command for life. Just in time, too, because her new owner was eagerly awaiting her arrival.

I still get e-mails from Glory's new mom telling me how great and well mannered her dog is. She says Glory's the most popular dog at the park and that they both love their early morning and evening walks. It always makes me feel good knowing that a dog I rescued went on to a new life with the skills to be a great companion. I'm especially glad that was possible for Glory, who had spent far too much of her life living in such profound neglect she didn't even know what a *SIT* was.

5

DOWN

If there's one command that's the most underrated, it's the *DOWN*. It has so many great uses, like getting your dog out of the way when company visits, or giving him a tool to handle being at an outdoor cafe, or ensuring he'll be a polite guest when you travel. It even comes in handy for the occasional photo op. Most importantly, this command is the ultimate form of control for even the most wild and crazy animal. Any dog owner can benefit from having some extra control from time to time—and we all know someone who needs it badly, like a friend or neighbor with an incorrigible pet who rules the house. I get about fifty calls a week from people in this situation, and I tell them all to start by teaching their dogs a reliable *DOWN*.

If teaching your dog to *SIT* is the canine equivalent of putting a car in park, teaching the *DOWN* is like shifting to park and also taking the keys out of the ignition. It's really a *DOWN* and a *STAY* rolled into a single command.

For most dogs, teaching the *SIT* first is an easy and obvious choice. Every once in a while, though, I meet a dog who needs an extra level of control before we can even get started. In those cases,

I start by teaching the *DOWN*. That was definitely the case with one of my rescues—a powerful, intense, large dog who'd managed to overwhelm every home that had tried to adopt him. This dog desperately needed a handler, not just an owner. And he needed the *DOWN* command to help him master the art of self-control. His name was Ari.

Meet Ari. *If you take two of the best working dog breeds on the planet—a German shepherd and a Malinois—and breed them, you get a dog like Ari. When I met this pup, he was a ninety-pound-and-growing adolescent. His jaws were so big and strong, he could chew through just about anything (and he had). He was very protective, and as soon as he came into a house, he'd scan the entire place, taking inventory of who was around. He was full of drive, energy, and determination. Ari was a perfect example of the kind of dog who needs a job; if he were a man, he'd be in the military.*

By the time I found Ari, he'd already been returned to the shelter multiple times, probably because he was just too much dog for most owners to handle. At his age, with so much strength and no Off switch, Ari was on a fast path to being branded unadoptable. I was his last chance to find a home, but I could see that this was a good dog—one with incredible potential—who just needed a

*way to stop and settle down when he was told. Teaching him the
DOWN command was going to give him the tool that would save
his life.*

Teaching the *DOWN*

Like any other command, there are lots of ways to teach a dog to
obey the *DOWN*. For me, the simplest, most reliable method is
always the way to go. There are three techniques I use most often
that are straightforward to teach and easy for most dogs to grasp.
One works best for big and medium dogs; one works best for small
dogs; and one is a quick, effective alternative for dogs of either size.

Big- and Medium-Dog Technique

Remember the instructions for the Double Leash Lock-Off in
Chapter 3? This method of teaching the *DOWN* starts with putting your dog in that locked-off position. You'll have him in a harness with an anchor leash attached to it and tied off behind him,
plus a collar with the guide leash attached and the handle in your
hand. Be prepared with your dog's favorite treats as you start this
process—and remember to train when your dog is hungry. Hunger
equals motivation. You'll need an optimal location to make this
work: a sturdy pole, fence post, or even a solid table leg will work
well to secure your dog's anchor leash, and in front of that you'll
want a flat area with about eight feet of clearance all around.

Step 1. Put your dog in the Double Leash Lock-Off position. Since
you're teaching a *DOWN*, you don't want any force encouraging
your dog to pull up, including the height of the anchor, so be sure
to hook it near the bottom. The easiest way to do this is to wrap

the handle end of the leash around the post, thread the clip end through the handle, and then attach the clip to the harness the dog is wearing. Now you're ready to let the magic begin.

Step 2. Using a treat, lure your dog toward you and away from the pole until he has pulled the anchor leash tight behind him. For an eager, intense dog like Ari, this only took a split second. With a more timid dog, you may have a short wait. Once your dog reaches the end of the anchor leash, hold the treat in one hand at the same level as his head and about six inches away from his mouth. Because he is secured to the anchor, he won't be able to lunge forward to grab it, so now you'll have his attention.

Step 3. Lower the treat straight to the ground while still holding it in your hand. At the same time, say the word *DOWN*. Some dogs will go straight into the *DOWN* position as they follow the treat. If yours does this, calmly praise and reward him with the treat immediately.

With your dog in the Double Leash Lock-Off position and the anchor leash secured low to the ground and taut behind him, hold a treat about six inches away from his mouth.

Lower the treat to the ground while saying the word *DOWN*.

Once your dog is *DOWN*, calmly praise and reward him with the treat.

While your dog is still down, I want you to step on the guide leash a couple of inches away from the clip and continue to praise him. This will deter your dog from popping back up. If he tries to stand, the resistance he'll feel will pull him right back to the floor. Very few dogs will try and fight to stand back up when you step on the leash because it takes too much energy and they want you to continue to reward them for being down. If your dog does resist and tries to stand, simply keep your foot on the leash, say *DOWN*, and wait until he relaxes. How long it takes depends on how headstrong your dog is, but you can definitely outlast him. As soon as he's back in the *DOWN* position, be sure to praise and give him a treat to let him know that's where you want him to be.

While your dog is still in the *DOWN* position, step on the guide leash to prevent him from popping back up, and continue to praise him.

Of course, it's not always quite that easy. Not every dog is going to give you a *DOWN* right away. Ari didn't. Like many willful dogs, he lowered his head and even the front of his body but kept his rear end in the air so he was bowing toward the floor. If your dog takes this position, it's time to utilize that guide leash in your hand. While your dog has his front half lowered, step on the leash and make sure it's pulled just snug enough that your dog can't stand back up. It's an awkward position for him, with his butt in the air and his head down, and that treat still out in front. Your dog probably won't like this pose much. As a result, he'll have to make a decision: hold the position, keep trying to stand up against the resistance of the guide leash, or lie down. Be sure to keep that treat on the floor just out of his reach as he thinks about it, and keep putting slight downward pressure on the leash and saying *DOWN* in a calm voice every few seconds. Very few dogs will stand. Most will hold their ground—some for a long time, and some for just a few seconds. Whatever the case may be for your dog, you're just going to wait him out. Trust me when I tell you that they all eventually give up and lie down—even big, strong-minded dogs like Ari who would rather not give an inch. At the exact moment your dog drops his bottom to the floor, be ready with calm praise and that treat that got his attention in the first place. And be sure to step on the leash right near the clip to prevent him from popping back up.

If your dog takes this position, keep the treat on the floor just
out of reach and exert enough pressure on the guide leash so he
can't stand back up. And then wait for his bottom to drop.

There are two key things to remember as you train this technique:

1. When your dog obeys the *DOWN* command, praise and reward him generously in a *calm*, *slow* voice and manner. You don't want your, "Good boy!" to rev him up and cause him to jump back to his feet.

2. When your dog obeys the *DOWN*, you want to give him rewards while he's in that position. Long, soothing strokes from his head to his back to let him know he did well plus food and praise—the whole nine yards. The more he feels comfortable and loved in the *DOWN* position, the more your dog will want to be there when you ask the next time.

Even the easiest dog to train will need some repetition to figure out exactly what behavior you are rewarding when you first teach the *DOWN*. Ari stood back up a couple of times during his first lesson, so I just repeated the steps. One lesson is never enough, so we kept working at the technique. You'll need to do this with your dog, too, until you're certain he's made the association between following the *DOWN* command correctly and all being right with the world.

After practicing for a while with the leashes on and seeing your dog master the technique while he's restricted, it'll be time to try this without leads. Rather than attempting to command a *DOWN* to a dog who's running loose and may not obey, start this change-over session just like you've been doing, with your dog secured to an anchor leash and a guide leash. After a few successful tries, quietly unclip the guide leash. If that goes well, then unclip the anchor leash, too.

This doesn't always go so well right away. In Ari's case, as soon as he figured out he was off-leash, he went straight for the treat instead of lying down to get it. And that's exactly the reason I always emphasize conditioning in training. It wasn't a failure—it was simply a sign that Ari wasn't ready, so he went back on the leashes and we went through a few more practice runs before trying again. Conditioning is the difference between a trained dog and a well-trained dog, so much so that even a big, willful adolescent like Ari can learn a totally reliable *DOWN* with a few days of consistent practice. Over and over, I conditioned his *DOWN* with the leashes on. And then one day when I removed them, his muscle memory was so polished that Ari didn't even have to think about the command. He dropped to the ground in a split second every time he heard it.

Small-Dog Technique

When it comes to training small dogs, we have to play by an entirely different set of rules because small dogs don't respond to the Double Leash Lock-Off the same way medium and large dogs do. Small dogs can be very tricky when learning the *DOWN* command because, believe it or not, even though they don't have that far to go to the ground, little guys usually put up more of a struggle against getting there than the big ones do. Large dogs tend to respond to leash resistance better than small dogs, so for this technique we are not going to use a leash at all. Without it, we need some other form of control. At the ranch, I use a pedestal. Since you may not have a training pedestal lying around—and since this technique works best if your dog is in a comfy spot anyway—you can use your couch or an easy chair as a substitute. The technique is very simple when we break it down.

Step 1. Place your dog on the edge of the couch. Make sure he doesn't jump off. If he does, put him right back up as many times as it takes until he's stable and staying put. The best way to keep your dog in place is by focusing his attention on a treat in your hand.

Use a treat to help focus your dog's attention.

Step 2. Take the treat and hold it about six inches away from your dog's snout. Now slowly lower it below the edge of the couch while giving the command *DOWN*. Naturally, your dog will watch the treat, following it down. Now here's the secret: You're only going to lower the treat about four inches below the edge of the couch, just enough so your dog's head will be hanging over the edge to follow. He can see it, but he can't take it in his mouth until his position changes or you move the treat—and you are not going to move it. From there, continue to say the word *DOWN*. It might take a little while, but your dog will eventually relax and lie down while still looking at the treat. If your dog is stubborn about this, put a little pressure on his shoulders to give him a hint where to go. The second your dog hits that *DOWN* position, calmly reward him with the treat and praise, telling him, "Good *DOWN*."

Lower the treat below the edge of the chair
while giving the command *DOWN*.

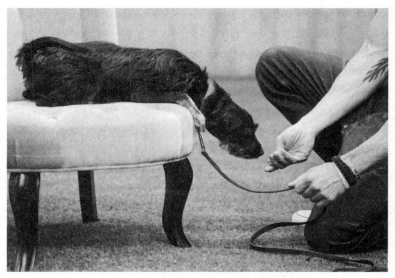

When your dog hits the *DOWN* position,
reward him with the treat and praise.

Step 3. Now this next part is very important. When they are down, most dogs will give you only a few seconds before they pop back up. You cannot let your dog do this from the *DOWN* position while you're training this command because a successful *DOWN* means your dog both assumes the position and stays put. It is vital you keep your dog where he is, so continue to "pay" your dog while he's in the *DOWN* position, petting him slowly and firmly from his head down the length of his back. This allows you to accomplish two things: giving your dog praise *and* keeping him in the *DOWN* with a firm stroke that guards against him trying to stand. If you feel your dog trying to push back up, that stroke you're giving him suddenly becomes a block for his movement. You'll need to use a little bit of pressure in this move. As soon as your dog settles again, continue to reward him with food and affection. Your goal is to keep your dog down for a long period of time—all the while rewarding him—because the longer he is down and the more he is rewarded, the better the *DOWN* will stick in his memory when you ask him to do it again.

This is an easy technique to teach. Here's why: Most small dogs naturally want to lie down on a soft surface, choosing the couch or bed over something like a tile or wood floor. Larger dogs often don't care as much, and you may notice they like lying on hard surfaces just fine. But ask yourself how often you've seen your small dog taking a nap on the wood floor. It's probably a rare event. For this reason, teaching the *DOWN* on a soft couch or chair is an efficient way to dovetail with your dog's natural inclinations. Trying to teach a small dog to lie down on a hard surface only makes more work for both of you. After a week of conditioning this command on the couch, your dog will most likely obey the *DOWN* anywhere you ask him. If he gives you any resistance, move back to the couch and gradually transition to other surfaces again.

The Grab-and-Slide Technique

This one is for the stubborn dogs of all shapes and sizes. The grab-and-slide technique is exactly what it sounds like, but it's all about *where* you grab and *what* slides. It's quick and simple:

Step 1. Place a bowl of treats next to you on your right side and sit down beside your dog either on the floor or on a raised surface like a couch or large chair. This puts you level with your dog and makes it easier to execute the technique.

Step 2. With your dog sitting to your left on the couch or floor, put your left arm around him and secure his collar with your left hand. Then extend your right hand, crook your elbow at a ninety-degree angle, and hook your forearm behind your dog's front legs, just under and behind the elbow joints.

Sit beside your dog and secure his collar with your left hand.

Step 3. Now say the word *DOWN* while slowly sliding your right hand toward you until your forearm is free. Your motion will gently slide your dog's front legs forward as you do this. Be sure to hold on to that collar the entire time. When your hand comes all the way free, your dog will be lying down on the surface of the couch.

Hook your forearm behind his front legs.

Say the word *DOWN* while slowly sliding your right hand toward you until your forearm is free. Be sure to hold on to your dog's collar the entire time.

Step 4. The second your dog reaches this position, grab a few treats from the bowl and reward him for being *DOWN*. From there, follow the instructions in Step 3 of the small-dog technique above to help your dog learn that the *DOWN* means both getting low *and* staying there.

As soon as your dog is *DOWN,* treat and reward him.

Training Tips to Remember

Stick to It. Just like when you're teaching any command, remember that it's up to you to follow through. This command, in particular, is one that relies on you giving the instruction and then outwaiting your dog until he gives in and does what you've asked. It can be frustrating and time-consuming at first, but I've never met a dog who can't learn the *DOWN*. I have, though, met owners who give up too soon, basically teaching the dog the opposite of what they intended—that the animal can outwait the person and bend him or her to his will. Needless to say, that's the beginning of a problem that can get much bigger than mastery of any single command. Stick to it, stay patient, and you'll be fine.

Stand Tall While Training Your Big Dog. Many people train the *DOWN* command from a kneeling position because it's easier for them to lower a treat to the floor that way. Keep in mind that you want to posture your body in a more normal (standing) position as soon as you can. If you continuously train the command on your knees, your dog will get used to that, and when you give the same command from standing, your dog may be thrown off by the change. So it's okay to start out kneeling to teach this command, but start inching back up to your normal position right away when your dog starts to grasp it. After a few days you should be standing all the way up while telling him *DOWN.*

Don't Back Away. Another common mistake people make when training a big dog the *DOWN* command with this technique is backing up when they first unclip the dog from the anchor leash. Many dogs will naturally start creeping forward when off the leash, and some people naturally back up when this happens. Don't back up. By doing so, you teach your dog to creep forward, which eventually leads to a bad habit of doing it every time. Simply give the command and stand still. Standing your ground will help ensure your dog will be ready and able to follow the command when he really needs it.

Use It or Lose It. This is the cardinal rule of training. If you don't condition your dog daily, he won't get good at the command. Always remember to lock in that muscle memory for your dog. Do several sessions a day for a week, and you'll be happy. Do it several times a day for months and you'll be blown away.

Variation

***Starting from* SIT.** Most dogs can learn the *DOWN* command just fine from a standing position, but if your dog resists lying down in favor of going after the treat, try starting him out in the

SIT position instead. For the majority of dogs, teaching a *SIT* is the logical first step in obedience training anyway—and the quickest way to ensure you get to the finish line of all 7 Common Commands in the shortest amount of time. Use the *SIT* command from Chapter 4 to help a dog who's struggling to go from standing to *DOWN*. Some dogs find it easier to stretch out from sitting, and they respond better to this slight change in technique.

Welcome to the World of Self-Control

Ari learned the *DOWN* command—but he learned something even more important at the same time. He learned some self-control. He was able, with the help of the Double Leash Lock-Off, to focus long enough to find out that he could earn rewards. And along the way he discovered, without ever hearing a raised voice and definitely without seeing a raised hand, that he couldn't win what he initially perceived as a game of will. Once he saw he couldn't win it—that cooperating was the way to get what he wanted—he decided it wasn't worth playing at all. Ari had undergone a very important attitude adjustment: he went from being a delinquent to being a student. After that, he was ready to learn more.

Your dog's case may not be as dire as Ari's was. Most of them aren't. But being able to trust that your dog's well-trained *DOWN* command will get a consistent response every time will give you an invaluable tool to keep him under control and safe anywhere and anytime.

Outtake

A few years back, I was training a service dog named Apollo—you might remember the story I told in Chapter 3 about our first meeting. One of the most important commands any service dog has to learn is the *DOWN*, mainly because service dogs go everywhere with their handlers and often have to lie next to them for long periods of time. When Apollo was learning this command, I would have him lie still for about thirty minutes at a time. After a while he got so good at it that I could put him in a *DOWN* by my feet while I watched TV, and he would not budge the entire time.

It was all going great until my student began to outsmart me. Apollo knew that when I put him in a *DOWN*, he was not to stand until I gave the command to do so. But his young, curious mind was always wandering, and if he heard something in the next room, naturally he would want to go check it out. He knew he couldn't just stand up and walk away, but he didn't let that stop him. I can't tell you how many times I looked down and discovered that the dog who was supposed to be at my feet was gone. Each time I'd go looking and find him in another room. This was happening every day, and I was racking my brain trying to figure it out. It's not like we're talking about a Yorkie here. I was sure I would notice—that *anyone* would notice—if a 120-pound Doberman stood up and walked out of the room.

I started paying closer attention to figure out how this great big dog was getting around the house, and I soon found out. Apollo *was* following my orders and staying in his *DOWN*, but while he was in it, he was crawling all over the house. I watched him slowly, silently crawl away and navigate from room to room. This was a dog who had learned his *DOWN* a little too well, so well that he figured he could go exploring on the technicality of crawling instead of walking. Even though what he was doing was wrong, I let it slide because I laughed so hard, and because it would never be a problem for the new handler who'd always have him on-leash in public.

I still think back to those moments with Apollo and smile at how he could be both so obedient and so smart. I knew then that he was ready for his new handler. It's times like that that make my job worth every minute I put into it.

6

STAY

I've heard countless testimonials from clients over the years about how the *STAY* command may have saved their dogs' lives. Many of these stories are about dogs who were in the yard or some other place off-leash, and then suddenly took off toward the street. The *STAY* command kept them in place—at or before the curb—and out of danger. Hearing stories like that from the owners of dogs I've trained makes my day, and knowing a command is saving lives raises my commitment to teaching it to as many dogs as possible.

This command can be a lifesaver, and so it's worth every minute you spend teaching it and any overtime you need to put in to ensure your dog really, truly knows what *STAY* means. If you take your dog anywhere off-leash, this is doubly important. It has been a critical skill for many of my rescued dogs, including a sweet boxer-bulldog mix who had a very important job waiting for her once she learned to reliably respond.

Meet Darby. *When I met Darby, it was love at first sight. This eight-month-old boxer-bulldog mix was so sweet she tried to fit her head through the bars of her kennel to kiss me when I walked up. She had the gorgeous shiny brown coat of a boxer and the smushed-in snout of a bulldog. And the second I stepped inside, she crawled up on my lap as if she were a tiny Maltese and not a fifty-pound mix of two much bigger breeds.*

Darby had a Zen demeanor, which is rare for a puppy, and especially rare for an energetic breed like a boxer. These dogs are known for being big jumpers, big chewers, and animated puppies. Calm is about the last thing you can expect from them. But Darby was different—like an old soul—and I could see right away that she had the foundation to be the special kind of dog who helps people. Within five minutes of meeting this girl, I had a good idea where she was meant to be.

A couple of weeks earlier, I'd received an e-mail from a teacher in Simi Valley who was looking for a dog. Her husband had recently passed away, and her only child was about to go off to college. It tugged at my heart to read how lonely her house was about to become. Then she threw me a curveball. She said she'd like a dog who could help kids in a program at her school. The program uses therapy dogs to assist kids who struggle with reading. Many of these students find it easier to read to dogs—who listen without ever judging—than to more intimidating human partners. When I heard this request, I was ready to make it my mission to find the perfect dog for this woman who was so committed to giving back to her students and community.

When I saw Darby in the shelter, I knew she was a great candidate to be both a companion and a help in the classroom. But training any dog to become a therapy dog is no easy task. These dogs need to have perfect manners—sometimes even better than the people they're helping. I quickly discovered that Darby had very few. She went 2-for-7 when I tested her on the Common Commands. Despite her lack of prior training, though, everything about this dog told me she could not only learn but completely master any skill with patient and consistent training.

One of the most important things to teach any therapy dog is the STAY *command. A dog with a solid* STAY *is a well-mannered dog, but a therapy dog might have to be able to* STAY *for periods of an hour or even more. This was a tall order for an eight-month-old puppy, but I was confident Darby could do it.*

Teaching the *STAY*

There are several methods I rely on to teach the *STAY*, depending on how each dog learns. My favorite of these, though, is a method called the cornered *STAY*. It's an effective technique with a unique logic behind it. I can't be sure I'm the first to ever execute this technique, but I can tell you that I came up with it through years of experimenting and learning, and I've never seen it used by another trainer. After you teach this technique to your dog, your days of worrying whether she might bolt into the street will be a thing of the past. Let's get to work.

The Cornered *STAY*

The only tools you'll need for this technique:

- A six-foot leash
- A bag of treats your dog loves
- An ideal location. Location is the key to this method so choose carefully. You're going to need an *enclosed* yard, empty lot, or some other large area with a wide-open space and a blocked or walled ninety-degree-angle corner. A yard with a fence is ideal because it offers a workable space with the fence creating right angles. A corner in a room of a house works, too, but make sure there's a clear space around the dog and no clutter.

Our goal is to make steady progress, but it's important not to get carried away on the first day. For the first session, I never recommend asking a dog to *STAY* for longer than six seconds at six feet. That's more than enough for one lesson. If you're able to get to that milestone, end the session in a successful *STAY* and call it a day.

As you begin your second session, start with a quick refresher of what you've already covered. This will go more quickly than it did the first time, but you still ask for a longer *STAY* only if your dog is reliable every time to that six feet for six seconds mark. At that point, you can continue to train the command for more time and distance.

Step 1. Clip the leash to your dog's collar and stow the treats in your pocket or bait bag. Now place your dog in that ninety-degree angle in the *SIT* position with her butt backed into the corner. If necessary, scoot her back or physically place her so she's right up against it. The situation you want to create is one where your dog has no options to run away. That's the key to this entire process—

starting your dog in a position where there's little else to do except focus on you and do what you ask. You'll start gradually giving her a little wiggle room as she learns the command.

Let's talk for just a minute about why we use a corner. Picture your dog standing in a wide-open space, at the hub of an octagon. From that position, your dog has eight different possible paths to use to get away. If you place your dog against a wall, you eliminate three of those paths and leave five of them open. If you use a corner, you block five and leave only three available. Once you stand in front of your dog, you've eliminated one of those last paths to freedom—and when you hold out your hands, you block the final two. Now your dog doesn't have many choices *except* to stay.

Step 2. Stand just a foot away from your dog and lift one hand, palm out like a traffic cop telling someone to halt. This is the *STAY* hand signal, and by the time we're done training this command, your dog will likely respond as well to seeing it as she does to hearing the command. Display that hand signal to your dog and si-

The cornered *STAY* with *STAY* hand signal.

multaneously say *STAY*. Remember that you are *telling* your dog to take this action, not asking. Use a firm, assertive, flat voice to show you mean this new word, saving your higher-pitched, more singsong voice for playtime later. Once you give the *STAY* command, hold your dog in position for one second and one second only. If your dog can be still for that single second, quickly pet, praise, and reward her with a treat, telling her, "Good *STAY*." If she budges before accomplishing the goal, correct her by taking your fingers and firmly tapping the middle of her chest. This generally gives a dog the idea to stop moving forward. Have her sit again, and repeat until she's still for just one second. You'll spend longer at this one-foot, one-second mark than at any other position because at this point your dog knows nothing about the command. Be patient and it will get easier as she figures out what you want.

A TIP FOR TOUGH CASES

If your dog struggles to make the connection at this first phase between your command and staying in place, there's an easy trick you can use to help her stay focused. All you need to introduce an extra measure of control is a chair. Place it in your training corner, and put your dog *on* it in a *SIT*. Obviously, if you've got a Great Dane or a rottweiler, this tip is not for you, but for most small, medium, and moderately large dogs, it works well. Adding a little height to her position encourages a dog to stop and think before making a move, and that will give you the extra edge you need to teach her the meaning of *STAY*. If necessary, the chair can move with your dog throughout the training of this command, right up until Step 6. At the end of the process, you may need to provide your dog with a quick review at ground level to ensure she doesn't make a distinction between a *STAY* up high and one on the floor.

Step 3. Next, you're going to back away another foot, making your distance from your dog two feet. This time you're going to tell her to *STAY* and wait for two seconds—so you're doubling both your distance from your dog and the amount of time you expect her to obey. I know it doesn't sound like much—being still for *two whole seconds*—but this gradual adjustment to the command is key. When your dog obeys, pet, praise, and reward her again. If she tries to move or take off, use your hands again to stop her. Typically a light tap to the chest stops a dog in her tracks. Start back at *SIT*, and repeat the process till you get that two seconds.

Step 4. Now it's time to try three feet for three seconds. As you get in position for this, you're going to be opening up gaps on either side of you that are just big enough for your dog to slip through, so we're going to make a slight change as we repeat Step 2. Hold both of your hands a little lower, so you're ready to stop your dog if she decides to bolt. The way you stop a runaway is important. I want you to keep your hand held out for a *STAY*, but if your dog takes off, use it to block her, pushing forward so she bumps right into your "stop sign" while you repeat the *STAY* command in a firm voice. Stiffen your fingers as you do this so your dog realizes she has hit a physical block. That will refocus her attention to you. This move serves the same kind of function as a gate lowering at the entrance of a parking lot. You may know you can drive through it, but you don't. You stop because there's something in the road ahead. Your dog will do the same thing when you block her path.

When your dog stays for three seconds, pet, praise, and reward her. If she budges, quickly use your hand to block the gap again while speaking a firm *STAY*. This is the point at which your dog will likely start figuring out what you're talking about. Once she masters this step, move on to four feet for four seconds, rewarding when your dog doesn't move and correcting when she does. Make sure to use your hands like a goalie to block your dog if needed, and move on only when she's mastered a distance with the corresponding time.

Step 5. When your dog can consistently and easily *STAY* on command in the corner for ten seconds at ten feet away, it's time to move on to the next big test. It may take a few days to reach this milestone, and that's okay. This is not the easiest command to learn, and it's much more important to focus on getting it right than on getting it quickly. When your dog is ready to move on, you're going to take her out of the corner and position her with a wall at her back. Choose a spot where there's plenty of wall space on each side of your dog—at least a few feet—and put her in a *SIT.* Your dog has a lot more paths of escape in this arrangement, so only open those up to her if she's proved she can be trusted to *STAY* in the corner.

From here, pick up where you left off, ensuring your dog is sitting with her butt against the wall, signaling and speaking a *STAY* command, and starting at the shortest distance and shortest time: one foot away for one second. Remember to use your hands like a goalie as you do this, prepared to stop a runaway with your hand in the *STAY* position. Most dogs who've already mastered this command in the corner won't challenge those hands. For those who do challenge, you'll once again stop them in place with your fingers.

Repeat the same pattern you followed in the corner *STAY*: two feet for two seconds, three feet for three seconds, and so on. After four feet, you're going to rely heavily on your voice to stop your dog because your hands will no longer be able to reach to do the job. Just in case you need something extra to keep your dog's focus, a good hard stomp of your foot is a great way to bring her to a halt. It will startle her for just a split second—long enough to remind her of what she's supposed to be doing.

Once your dog has mastered the cornered *STAY,*
place her against a wall and put her in a *SIT.* Then begin the
steps again, slowly increasing the distance and the time.

Be prepared to use your fingers to block your dog if she tries
to take off. A light tap to the chest is all that's needed.

Step 6. Once your dog has mastered the *STAY* against the wall, it's time for the final step. Bring her out into the middle of an open area. Away from all barriers, her options for getting away will be unlimited. And this is where you're going to find out if she truly understands and accepts the command. Repeat Steps 2

The final step: training the *STAY* in an open area.

and 3, moving on as your dog successfully obeys at one foot, two feet, and so on. Use that foot stomp if necessary to refocus her attention. At this point, all the conditioning you've already done should pay off, and your dog should *STAY* each time she's asked. If she doesn't, that doesn't mean she can't learn this command; it just means you moved too soon. Go back to the corner and review until your dog has got it.

Every minute you put into training this command is worth it because it's a critical tool to use to keep your dog safe.

Training Tips to Remember

As always, training is in the details, and there's a lot to point out with this method.

Start with a Tired and Hungry Pupil. If your dog is hyper with a ton of energy when you start teaching this command, she's going to be running around like a maniac, you're going to be frustrated—and the whole process will be hard on both of you. Instead, it's always a good idea to teach the *STAY* command when your dog is tired. That way she'll be less likely to run and she'll condition much faster. After a walk or at night is an ideal time to start working on this command. Also remember that training a hungry dog is always easier than training one who is full. You want your dog's attention to be focused on you and the great treats you'll be willing to share if she follows the command when you give it.

Keep Calm. Just like when you're teaching the *DOWN* command, you want to stay very steady and calm while you teach the *STAY*. If your body language and voice are animated or excited, your dog will pick up on that and get animated and excited, too—a bad recipe for teaching her to be still. When you praise and reward her, do so with a soft, positive voice and use slow, smooth strokes when you pet your dog. Remember, the face you show your dog is the face that's shown back to you, so if you have a lot of energy and anxiety while training, your dog might, too.

Block Carefully. The hand halt needs to be done correctly. I don't want you to slam your fingers into your dog's chest—and I know you don't want to do that, either. I want your dog to run into your fingers. There's big difference. Your hand should be like a fence standing in your dog's way—not something that's charging at her. Once your dog bumps into your hand, she's not likely to do it again. Think of it this way: no creature wants to keep running into the same obstacle over and over again, but there are many—including most dogs—who love a good chase. Be an obstacle, not a pursuer. For larger dogs it might be better to simply block their path by stepping into it. In that case, your whole body is a better block than just your hands. The only drawback with this is that it takes a little bit longer to move your whole body than to raise your hand, and you must get in position in time. Focus on being speedy and your dog will quickly figure out what you're up to.

About That Stomp. A foot stomp is a great way to stop your dog if she decides to move when you're a significant distance away. This gets her attention just for a split second so you can get her mind back on you. I strongly advise you to use this tool—it's one of my favorite ways to stop a dog in motion.

Take It Slow. I know you hear me say this a lot, but I only repeat it because it's important: do not move on to a next step in this process *until your dog is ready*! Moving too quickly is the main reason people get frustrated and eventually fail at teaching this vital command. You may see really quick progress in the first few minutes and figure you can skip a few feet or seconds and go for the gold.

Please don't. It takes a few days to train this technique correctly, and *very* few dogs ever get to the final step on day one. Take it slow and your dog will learn to *STAY* like a pro.

Variation for Tough Cases. Instead of using a corner, place your dog on a *SIT* in the doorway of a dark room (so the lights are out behind her). Naturally, your dog will want to leave, but you will be blocking the doorway and giving the *STAY* command. Using the same process as above, back up by one foot and add one second at intervals until you're at ten feet for ten seconds. Do a few fifteen-minute sessions each day of this and you'll see results. The pros of this method are that it's fast and simple and works with all dog sizes. The cons are that any technique that's as fast as this cuts corners and can result in a sloppy *STAY*. This method teaches the absolute basics, but you'll still need to bring your dog out in the open eventually to help her become more advanced and reliable.

Variation for Slow Starters. Place your dog on a couch. Have her *SIT*, and then follow the steps above, backing up and adding a second for every foot. This one is a home run because most dogs prefer to be on a comfy couch rather than on a hard floor. Pros: It's fast and simple, and the couch gives you a lot of control. Cons: This teaches a kindergarten version of *STAY*. It works to convey the absolute basics, but I highly recommend moving on to the cornering technique once your dog has mastered this.

Teacher's Pet

For Darby, learning the *STAY* involved mastering all the steps of the cornered *STAY* and then some. Before I could allow her to take her certified therapy dog test, she had to prove she could obey the *STAY* command under any circumstance: in different places, for long periods of time, and without becoming unsettled by any distraction. Darby showed me she could do it all. When I finally took her to her new owner's school to make the adoption official, they bonded immediately. Sarah crouched down in her classroom, and Darby scooted up close, stood on her haunches, and gently put one paw around each of her new owner's shoulders, resting her head on Sarah's shoulder. It was a classic boxer move—their own distinct and loving kind of hug—and at that moment everyone in the room understood that this sweet dog and this kind, generous teacher were going to be a perfect match.

7

NO

I f there's one word you'll be saying more than any other when you get a new dog, it's *NO*. It's only natural for any newcomer not to know your house rules. A rescue will come from an environment with a completely different set of rules or none at all. And a puppy—a puppy will come to you knowing absolutely nothing. Regardless of where your dog comes from, though, teaching him the *NO* command is a vital tool in stopping unwanted behavior like chewing, excessive barking, or any mischievous behavior a young (or old) dog might get into.

Teaching the *NO* is also a matter of safety. One of the safeguards I rely on this command for is keeping dogs from scarfing up "treasures" they find during walks. Anything your dog is picking up from the sidewalk or bushes while you're out is probably not loaded with vitamins and minerals—and many found items can be dangerous to his health. Plus, if you've ever had to pry a dead bird, toad, or squirrel from your dog's jaws, you know it can feel like a pretty unhealthy situation for you as well.

Another place where *NO* helps keep your dog safe is in the

kitchen. Lots of foods that are safe for people are harmful—even potentially toxic—to dogs. Common foods like onions, chocolate, chicken bones, grapes, some kinds of nuts, and coffee are all bad news for dogs. Your best tool to keep your dog safe from toxins is the *NO* command. Any dog can learn this command, even one with no previous training and a ridiculously strong food drive. I know because I had to put in overtime to teach the *NO* to a dog I trained for a family member who means the world to me.

Meet Poppi. *Poppi was a special dog for me. I adopted him for my aunt, who was holding my own dog Lulu "hostage" until I found her a replacement. This three-year-old cocker spaniel seemed like an ideal candidate. He'd been overlooked at the shelter, probably because he was missing half of one of his ears—at some point in his life it had been badly injured or infected and he'd lost it. A lot of people see a dog like Poppi in a shelter and only see what's wrong with him, overlooking more important qualities like personality and temperament. As soon as I met him, though, I could see that Poppi had these two most important assets in spades. He was a joyful dog with a tail nub that never stopped wagging. He had this great goofball expression—somehow sweet and nerdy at the same time. And he had a big tuft of hair that stuck up on the back of his head,*

making him look like he just might be wearing a toupee. It added yet another facet to his sweet, comical character.

Poppi started his training with no understanding of any of the 7 Common Commands, but because he was incredibly motivated by food and eager to please, he was a quick study. The only problem was that Poppi was so food motivated, he quickly showed me he could strike at any fallen food with the speed of a rattlesnake. He was always hungry, and always looking for any morsel he might be able to beg or steal. My aunt is a great cook who loves to prepare gourmet meals in the kitchen and on the grill. But a lot of the ingredients in her kitchen—and in most kitchens—could harm a dog. Before I could even think about handing Poppi over to my aunt, I had to teach him a 100 percent reliable NO command. Otherwise, I might never get Lulu back!

Teaching the *NO*

If trained effectively, a reliable *NO* can make life easier for you and your dog. Some people use the command *LEAVE IT* instead, which is fine, but personally I prefer *NO*. As always, there are many ways to train a command, but this is the one that works best for most dogs. The only tool you need to teach this technique is treats. Have handy several different kinds that your dog loves, and be sure he's hungry.

Step 1. Hold one of those favorite treats flat out in your hand at eye level and about six inches from your dog's mouth, and say the word *NO* right away. Unless the dog cares nothing about the treat, he'll naturally try to take it. When this happens, simply say the word *NO*, then quickly close your hand into a fist with the treat still inside. Be sure you deliver your *NO* command with a little conviction. You don't want to yell, but you want to make the point with your tone that this is not a game or a negotiation. A lot of dogs will keep trying to mouth the treat in your closed hand. Most will stop after a few seconds. If your dog does not stop, simply pull your hand away and give him a few seconds to reset and calm down.

Hold a treat six inches from your dog's mouth and say *NO*. If he lunges for it, say the word *NO*, then quickly close your hand.

Step 2. Once your dog is calm, place your open hand with the treat at his eye level again, about six inches from his mouth. When he goes for the treat, close your hand into a fist again, saying *NO*. Repeat this process five times, then stop for five minutes. The five-times, five-minute-break routine is a single session for training this command. It's very important to train in short sessions so your dog's brain can have a little time to process this concept. Most dogs need five to ten sessions over the course of a day or two to grasp it.

Step 3. As your dog progresses, he'll stop lunging and mouthing at your hand. At that point you can repeat the same steps with your palm open, using the *NO* command to control your dog. But keep sharp because some dogs can be sneaky when they have their eyes on the prize. When your dog can be trusted to respect the *NO* command with your open hand, he's ready for the real test. Place the treat on the ground between the two of you and say *NO*. When your dog no longer seems tempted to lunge out and take that treat, you've taught him the command.

When your dog respects the *NO* with the treat in your open hand, place the treat on the ground between you for the real test.

Step 4. Now that your dog has the *NO* at point-blank range, it's time to teach the command from a distance. Picking up from the end of Step 3, place a treat down in front of your dog, say a firm *NO*, and then back off. Be sure to back up only a foot for the first few seconds. Feel your dog out from that distance, and if you don't see him going for the treat, then move another couple of feet back.

You're going to keep moving back while saying *NO* until you hit ten feet. From there you'll slowly move back until you're right next to your dog again.

Step 5. Once your dog has grasped the concept of *NO*, you get to teach him something he'll like better: *OKAY*. This is the flip side of *NO*; *OKAY* gives your dog permission to take the treat. Move on to this only when your dog has learned to respect *NO* and its meaning. Once he's restrained himself for the *NO* correctly several times, simply say the word *OKAY* and put the treat right up to his mouth. This process teaches basic manners and respect. *NO* means *NO*, and it's nonnegotiable. *OKAY* means, "Go ahead. I give you permission." The beauty of teaching this command is that your dog will eventually understand it enough to look to you when a situation comes up where he's not clear on what's allowed. At that point, you can give him either a *NO* or an *OKAY* to help him sort it out. This command translates to many areas of your dog's life and far beyond just the kitchen.

Training Tips to Remember

Be Speedy. It's important to be quick on the draw when closing your hand. If you allow your dog to grab that food away too many times while training, you'll be teaching him he can beat you at this game, and he may even start challenging you in other areas of training. This is the last thing any dog owner needs. If you notice your dog is too quick for you the first couple of times, hold your hand a little farther back when holding that treat out. A foot should be plenty.

Use Noise as a Distraction. When you start placing the treat on the ground, your dog may be sorely tempted to go ahead and snatch it away. A good way to refocus his attention on you and the *NO* command you've given is to slap the ground right next to the treat with your hand if he starts to move toward it. The movement and the sound of your hand will momentarily break your dog's focus on the treat and help him resist temptation. A penny bottle or a Shake & Break works very well as a noise distraction, too. If you're struggling to maintain control as you start teaching this command and aren't getting the response you want with just a slap, try utilizing a noisier alternative.

Break Out the Leash. For dogs who are really stubborn about learning this technique, continuously going after the treat without heeding your *NO* command, put them on a leash and use it to cor-

Use a leash to correct a dog who continues to lunge forward.

rect them as they lunge forward. You'll accomplish this by holding the treat in one hand up close to your body and extending your other hand to hold the leash behind your dog's head. This will stop even the most difficult pups with this problem. Remember: You need to win at this game more than your dog does. This is how the command is set in stone. As soon as your dog realizes he is on the losing side of the game and that you will offer up that treat only when the *NO* command has been respected and you've given a clear *OKAY*, he won't challenge you on the issue anymore.

Variation for Tough Cases. If your dog is challenging you on this command, you can take my tip about using a leash one step further. In this case, you're going to "ground" your dog while you teach the *NO*. Simply loop a leash around a leg of a heavy table or sofa and attach it to your dog's collar. Place him so the leash is taut behind him and he's facing you. Next, place a treat on the floor just out of reach of his snout (about six inches away) and firmly say the word *NO*. Your dog is probably going to struggle and lunge to get the treat, but you won't have to hold him back—the leash tied off behind him will do it for you. As your dog tries to get the treat, repeat the word *NO* every few seconds until he calms down and stops struggling. When he does settle, wait three *full* seconds (start at zero and don't count fast!), then praise, give him the treat, and tell him *OKAY*. Repeat this process, adding one second each time. Remember to say the word *NO* right as you set the treat down and to keep it just out of your dog's reach. Also, remember to wait until your dog *completely* stops struggling before starting your count. After a few days when you feel he's ready, simply unhook the leash from the collar and repeat the steps. If he goes for the treat right away without respecting the *NO* command, then it's too soon. If he respects the command and waits for you to give the *OKAY*, then he's mastered the *NO*. This variation often works for the dogs who are a little too unruly to grasp my first technique.

**For a tough case, "ground" your dog while teaching *NO*
by attaching his leash to the leg of a heavy table or chair.**

Variation for Really Tough Cases. Follow the same steps in
"Variation for Tough Cases" above, but add a penny bottle or a
Shake & Break to the process. If your dog lunges for the treat, say
NO, shake the bottle, and say *NO* again. The bottle will help make
your point and train this skill.

One Final Note. It's important to remember that the *NO* command is only effective when you say it. It's possible that this
command may discourage your dog from engaging in a specific
behavior if you use it consistently and over time—in other words,
that it may sink in that a particular action is not acceptable. In
general, though, the *NO* can't be relied on to stop your dog from
engaging in unwanted behaviors when you're not around to give
the command. For that, you'll have to work on each behavior,
teaching your dog that it is not acceptable and then making sure
he knows the rules apply even when you're out of sight. You'll find
a number of examples of how to do this in Part Three a little later
in the book.

It might take a few days of consistent training to get this command down, but your dog will get there. I've done this with thousands of dogs over the years, and I've never met one who couldn't figure it out. That said, I've definitely seen a few dogs take longer than others. If your dog is slow to grasp the *NO*, just stick to it.

Welcome to the Family

When I'd taught Poppi all of the 7 Common Commands—including that *NO* he'd resisted at first—I was able to deliver him to my aunt Patti. She took one look at the one-eared cocker spaniel that had been passed up at the shelter by so many potential forever families, and she saw just what I had seen: a perfect dog. Patti put her arms around Poppi and said, "Look at you—you're *gorgeous*!" Ever since, he's been a part of the family.

In case you were wondering, my aunt liked Poppi so much that she finally let me have my dog back that day, too. Lulu came home with me. There are always lots of dogs in my life, but things just hadn't been the same around the ranch without her there.

8

OFF

Jumping up on people is one of dogs' most common—and most offensive—bad habits. Not only can a jumping dog mess up clean clothes or scare friends and visitors who are animal shy, but she can also trip, scratch, knock down, or even unintentionally injure someone. Every dog with this bad habit needs to learn the *OFF* command. Once your dog understands that jumping up on people is a bad idea, you'll still want to keep the *OFF* command fresh in your arsenal because it serves the dual function of getting your pup off the furniture, too. You'll most likely be using this command just about every day.

Now I know most of us swear we *never* allow our dogs on the furniture, but I also know many of us bend the rules in this area. I'm right there with you. I'm not one of those trainers who feels the need to be vigilant about keeping my dogs on the floor. As far as I'm concerned, my house is their house, too—even if they're only living with me for a little while during training. I'm especially soft on the furniture policy because many of the dogs who stay with me are rescues, and they've just come from a place where a cold concrete floor was home. I want them to feel safe and comfortable with me—to be able to trust that their lives are going to be better.

There are very few things I can do that convey that message as easily as letting a dog sit beside me on the sofa and putting my arm around her. To that end, my rules are simple: as long as a dog isn't possessive or aggressive of the furniture, that dog is welcome on the couch or bed anytime. To cut down on the shedding problem, I designate one area as dog friendly with a blanket that doubles as a fur magnet. When I want to make it even easier for a new dog to know she's okay, I put a dog bed right on the sofa. That way the newcomer knows she's definitely allowed to lie in that area.

My Lulu sleeps on just about every bed, sofa, chair, and chaise in the house—I think she likes to enjoy them all in turn. If I need her to move, though, I just tell her *OFF* and she clears out. It's an easy command to keep her in check if I have company or need the space she's using. Of course, it's not that easy with every dog—like the seven-month-old puppy I rescued a while back who quickly showed me she needed to learn the *OFF* more urgently than any other command.

Meet Jemma. *When I met Jemma in the shelter, she was one sad puppy—a shepherd mix with downcast eyes who retreated to the corner of her kennel when she saw me coming. Jemma and a sibling had been rescued together, but the dog who had been her companion since the day she was born had been adopted, and now this girl was in the shelter alone.*

When I walked her outside, Jemma put the brakes on at the end of the sidewalk, freezing in place and bracing herself, most likely from fear of where she might be going next. Getting her into my truck was a challenge because even though she was a puppy, she was a big puppy, and she slumped down like dead weight to avoid getting in. Back at the ranch, it was more of the same. Jemma wouldn't even pick her head up to look out the window, and I had to lift her out of the truck and put her on the ground. I figured she'd need a few days to get settled in before we could start training. Whether she was suffering from grief over the loss of her littermate or shelter shock—or both—she needed some time and space to process everything she'd been through.

As it turned out, all it took was one night to turn this sad dog around. In the morning, the timid animal I'd had to carry away from the shelter had been replaced by a puppy with a completely different personality. Jemma made the fastest recovery from down-and-out to party animal I've ever seen. She was jumping all over the furniture—not just couches and beds, but coffee tables and nightstands and piano, too. If she had feet like a lizard, I think she would've climbed the walls. And Jemma's wild antics didn't stop at the furniture—she jumped all over me and everyone else at the Lucky Dog Ranch. That was when I knew for sure that not only did this dog have no training in her history—she also had zero manners. In order to start making her adoptable—and to save my furniture—I needed to teach her the OFF command, stat.

Teaching the *OFF*

Since this is a multipurpose command, I'm going to give you techniques specialized for various situations: jumping on you, jumping on other people, and jumping on furniture. There are countless techniques and methods to teach the *OFF*, and a wide range of responses to them among different dogs. As a result, it sometimes takes a few tries to find the right one for a particular animal. None of the techniques I use are very time-consuming, so I'm going to list them from the simplest to the most complex. Always keep in mind that where one method fails, another one prevails. If one doesn't work for you, move right on to the next. I'm certain one of them will be successful.

One of the easiest techniques to discourage jumping is to turn your back.

Teaching *OFF* for Jumping on You

Technique 1

Turn Your Back. This is the easiest technique to discourage jumping up, but it doesn't work on every dog. The only way to find out is to give it a try—and if it doesn't work, move on to the methods below that require a little more time and effort. It doesn't get any easier than this.

Wait for your dog to jump up on you—if she's a frequent jumper, you won't have to wait long. The instant she jumps up, say the word *OFF* in your firmest voice and turn your back. Have no further interaction. The second the command is given in a cut-it-out voice and attention is withdrawn, many dogs go back down on all fours. Repeat again and again over a few days, and most dogs who are motivated by the attention they receive from jumping will simply give up the habit because they stop getting what they want.

Technique 2

Hold Those Paws. Grabbing a dog's paws and holding them for about thirty seconds after each jump is a technique I've found over the years to be effective for teaching *OFF* to many dogs. Unfortunately, it only works on large and medium-size dogs, so if you have a pint-size jumper, skip ahead to the next technique instead. Like many effective training methods, this one relies on reverse psychology. Just as a human with a bad habit can sometimes be persuaded to change behavior by getting too much of a "good" thing, reverse psychology tends to work on dogs because the fun habit they love starts to get annoying.

Let's break this down. When your dog jumps up on you, I want you to grab her paws, hold them, and give the *OFF* command.

Now brace yourself, because here's what's likely to happen: After a few seconds your dog is going to try to pull away. Do not allow that; this is vital to the command. I want you to keep repeating the word *OFF* every couple of seconds, embedding it in your dog's mind while you stand toe-to-toe in this awkward position.

Holding your dog's paws is another effective *OFF* technique.

In addition to pulling away, some dogs may have temper tantrums or cry when you use this technique. Don't give in. You are not injuring your dog by holding her paws, I promise. You are only going to hold this position for a matter of seconds—but in the process you are taking away your dog's control, and she's not going to like it. I've even seen dogs who try to nip at my hands while I'm holding their paws to teach this command. What's going on in this very important thirty seconds or so is on par with a toddler's temper tantrum. Your dog is like a two-year-old throwing a fit over the "right" to pull her brother's hair or not wear a seat belt. You can't give in on that kind of thing, and you can't give in to your jumping dog, either. This is a potentially dangerous habit, and you can break it if you just stick to the plan.

So hold on and keep repeating *OFF*. While you're holding your dog's paws, her young, inexperienced mind will be processing the situation and figuring it out. It takes a little time—usually twenty to forty seconds. After that, your dog will calm down. The tantrum will stop, and she will be standing on her hind legs looking at you and hearing the word *OFF* repeated over and over in your calm, firm voice. Once your dog is completely settled and not resisting, wait just three more seconds, say *OFF* one last time, and then let her paws go. That's all there is to this reverse-psychology technique. Your dog might jump on you again after a few minutes, testing the waters—and that's normal. Just go through the lesson again. Most likely your dog won't jump a third time. Suddenly, jumping up will have lost its appeal.

Technique 3

Use a Penny Bottle or a Shake & Break. This technique is great for super stubborn dogs. People who know me and watch my show know that I swear by these simple yet incredibly effective tools. The penny bottle and the Shake & Break are basically universal correctors that can be used to help solve almost any behavior problem. These simple training tools are among the easiest ways to bring jumping to a halt. This is how it works: With the bottle in hand (preferably hidden behind your back), wait for your dog to jump up. When she does, give a firm *OFF* followed by a shake of the bottle, then another *OFF* command. The sound of the clanging

For a stubborn dog, use a penny bottle or a Shake & Break.

metal will startle your dog, and she'll get down. Repeat this process as needed. Like the paw-holding method, most dogs don't challenge this one too many times before grasping it for good. Throughout your week of training, you'll need to utilize the bottle—always pairing it with the word *OFF*—less and less until your dog responds to just the command without the jarring, unpleasant noise. By the end of the week, the bottle should be eliminated altogether and your dog should be responding to your verbal command alone.

Teaching *OFF* for Jumping on Other People

Technique 1

Use a Penny Bottle or a Shake & Break. With the bottle in hand, wait for your dog to jump up on someone else. When she does it, give a firm *OFF* followed by a shake of the bottle, then another *OFF* command. Make sure you're close to your dog (a foot or two away). The sound of the rattling metal will startle your dog, and she'll get down on all fours in response. Encourage the person your dog is jumping on to say a firm *OFF* as well.

Technique 2

Correct with a Leash. They may not be able to understand hard science, but most dogs understand simple physics enough to know that when a leash gets pulled one way, it's better to go with it than to fight against. If your dog is generally cooperative on-leash, this method may be the easiest for her to learn. It works best with dogs who weigh twenty-five pounds or more. If you know you're going to have visitors, attach a leash to your dog's collar before anyone arrives. With the leash in hand, wait for her to jump up. When she does, say the word *OFF*, then pull the leash straight down or down and to the side. Timing is everything here. Correcting your dog right as she's about to jump is best. Correcting her after she's made it onto the person also works but not as well. So treat this like a game, and don't let the dog win.

Technique matters. Be sure your pull isn't too harsh but also not too light. To get it just right, choke up on the leash with your hand, then stiffen your arms in a downward motion. The idea is not to yank at your dog, but to stop her forward momentum and direct her away from her jump.

Say the word *OFF*, then pull the leash straight down or down and to the side to correct jumping on another person.

If you have a large dog and a simple pull isn't getting results, take the end of the leash, hold it firmly against your hip, and take a step back. That way your body weight is doing the pulling, not your arms. This is a basic collar correction and with enough conditioning most dogs learn from it. The drawback to this technique is that most dogs will grasp it with the leash on, but they may revert to their old bad habits when the leash comes off.

If you're not getting results with a large dog, hold the end of the leash firmly against your hip and step back.

Teaching *OFF* for Jumping on Furniture

As I mentioned, I don't enforce a no-dogs-on-the-couch policy. My home is my dog's home, too, so she can pretty much get comfortable wherever she wants. But when I have friends over and my seven-pound Chihuahua somehow manages to take up half the couch, then I expect her to get off on command. This is just the circumstance that makes the *OFF* useful on an everyday basis. It's fine to let your pets on the furniture, but when they don't want to budge so your grandma or your date can have a seat, there has to be a command for that. The process of teaching *OFF* in this context is so simple and effective that I'm only going to give you one technique to use. And that technique utilizes . . . drum roll, please . . . the penny bottle or Shake & Break! Please hold your applause until after you've used this quasimagical training tool to teach your dog to obey the *OFF*.

With your noisy training tool in hand (again, preferably behind your back), approach your dog while she is in the spot you want her out of—the couch, the bed, or if she's got bigger issues like Jemma did, the coffee table. Say *OFF*, give the bottle a one- to two-second shake, then say the command one more time. Very few dogs remain in place after this. They just don't like those jarring sounds. For the ones who stand their ground, repeat the process until they move at your request. Even the most stubborn dogs eventually move because the sound of rattling metal is not exactly soothing. After a few times through this routine, your dog will learn to respond to the *OFF* command without a noisy reminder. It's that simple—so simple I've actually given this advice via e-mail to dog owners all over the world. More often than not, I get an e-mail back within a matter of days raving about the results. A few enthusiastic owners have even joked about how the technique worked so well on the dog, they're going to try it on a spouse next! I do *not* recommend that.

OFF the Furniture and on to a New Home

Once Jemma learned the *OFF* command—as it applies to jumping on people and on furniture—she was ready to go to her new home at a California bed-and-breakfast. Jemma's manners were great before she left me, but she was going on to study advanced B&B etiquette with the elderly mascot dog already in residence in her new home. I'm sure she has a long, thriving career ahead of her in the business of making guests feel welcome and at home.

Outtake

About ten years ago, I had a client with a yellow Lab named Jack. Jack had a terrible jumping habit. We worked on the problem for days at the client's house, and he mastered the art of staying *OFF* there, but his owner said she was still having trouble with him out in public. In order to work on the issue at the "scene of the crime," I met them at a local dog park. Sure enough, within minutes Jack had walked up to a stranger and jumped on him.

I told my client to say *OFF*, but Jack just kept romping around, jumping wherever he wanted. That's when I was finally able to pinpoint the problem: Out in public, surrounded by people and dogs, Jack was getting a lot of sensory input. He was hearing all kinds of voices, and even a lot of commands because a dog park is full of people telling their dogs what to do and what not to do. Jack's owner's voice was getting lost in the activity and noise of the place. I told my client to raise her voice, first saying her dog's name, and then following it up with the command. So in a loud, assertive voice, she followed my instructions, saying *OFF* over and over as she followed Jack around the park. As the scene unfolded, I realized that this dog's name and the *OFF* command wasn't the most family-friendly combination, but the owner carried on in the name of finally gaining some control over this bad habit. The good news is Jack did listen, and he's been a pro at obeying the *OFF* command ever since.

9

COME

The *COME* command is not only a cornerstone of obedience training; it can also be a lifesaver. I've lost count of how many times I've seen people hiking in the hills around Los Angeles, yelling at the top of their lungs for their dogs to come back. Meanwhile those "lost" dogs are just trotting along . . . in the opposite direction, oblivious to the fact they're being called back *and* to any dangers that might lie ahead. That scenario is a recipe for disaster. Whether the threats in your community are traffic, snakes, coyotes, other dogs, or something else entirely, your dog needs the skill professional dog trainers refer to as *recall*—what most of us know as the *COME* command.

This command can be one of the most challenging to teach, especially if you're working with a puppy. After all, puppies are basically as loyal as their options. A young dog's mind works like a perfectly timed clock: every ten seconds it resets and is on to the next best thing. This makes it tough to teach a command that requires more than a little bit of focus from a young dog. Despite its challenges, though, I have a method for teaching the *COME* command that works on dogs of all ages and sizes. I've used it to train dogs of all different breeds, too, including a golden corgi I found in a local shelter who had to demonstrate near-perfect recall before I could let her go to her new home.

Meet Leah. *Leah was a one-year-old golden retriever–corgi mix, a beautiful dog. She'd ended up in a shelter after being found on the street, and despite being a mix of two popular breeds, that was where she stayed. No one came to pick her up, she didn't have a microchip to help the shelter track down an owner, and no one chose her for adoption. After a while, the shelter manager called me.*

In Leah's kennel, the first thing I noticed was her calm, friendly demeanor; she curled right up to me when I sat down. I knew then she was going to make a great pet for some lucky family. The second thing I noticed was that Leah was covered in fleas and ticks, and her skin was red and raw. I wondered, for about the millionth time in my life so far, who could neglect a dog like this, and then I filled out the paperwork to take Leah home.

Back at the ranch, Leah's tail wagged constantly, and she seemed determined to show she was a devoted, good dog at any cost. In her assessment, she did well with SIT *and* DOWN, *and she picked up* COME *pretty quickly. But the home I'd found for her was with a family who wanted to be able to take their dog hiking—*

off-leash. This mom and dad already had two young boys to keep track of, and the last thing they needed was a dog who couldn't be counted on to stick with them when she was called.

Not every dog is meant to be an off-leash dog. Every now and then I have to make a decision about whether one of my rescues is fit to take on this role. It's an important decision because I invest a lot of myself in these dogs, and I never want to make any of them vulnerable to getting lost or injured by giving the okay for off-leash activities if they can't handle that much freedom. Just because a dog has a recall doesn't mean she'll be reliable in every situation. Leah was on the cusp. She was great at responding to the COME command in the training barn, but in the yard outside she had a bit of a wandering eye. That raised a red flag for me about whether she'd be reliable on a hike with no fences and unlimited distractions.

I wanted to believe the forever home I'd chosen for Leah would work out, but before I could entrust her to the loving family she had waiting, she'd have to prove to me she could obey the COME command at any time, in any place, and despite any distraction . . . and the world is chock-full of distractions for a dog.

Teaching the COME

The technique I'm sharing here is one I devised and have used on hundreds of dogs over the years. We're going to start small—in the same room with your dog—and work up to teaching the COME command at greater distances. The tools you'll need:

- A twenty-five-foot leash
- A harness
- A clicker
- A variety of treats your dog really likes

You can find a quick refresher on using the clicker in Chapter 3, if needed. If your dog is out of practice with this training tool, you can get her reacquainted with the habit of responding to it in a few short sessions. This is the easiest lesson you'll ever teach. Simply take a handful of treats and give them to your dog one at a time, clicking before giving each one so she learns to associate the *click* sound with good rewards.

In most cases, the 7 Common Commands can be taught in any order, although it makes sense to start at the beginning with the *SIT* for most dogs and work your way through the commands in the order I've given them here. However, teaching the *COME* command is most effectively done if your dog already has a good understanding of *STAY*. For that reason, if you haven't taught the *STAY* yet, I recommend going back to Chapter 6 and helping your dog learn that skill before this one. Taking that preliminary step will help both you and your dog master this command more quickly and easily. Now that you're geared up, let's break this down.

Step 1. With treats in your training bag or pocket and the long leash hanging loose from your dog's harness, start in a single room where your dog has a little space to roam but not so much that she can get more than a few feet away from you or out of sight. This should be a distraction-free zone, with no other dogs or people, no toys, and no other activity going on. You want to set your dog up for success so her first association with the command is an easy one to make. When your dog is a few feet away, say the command *COME* in a cheerful voice (you can even clap your hands), and watch what she does. If she turns and looks at you, click the clicker. If she walks toward you, click again. If she comes all the way to you, click, praise, and give her a reward, telling her "Good *COME!*"

In one room with treats at the ready, this should go pretty easily. If your dog does not turn toward you or come to you, though, you'll need to help her figure out what you want. If this happens, pick up the leash and give it one quick tug toward you, then drop it. Your tug should not be a hard jerk—its purpose is solely to change your dog's direction. The power of your tug should be relative to your dog's size; small dogs need very little tugging, but a larger breed may need a bit more. The tug will turn your dog in your direction, and as soon as that happens, click the clicker, give the *COME* command again, and then reward her when she gets to you. Repeat this step several times until you can see your dog make an association between the command and coming to you.

Owners of dogs who are highly motivated by rewards won't need long to figure out why the *STAY* command is a good one to have in their arsenal once they start teaching a dog to *COME*. When your dog knows you have treats or toys and that the way to get them is to come to you, you're going to find yourself with a *very* close companion. Many dogs choose this moment to become glued to their handlers' sides. Unfortunately, that sudden closeness can cut way down on your training efficiency. The fact is if you've got a fifteen-minute session planned and your dog spends twelve of those minutes trying to stay close to you to earn rewards, then you're not going to accomplish a whole lot of repetitions of the technique.

To streamline your sessions with a dog who's hovering at your side, put her in a *STAY* at the distances discussed in each step here, then give the *COME* command when you reach your desired distance away. That way your dog will get the full fifteen minutes' worth of work in each session—and you'll spend a lot less time teaching this command.

Step 2. Now that your dog has mastered the *COME* command when you're close-by, it's time to teach her to keep up the good work when you're a little farther away. For this step, leave that long leash attached to your dog's collar just in case you need to pull it or step on it. Keep the clicker in your hand and treats at the ready, but move to an area where your dog has the freedom to roam into the next room and out of your sight. A spot where she'll be around a corner from you is ideal, so you can peek at her but not be front and center. Once again, give the *COME* command in an upbeat voice. If she turns toward you, click. When she gets to you, click and give her a good reward.

If your dog doesn't come when you give the command, give her leash a tug again to get her going in the right direction and click as soon as she's turned your way. Repeat this step until your dog's response to *COME* is reliable from a room away.

Step 3. The next step in this exercise is where the length of that leash comes into play. You're going to repeat the same process as you did in Steps 1 and 2, but I want you to let your dog roam farther. Test her response to the *COME* command from different areas of the house—a room away, two rooms away, etc. Be sure you move from place to place, too, so your dog learns that the command means to come to you wherever you are—not just in the one place you're training. If she struggles with any distance or location, work from there using a tug on the leash to remind her to move toward you.

Step 4. Once your dog masters the *COME* command inside, it's time to take your training to the great outdoors. This is a critical part of training this command because if you ever *really* need your

It's okay to clap your hands for emphasis when training the *COME* command.

As soon as your dog turns and looks at you, click the clicker.

If she gets all the way to you, click, praise, and give her a reward.

dog to answer to *COME* for her safety, it'll likely be somewhere outside your home. Training outside is not the same as inside because even though you've controlled for distractions up until now, there will be things you can't control outdoors. That whole environment feels different to your dog.

Always train the *COME* command in an enclosed space—a fenced yard is a perfect spot. Once you're there, lay your dog's twenty-five-foot leash down and let her go. Chances are, she'll start wandering, looking for something to see or smell or do. When she gets about ten feet away, say her name, then say *COME* in a loud, cheerful voice (again, you can clap your hands for emphasis). As soon as your dog turns and looks at you, click the clicker. If she steps toward you, click again. And, finally, if she gets all the way to you, click, praise, and give her the reward.

Of course, it's not always *that* easy. Even if your dog has done well with the command indoors, she may be distracted by nature's temptations and not immediately head your way. If she doesn't, give the leash a tug to turn her momentum toward you. The second she starts changing direction, drop the leash and click. When she gets to you, click again, praise her, and give a reward. The clicker lets your dog know what she's doing right each step of the way, even as you start training at longer distances.

You're going to repeat this process over and over, letting your dog get another foot or two farther away each time. Eventually, when she has demonstrated that she understands the *COME* command and responds every time, you're going to let her wander past the entire length of the leash. This process needs lots of practice—plan to repeat it a couple times every day for a week.

Step 5. When your dog has the *COME* command down pat, you'll need to make sure it's set in stone before you can trust it in any open areas. To do this, I want you to add in some distractions. If you have another dog, let him join you. Have someone ring the doorbell. Enlist a friend to be in the yard so there's some competition for your dog's attention. Through it all, keep practicing the command.

If your dog passes all these steps and you want to see if she's capable of being reliable off-leash, you can move to a safe open space and start again on Step 4, keeping the long leash within reach as you train. Please know that not every dog is capable of being an off-leash pet. We'll discuss this in more detail in the "Training Tips to Remember" section below. The most important thing to recognize here is that if your gut tells you your dog is likely to bolt at the first big distraction, trust that instinct and stick to using a leash when you're in the field, woods, or park. Better safe than sorry.

Step 6. As your dog grasps the command better over a few days, start giving her fewer treats and more praise. This tapering down on how often you give rewards will keep her from becoming totally dependent on food to work. You don't want to train your dog to respond to commands only when you've got a handful of treats. So as your dog masters the command, you're going to switch from a one-action-one-reward system to a lottery system, where your dog gets rewarded sometimes, but not every time, for obeying. This way your dog will eagerly follow your commands, always wondering if this is the time she will earn a food reward.

Training Tips to Remember

Safety First. The supply list for this technique includes a harness. It's important to use one when training the *COME* command. A choke chain, pinch collar, martingale, or even a regular flat collar is not recommended for this technique. Any collar that lies directly on your dog's throat could pose a danger to her trachea if you have to pull the long lead when she's running in the opposite direction. This is a rare instance in which I recommend doing as I say and not as I do. If you watch *Lucky Dog*, you may have seen me teach this technique on dogs wearing martingale or flat collars. I've had decades of experience training dogs—enough to develop an expert sense of when to pull a leash and how much pressure to apply. When you're working with such a long leash and fewer years of experience, though, it would be all too easy to accidently overcorrect and injure your dog. To eliminate that possibility, I recommend sticking with a harness.

Start with the Fewest Possible Distractions. Using this technique to train any dog—*especially* a puppy—with a lot of distractions around is difficult. I recommend doing the first few days totally distraction-free. After that, you can start adding in distractive elements. This way you give your dog a chance to grasp the concept before taking her to the next level. You don't want that brain of hers working too fast because that's what can cause it to shut down. Slow and steady wins the race.

Make Yourself Look and Sound Inviting. When teaching a dog to *COME*, the last thing you want to do is use a stern voice. Dogs generally equate that with being in trouble—and most know better than to come running to receive a punishment. Use a light, inviting voice. If need be, you can kneel down while giving the command. I usually don't like doing that, but sometimes we need to use all the tools we have at our disposal in the early stages of training a command—and then make up for them later. As your dog learns to come through conditioning, slowly go back to your normal voice and give the command from a standing position. Remember: If your dog is not coming when called, never yell at her. If you turn the *COME* command into a negative thing, you may prevent your dog from wanting to learn it at all.

Food Is a Dog's Currency. Be sure your dog is hungry when you start to work. I highly recommend training this command at mealtimes so your dog is motivated to return to you. Training a dog who just ate is kind of like offering a minimum-wage job to a millionaire. Motivation drops dramatically once most dogs' bellies are full.

Keep in mind that when teaching the *COME* command, you're in competition with every squirrel, kid, sound, and smell around. Since food is money to a dog, have multiple denominations ready to compete with any distraction. This will keep your dog's attention squarely on you. Use your hottest bait only if absolutely needed. Also keep in mind when praising and rewarding that a longer recall deserves heavier praise and better rewards. If your dog successfully responds to the *COME* command at twenty feet, reward her at a level 5. If she responds at fifty feet, reward her at a level 10. Use your dog's absolute favorite treats only when she's performing at a top-notch level. In other words, if your dog is a bacon lover, give her a piece only if she comes to you when called from a far distance and through a ton of distractions.

And while we're on the subject of compensation, remember the lottery system we talked about in Chapter 3. As you taper down on how many rewards you give, it's still vital to reward the first and last successful effort your dog makes when learning any command. That first reward gets your dog's mind in gear to train. After that, you can randomly give rewards throughout the session, keeping your dog guessing about which time she's going to get the prize. At the end of the session, *always* give a reward. This leaves a good impression of the command and will make your dog eager and willing to work the next time you train. This is an important rule to follow because your eventual goal is to wean your dog off the treats so she won't be completely dependent on them.

Use Toys. Remember that your dog is a prey-driven animal, and toys are the best way to bring that instinct out in her. Toys are often a better training tool than food when training recall because they squeak and get the attention of your dog even when she's distracted—which makes them basically a distraction *from* a distraction. I like using both food and toys, but it's a trial-and-error process to find out what works best for the dog.

Don't Give Too Much Freedom. I want to make one thing very clear: not all dogs are meant to be off-leash dogs! I can't stress this strongly enough. This is the unknown with every dog I work with because I can't know if a dog will be good off-leash until I start training for it. Even a dog with a good *COME* command may not have a reliable recall in an open field—because that's where the rules change. As you train, you'll have to make the decision about whether your dog can be safe off-leash, and I urge you to err on the side of caution—anything short of 100 percent recall is not enough. Keep in mind that young puppies are rarely up to off-leash freedom. Any dog with a wandering eye who hasn't truly mastered bringing her focus to you on command is also a significant risk. Neither of these things means your dog won't ever learn this technique, but they do mean the open wilderness needs to stay off-limits for now.

The bottom line is that this final step of the recall command is advanced, and many dogs won't graduate to that stage ever, let alone in a week. Proceed with caution.

Right at Home

I trained Leah with a long leash for several days, and in the end she was able to show me she could be trusted 100 percent to return each time she heard the *COME* command. When she met her new family, Leah seemed to instinctively know that they were hers. We took her for a long walk in the hills so she could demonstrate her off-leash skills, and she ran alongside each of them in turn—Mom, Dad, and their two young boys. When I left her that day, Leah was curled up beside them, tired from her hike and secure in her forever home. To this day I get pics and videos of the family hiking together in the hills and feedback about how much responsibility the kids have learned through having a dog. Making a placement like that is my personal equivalent of hitting a home run.

10

HEEL

One of the joys of having a dog is taking walks together—unless your dog pulls your arm nearly out of its socket or trips you up every time you try. The *HEEL* command teaches a dog to walk beside you, matching your pace, without plowing ahead or lagging behind. I often meet dog owners who are so accustomed to push-me, pull-me walks they're not even sure if a side-by-side stroll is possible, but it is. Any dog can learn to *HEEL*.

If you have a small- or medium-size dog, the *HEEL* is a convenience and a fail-safe for keeping your dog beside you when you need him to be. But if you have a big dog, this command is an absolute necessity. There are few experiences more stressful than trying to walk a dog you can't handle. And too often, dogs who don't learn to *HEEL* end up not getting the exercise they need—which makes them all the more crazy when they do get put on the end of a leash. It's a vicious cycle that can lead to an out-of-control, pent-up dog and a frustrated, unhappy owner.

When I train a dog to work in a therapeutic setting or to be a service dog for a disabled veteran, I have to know he will *HEEL* every single time he's asked without fail. This was especially important for Sandy, a dog I rescued and trained to assist a brave young marine who lost both of his legs in an IED blast in Afghanistan. Back in the United States, he received prosthetics and began the long, difficult process of relearning to walk. A well-trained service dog had the potential to make his transition a little easier.

Meet Sandy. *In my line of work, I meet a lot of dogs who've been beaten down by their time in animal shelters. Many withdraw or become depressed. But when I met two-year-old Sandy in an LA shelter, my gut told me something very different had happened to this golden retriever during his stay. Sandy had been turned in after his owner passed away. This was a pedigreed dog who'd had a very easy life before his change of fortune. You could see it in his manner—he was out of shape, a little pampered, maybe even a little lazy. He'd been taken out of his Beverly Hills home and placed in a cell, and he didn't know why. Rather than causing him to psychologically retreat, though, Sandy's experience in the shelter seemed to have ignited a slow burn inside him. He had developed an edge, and he'd drawn on all the strength and fire he had within*

him to get through his ordeal. Instead of losing confidence, he seemed to have gained it. When he looked at me, I could see that this was a dog with drive.

Even though I hadn't even assessed his skills yet, I knew a dog with that unique quality would be eager to work and learn new things—it was all I needed to know to decide he was a potential candidate to train as a service dog. My gut told me Sandy was the dog I'd been waiting for—a dog to place in a very special forever home. Sandy's new owner would respect the inner strength hard times had brought out in this dog. Tim is a young man who was digging deep to overcome his own hardships.

I love training dogs and helping them find their forever homes, but training a dog like Sandy to be a service dog for a man like Tim—that's something I live for.

It was going to take a lot of work, but I knew that while Sandy and I were training in California, Tim would be working even harder on the other coast, learning to better balance and walk with his prosthetic legs and figuring out how to approach his new life as a disabled veteran.

Teaching the *HEEL*

The *HEEL* command is a must for every dog, but it can be one of the more frustrating commands to train, especially if you're a novice dog owner working with a big, powerful, or high-energy dog. I'm going to share two methods here—one that works best for big dogs and one that's better for smaller dogs. If you need extra guidance, you'll find a number of ways to customize it for your dog's unique challenges in the tips section at the end of the chapter.

Big-Dog Technique

First things first, you'll need:

- Some really attractive treats, and you'll need to train this command when your dog is hungry. Ideally, you want him to be hungry enough to be motivated, but not *so* hungry he's ravenous and unable to focus.
- A four- or six-foot leash

Step 1. Hold a treat in your right hand and position your dog on your left side. (You can swap sides if you like, but traditionally dogs are walked on the left.) The leash will be in your left hand coiled up so the dog has just a little slack. Hold the treat in your right fist with a closed hand about six inches from your dog's snout.

Hold a treat in your right hand and position your dog on your left side.

Step 2. Begin walking at a normal pace and say *HEEL*. Most dogs will naturally start jumping up and mouthing at that treat in your closed hand. This is completely normal, but your goal is to keep your hand closed and wait your dog out till he stops, so get ready to endure a little slobber for a good cause. Most dogs stop after ten seconds. Some take a little longer. Whatever the case, wait your dog out, and when he stops this behavior, he'll be walking perfectly for a few seconds before he starts jumping and mouthing again. The trick is in the timing; you need to praise and treat your dog during that short interval when he has stopped mouthing and is walking normally. Like most animals, dogs are trial-and-error creatures, so they'll quickly learn they get rewarded when they stop mouthing and walk at your speed. Do this over and over, and your dog will mouth less and walk normally for longer periods of time. Your goal is to add a couple of seconds of good walking behavior every time you have a training session.

Step 3. It won't be too hard for your dog to figure out that walking straight ahead alongside you is earning rewards, but a proper *HEEL* has to mean more than that. Your dog has to make the association between the command and sticking by your side no matter which way you go. In order to start teaching this more complex understanding of the command, start mixing up your walking pattern, turning left or right, doing an about-face, and moving in ways your dog can't predict. As you make a turn, hold that leash in your left hand close to your hip so your dog doesn't have a lot of wiggle room and give the *HEEL* command again. Your goal is to keep your dog moving at your left side as you go. Be patient. This is a complicated concept, but your dog will get it with steady practice.

Step 4. You don't want a dog who constantly requires food to do the things you want, so once your dog has gained an understanding of the command, it's time to start the process of weaning him away from getting a food reward every time. Here's how to do it: Start by going back to Step 1, but have a treat in your hand only eight of ten times. The two times you don't have a treat, heavily praise your dog and let him know what a good job he did. Always make sure that both the first and the final time in a session are paid with a treat. You do not want to end a session without giving a reward—that will leave a lasting impression with your dog and might impact his motivation level the next time you work with him. Your goal is to slowly use fewer treats over the course of a week until you eliminate them completely.

Step 5. In addition to weaning your dog from receiving a treat each time he correctly obeys the *HEEL*, you also need to help him adjust to heeling without your hand in front of his snout. Over the course of the week, begin moving your hand a little closer to a normal position each day. You started at about six inches from your dog's snout, so it'll take a few days to bring that right hand back to resting at your right side. Keep in mind, though, that your dog has been relying on that hand as a signal, so if he falters at all with the command, give him a little extra clarity and motivation by putting your hand back in front of him.

Small-Dog Technique

If you have a small dog, it's not practical or comfortable for you to be constantly bending down while teaching the *HEEL* command. And it's not effective, either, since you want your dog to be focused on the treat at first, so it needs to be close. To make things easier on both of you, you can use an inexpensive training tool called a lure stick. Long before I started using these sticks for dogs, I used them to train big cats like tigers for commercials and movies. A good rule of thumb in that kind of training is that you don't want to feed a tiger with your hand unless you don't mind losing it! Any tiger treat—think big cuts of red meat—goes on the end of a lure stick, and that keeps the trainer's hands a safe distance away.

When you use a lure stick for teaching the *HEEL* command, it'll bridge the gap between your hand and the dog's snout.

Step 1. Position your dog at your left side and hold his leash coiled in your left hand so there's just a little slack. Hold the lure stick in your right hand and attach a dog treat to the end.

Step 2. Now comes the tricky part. Start walking at a normal pace and hold that treat on the lure stick a few inches in front of and above your dog's snout, but *don't let him grab it.* If your dog lunges for the treat, lift it out of reach, pull back on the leash to stop him from lunging, and keep walking. Keep repeating. Eventually, your dog will end up just walking beside you—even if just for a few seconds—without lunging or jumping for the treat. At that moment, say "Good *HEEL*," and give him the reward. Do this repeatedly and your dog will soon figure out that he gets a reward when he stops jumping and walks at your pace. Once he grasps the concept, start waiting for another second or two each time before giving him the treat.

A lure stick is a useful, inexpensive tool for
teaching the *HEEL* command to a small dog.

Once your dog masters these first two steps, jump to Step 3 above and follow the remaining instructions for training this command. At the last step, you'll be phasing out the lure stick instead of just readjusting your hand position, but the logistics are just the same.

Training Tips to Remember

Narrow the Options. If your dog has a hard time grasping the *HEEL* command, make it easier for him by giving him fewer prospects for roaming. At the Lucky Dog Ranch, I do this by setting up a temporary barrier about two feet from the wall of the training yard, creating a corridor that keeps dogs next to me—even before they understand the *HEEL* command. At home, you can do the same, using a row of folding chairs or card tables turned on their sides. As your dog starts to grasp the command, move that barrier back to three feet, and then four. Eventually you can remove it altogether.

If your dog has a hard time grasping the *HEEL* command, use a temporary barrier to create a corridor. This gives him fewer opportunities to roam.

Teach Your Dog Not to Crowd You. Some dogs just want to be close to you—even on a walk. If your dog has a habit of leaning in or getting underfoot, you'll want to make it clear that the *HEEL* command means walking *beside* you, not on top of or beneath you. To teach your dog to walk politely beside you, you'll need to make a temporary adjustment to your own gait. Start with your dog walking next to you on your left. When he starts to crowd, straighten your left leg and step it out in front of him , basically taking one very wide, awkward step. This movement will give your dog a light bump and push him out a few inches from your side. Say *HEEL* at the same moment you claim that space so your dog starts making an association between walking next to you and the command. Continue to repeat this process until your dog gets the hint that walking beside you is great, but crowding up against you just doesn't work. Be sure to praise him when he's walking in the correct place so he understands what he has to do to get this command right.

If your dog starts to crowd you, straighten your left leg, step it out in front of him, and give him a light bump to push him a few inches from your side. Say *HEEL* at the same moment you claim that space.

Special for Dogs Who Race. One question I hear a lot is, "What can I do if my dog is racing ahead?" The first step in solving this problem is a simple one: make sure your dog is hungry when you start training. Learning to *HEEL* is real work, and just like you wouldn't want to work for free, your dog doesn't, either. If he's hungry enough and you have a treat, he'll figure out he needs to stay right at your side to get it. As you teach this technique, be sure not to wean your dog off the food rewards too quickly. Training is a marathon. If you teach your dog quickly, he'll be trained. But if you teach him slowly, he'll be well trained.

You can also get control of a dog who tends to want to lead with a technique that requires a little clever footwork on your part. This technique is *not* for use on heavy pullers—and if you try to use it for one you could get knocked off-balance. Despite that limitation, it can be very effective for dogs who always seem to be trying to get just a few inches out in front. Here's how it works: Get your dog walking beside you on the left at a slow, steady pace. When he

For a dog who races ahead, pivot and place your right foot
directly in front of his chest. Your foot should not physically stop
your dog but instead act like the mechanical arm at a gate:
a barrier that causes him to hesitate to push through.

starts to take the lead, pivot on your left leg, lift your right foot, and place it directly in front of your dog's chest, giving the *HEEL* command at the same time. You're not actually using your foot to physically stop your dog—if he's going to plow into it, skip this technique and move on to the tips for dogs who pull. Instead, with this method you're using your foot like the mechanical arm at a guard gate: when you put it in place, your dog will hesitate to push past it, giving you a chance to remind him that *HEEL* means staying next to you and not in front.

Special for Dogs Who Pull. For severe pullers, you'll need to get a little bit creative to teach the *HEEL*. As in the tip above, starting with a hungry dog is key, but let's talk about technique. To teach this method, I recommend using a martingale collar and some sort of makeshift alleyway. It can be a hallway or a sidewalk with a wall on one side—anything that forces your dog to at least walk a straight line.

With the dog on your left and the collar high on his neck, say *HEEL* and begin walking. Chances are your dog will start to pull immediately. When that happens, place the leash on your upper right hip, turn your body clockwise (be sure to turn your head, too!) and walk in the opposite direction. When you do this, your dog will change directions with you—and most likely start pulling in the new direction. Once again, you're going to say *HEEL*, put the leash on your upper right hip, turn your entire body and head clockwise, and quickly walk in the other direction. This process gets repeated over and over. You'll notice after a few minutes that your dog will not only be pulling less but also looking at you more because he's actually waiting for your next move in the opposite direction. Now it's very important that you praise and reward your dog for his "Good *HEEL*" when he's walking with you correctly for those few seconds while he's trying to figure out what you're up to. This lets him know what he's doing right.

It's vital to train this technique in a narrow passage of some kind. That way, your dog will have a limited choice of directions of travel. Also remember that timing is everything. Have those treats ready in your bait bag or pocket. When your dog is walking correctly, reward him in that moment. If you wait too long and he's out of control again, he'll be under the impression he's being rewarded for pulling—and you definitely don't want to reinforce that.

If your dog starts to pull, hold the loop of the leash in a fist behind your back and place the leash against your upper right hip.

Turn your head and entire body clockwise.

Walk in the opposite direction.

Special for Severe Pullers. The method for teaching any dog who pulls is the same one I just described, but some dogs require a little extra help before they're able to achieve even a small measure of improvement. For these dogs, there are a couple of training products that can be useful tools to help you. To be honest, in my mind, animal training is always about technique. Training is the ultimate problem solver, and I don't believe that any product is a substitute for truly teaching an animal. However, there are times when the first problem that needs to be solved is how to get a dog under control enough to be able to start training. If that's how you're feeling about teaching your dog to *HEEL*, a head halter or an anti-pull harness may help bridge the gap between the crazy puller at the end of the leash and a dog who can be dialed down enough to learn to *HEEL*.

The first of these tools is a head halter. These are one of my favorite picks for working with heavy-pulling dogs. One of the most basic tenets of controlling any dog is that where the head goes, the

A halter-style head collar is one of my favorite tools for severe pullers.

body goes, and the design of this type of collar gives the person at the end of the leash excellent and gentle control over where the dog's head is. The problem is that this tool takes some getting used to for both dog and owner. If you don't put the collar on correctly, the dog can back out of it—and the next thing you know you've got an even bigger problem than pulling. In addition, it takes time for a dog to get used to having the strap over his snout. This kind of collar can be a great tool, but if you're going to use one, be sure to take the time to get a demonstration from someone who's experienced in using it, watch a tutorial video, or both.

The second tool that may help you get your pulling dog ready for *HEEL* lessons is an anti-pull harness. These harnesses are simple, effective, and user-friendly. Even though a harness will help you get your dog under control, though, it may ultimately mean you'll have to spend a little more time training the *HEEL*. The reason is that the harness controls your dog's torso but not his head. He'll learn the command more slowly when his whole body (which naturally follows where his head goes) is not engaged in the training.

Private Sandy Reports for Duty

In over twenty weeks of intensive training, Sandy proved my instincts about his ability to be a working dog were right. He was an obedience champ, first learning all 7 Common Commands, and then moving on to more complex instructions like picking up and retrieving objects when he was asked. Sandy learned the basics of the *HEEL* command in a few days, then polished it to service dog perfection over the next several weeks. Along the way, he took things one step further by learning to brace himself on command so he could offer support if Tim needed to lean on the harness to maintain his balance or negotiate stairs.

The day I introduce any dog I've trained to a new owner is

always bittersweet, but the relationship I develop with the service dogs I work with is especially close. We are constant companions for months during their training. Sometimes it can be a little difficult for the dogs, too, because they become closely bonded to me. I took Sandy to meet Tim for the first time with this on my mind. I wanted the two of them to hit it off, but there was a possibility Sandy would cling to me.

It turned out I had nothing to worry about. Sandy went straight to Tim's side and stayed there. Tim stroked his new dog's head while we talked. I'm sure anyone who saw the two of them together that first day would have thought Sandy had been Tim's dog all his life. The next day as Tim learned to work with Sandy, they had the kind of natural partnership that can't be taught. When I asked Tim to try out a couple of steps using Sandy's help, the two of them blew me away by climbing not just three or four steps, but the entire thirty-step flight. Tim once again proved himself to be a warrior, and Sandy showed he was equal to any task.

To this day I still talk with Tim all the time, and he tells me Sandy has only gotten better with experience. Sandy assists Tim just about everywhere they go, and people are always impressed by how they work perfectly together. I'd never say any dog is my favorite, but I can admit that having a hand in creating this incredible partnership is some of my proudest work.

PART THREE

CURES FOR
7 KINDS OF
BEHAVIOR ISSUES

11

HOUSEBREAKING AND INDOOR MARKING

Nobody knew how the five-month-old pointer mix ended up flea infested and wandering the mean streets, but there was no doubt this puppy needed a home. He was too young and much too sweet for people to have given up on him so soon. When I met Chance at the shelter, he was exceptionally calm for a puppy, but he'd never had a minute of training. I wondered if he'd ever had a real home. I did a very basic focus exercise to see how long I could hold his attention—and got all of about three seconds before something more interesting caught his eye. At the ranch, he didn't do much better—his cheerful, curious, slightly dopey demeanor meant that everything new he encountered grabbed his attention. And every single thing was new to this dog. This is completely normal for a young dog with no experience of the world. Think about it like this: When you see the Empire State Building for the first time, you're in awe. But when you live in NYC and see it every day, the glamour wears off and it becomes just another building. Chance's young, inexperienced mind was still getting first impressions of a lot of new things when I met him, but I knew he'd settle down over time.

Luckily what Chance lacked in focus, he made up in willingness to learn. He picked up the *SIT* command quickly, but then took his sweet time learning the *DOWN*. A slow learning pace is common in pointer breeds because they tend to be both sensitive and strong-willed. In other words, you sometimes have to do a little more convincing with them than with a dog bred for a less independent-minded job. Once he got over the hump with the *DOWN*, though, Chance picked up *STAY* and *NO* in no time.

Chance and I celebrated these first accomplishments by lounging on the couch. But when I stepped into the kitchen to get a bottle of water, I came back to discover this dog's biggest challenge wasn't going to be learning any of the 7 Common Commands—it was going to be housebreaking. I'd wrongly assumed that Chance had already learned basic indoor manners. This dog was well past prime housebreaking age, but he didn't know the difference between the carpet and the grass. The world was his toilet—and that's a problem that could keep any dog from finding (and keeping) a forever home. It was my mistake to give a new dog too much credit, and it was going to be my responsibility to teach Chance what he needed to know.

Of all the common behavior issues, house-training is one of the simplest to fix because the training for this issue falls right in line with a dog's instincts. Even though house-training problems don't have to pose a big, long-term challenge to pet owners, they are still one of the main reasons dogs get taken to or returned to animal shelters. Nobody wants a dog who ruins rugs or couches or requires constant cleanups, so people are quick to give up at even the hint of a housebreaking problem.

The owner I had in mind for Chance had permission to take

her new dog to work every day, but this puppy's anywhere-will-do philosophy could ruin his big opportunity. I put his 7 Common Commands training on hold and turned my attention to housebreaking.

The Problem: Housebreaking

Whether you're dealing with a puppy or an adult dog, housetraining issues are always a serious problem. Data from animal shelters all over the country suggests that as many as 20 percent of dogs who wind up abandoned at shelters are dropped off because of housebreaking troubles. In some cases, these issues may be caused by undiagnosed or untreated health problems, but for most dogs, this is a training issue, pure and simple. It's a tragedy that so many dogs with the potential to be great pets—sweet, trainable dogs like Chance—end up abandoned, homeless, or even lose their lives because they haven't yet learned where and when it's okay to answer nature's call.

For puppies, this is particularly unfair because one of the main reasons they have so many accidents in the house is that a young puppy's bladder is not strong enough to retain urine for as long as an adult's. Those muscles develop over time and with practice. Think about how your own muscles developed. If you squeeze something in your fist, you've got a solid, tight grip. But babies and toddlers don't have that kind of grip strength. Over time, their muscles develop and become trained to hold on. The same theory applies to a puppy's bladder. The more he learns to hold it, the more his muscles are working and getting stronger, till eventually he can go for several hours without losing control.

Even though house soiling and marking are very serious issues— potential deal breakers for almost any indoor family pet—they are problems that can be solved through careful, consistent training.

The Approach: The House-Training Triangle

I probably get more calls about house-training than any other problem behavior, so I've put a lot of energy into figuring out a solution that works. Some of the dogs I deal with are puppies, some are adolescents, and many are adults. Each case has its unique challenges, but the training principle I use, a technique I call the house-training triangle, is the same. The reason I like this system better than any other is because it effectively helps a dog understand what he's doing right when he does his business outside—instead of just punishing him when he makes a mistake.

Later in this chapter, I'll share a separate technique to deal with dogs who have a marking habit. Even though that problem is technically also a housebreaking issue, it's one with different origins. A dog who indiscriminately does his business in the house hasn't learned where the appropriate place is to go. A dog who marks your furniture or walls with small amounts of urine as a habit knows what he's doing—though he surely does *not* know how wrong it is to treat your things that way. Like a small child who writes his name on everything he owns, a marking dog is labeling everything in his personal space as *mine, mine, mine* by putting his scent on it.

First things first, though. Let's start with a technique for general house-training.

A Step-by-Step Plan

Of all the methods available to housebreak a dog, I find the most effective ones are those that utilize some version of crate training. Why do they work? The biggest reason is because they take advantage of a dog's instinct to keep the areas where he eats and sleeps clean. This is a basic rule among dogs with very few exceptions.

That said, just crating a dog is not enough. You've got to provide him with opportunities to do the right thing to really teach and reinforce reliable house-training. The three-part process of my house-training triangle is easy to follow—and if you do it correctly, it's very effective. Most dogs will pick it up in a week or less, and even the most stubborn and slowest learners will master it after a couple of weeks of consistent practice. My system gives dogs separate opportunities for free play, for confinement in the crate or pen, and for doing their business outside. It also helps prevent accidents during training, which is a key factor in success. The more accidents a dog has in the house, the more the floor smells, and the more normal it feels to the dog to make another mistake. More accidents mean more reprimands, and who needs all that negativity? Bottom line: the more your dog goes to the bathroom in the house without being caught in the act, the more normal it feels to him and the more he'll do it. This is one of the main reasons so many dogs end up not house-trained.

To teach this method to your dog, you'll need:

- A crate or small indoor pen
- A leash
- Some treats
- A healthy supply of patience

The right choice of crate or pen is a big deal for this method. You want one that's not too big and not too small. Ideally, you want your dog to be able to sit, stand, and lie down comfortably when he's confined—but that's it. If he can walk around or, more importantly, do his business in a corner that he can avoid, that's too much space. If you're planning to use the crate for different purposes later and want it to be bigger, or if you've got a growing puppy and want to buy only one crate, you can easily block off a portion of it with a divider or even a cardboard box to make it the right size—the size your dog is now. Your goal is to create a space just a little larger than your dog's height, length, and width. For Chance, I put up a small, open-topped dog pen in my living room. Most dogs quickly adjust and are perfectly happy in a crate, but if you have the rare dog who can't handle being closely confined, an older dog who's never been crated, or even if you just prefer the idea of using a wire or plastic playpen, a small pen is an effective alternative.

The ideal age to start this training is around twelve weeks, when a puppy is physically able to hold his bladder overnight. A puppy's system slows down and can last longer when he's asleep than during the day when he's active. If your pup is younger than twelve weeks, you can still use this house-training method, but you may need to take your dog out to relieve himself once during the night for a few more weeks. After twelve weeks, many dogs will still cry in the middle of the night out of loneliness or protest, but most fall back asleep after fifteen minutes. If your dog keeps crying and you're going to take him out to pee, wait

This crate is the perfect size for Lulu. She can comfortably sit, stand, and lie down—but that's it.

until he's quiet for a good thirty seconds so you don't reinforce the idea that crying in the night will get your attention and get him out of the crate.

Step 1. To help ensure your dog doesn't have a full bladder after bedtime, stop giving him water about two hours before lights-out. At the end of the day, after your dog goes outside for the last time before bed, confine him to the crate or pen. First thing in the morning, take him out of the crate and go *directly outside.* Do not pass Go or roam around or stop in the kitchen or give any treats along the way—not even for a few seconds. Your dog *will* have to go at this time, and you want to take advantage of that urgency. Besides, there's nothing worse than starting your day by scrubbing pee out of the carpet. So either pick up your dog and go straight outdoors or attach a leash to his collar and hustle him out the door. Preventing an accident is your goal.

Step 2. Once you're outside, tell your dog to *GET BUSY* and wait him out. You can use a different command if you like, but choose a word or phrase you can use consistently every time you want your dog to do his business. While you wait, keep giving that command, knowing your dog does have to go because he's been cooped up overnight. When your dog relieves himself, wait for him to finish, repeat the command once more, then praise him and give him a treat. Timing is key, so give the treat right after he does his business. Waiting too long will have no effect because he won't make the connection between his action and the reward. Have that treat locked and loaded, but in your pocket, not in your hand. If your dog has his eyes—and mind—on a treat, he may get distracted from doing his business.

Step 3. Once your dog has finished his business outside (preferably both kinds), he can go back in the house for some well-earned supervised free time. The key word here is *supervised*. Just like in Step 1, one of your most important jobs is to make sure no accidents happen. Keep your dog in the same room with you, keep an eye on him, and set a timer for an hour (thirty to forty-five minutes for small breeds). At the end of that free playtime, put your dog back in his crate or pen. Set your timer for two hours, and at the end of it, put the dog on a leash and go straight outside to begin the process again. If necessary, you can adjust these times to be a little bit shorter or longer based on your dog's track record for being trustworthy in the house and his size. In general, large dogs can handle longer periods of time between trips outdoors than small dogs.

This three-part rotation of crate time, outside time, and indoor free time is the house-training triangle. If you follow the steps consistently for several days, your dog will learn not only that outside is the only acceptable place to do his business but also that the command *GET BUSY* means he needs to do so sooner than later. If you live in a cold or rainy climate, you'll be glad to be able to speed up that whole part of the process in bad weather.

Step 4. There's an important tweak you'll be making during the process of gradually training your dog to understand the larger concept that outside is the only place where it's okay to relieve himself. Every day, your goal is to eliminate a little crate time and add a little free time to his schedule. If your dog does well with the one-hour increments of free time on day one, increase to ninety-minute increments on day two, then two hours on day three. After that, start taking fifteen minutes away from the crate time and adding thirty minutes to your dog's free time each day. By the end of a week, your dog should be spending thirty to sixty minutes in the crate and around five hours free in the house. Once he's reached that milestone or a similar pattern, you can start to eliminate the crate completely.

Training Tips to Remember

As always, there are a few tips that can help make the technique successful.

Supervise Your Dog's Free Time Until He Learns It's Only Okay to* GET BUSY *Outside. This is a must! If your dog does have an accident and you catch him in the act, give him a quick, stern *NO*. You can also use the technique I outline below for marking to combat this problem. However, if you don't catch your dog in the act and happen to find a mess an hour or two after the fact, you may as well just clean it up because reprimanding after the fact is pointless. Your dog will have no idea what he's done to make you angry. So, for best results, don't let your dog out of your sight for the first few days of training.

Feed Your Dog in the Crate about Ten Minutes Before You Take Him Outside to Do His Business. Most dogs' (especially puppies') digestive systems get moving pretty quickly after they eat, and if you time this correctly, you'll help your dog learn the *GET BUSY* command more quickly and save yourself any unpleasant cleanup.

Make the Crate an Inviting Place to Be. A crate isn't supposed to be a dungeon; it's a place to learn and rest and have a positive experience. Toys, chews, and comfortable blankets and dog beds all help convey that to your dog. (I'd recommend staying away from chews that dissolve or real bones with meat on them during this training. These tend to speed up a dog's digestive system and can make them have to go more often or more urgently.)

Stick to the Plan. Many dogs—especially puppies—quickly decide that the first couple of days in a crate are a great time to stage a protest. These dogs will bark and bark (and bark). You have two choices for dealing with this—and neither of them is giving in and taking your dog out of the crate. Either go to your inner quiet place and ignore it, or use a penny bottle or a Shake & Break to teach your dog the *QUIET* command (you can read how in Chapter 14). A lot of people give up on house-training because of this complication, but that only teaches the dog that barking excessively gets him what he wants. Stick to the plan and win this battle of wills.

Be Motivating. Maintain a positive outlook when you put your dog into and take him out of his pen. So many people get caught up in yelling or punishing their dogs during housebreaking, but in the end, that approach just slows the process and upsets both owner and dog. You want to make the teaching of this—the most important of all dog etiquette lessons—as positive an experience as possible. That way your dog will not only master it but also continue to view you as both a teacher and a friend.

Let's follow up on those bladder muscles. Being in the crate all but forces your dog to hold his urine, which in turn strengthens his bladder muscles. This is one of the secrets to this method's success. By enforcing regularly scheduled crate times, you give your puppy's bladder muscles a chance to get stronger and more controlled.

Variation for Indoor-Only Training. I've been asked by a number of dog owners if there's an alternative version of this training for dogs who use indoor house-training pads. I don't use this tool in my own training, but if you are dealing with circumstances like inclement weather or a ninth-floor apartment, they may be a key part of your house-training routine. If you use these pads, you can substitute them for the outdoor section of your dog's house-training triangle.

To start, put the training pads directly outside your dog's crate or exercise pen, leading him to them each time he leaves his enclosure and using the *GET BUSY* command just as described above. Once your dog becomes habituated to the pads, move them a short distance away and make sure he gets to them each time he relieves himself. Eventually, you can set up a sizable exercise pen for your dog with a sleeping/play area on one end, and the house-training pads on the opposite side.

If you're using training pads as part of your house-training routine, start by placing them immediately outside of your dog's crate or exercise pen.

One Final Note. If you follow these steps carefully and consistently, the house-training triangle works on upwards of 90 percent of dogs in a week or so. However, when it comes to this critical skill, a lot of variables can affect how long it takes for a dog to become reliable. For example, size matters in housebreaking. If you have a very small dog or a very big house, it may take extra time for your dog to get the hang of the rules. It only makes sense that a small dog like a Maltese, Yorkie, or Chihuahua would need a little more time to understand that *all* the indoor space around him is off-limits for relieving himself. After all, he doesn't need much space at all. Ditto for a big dog in a really big house. If you've got a dozen rooms and you want to teach your dog that all of them are part of his living space and none of them suitable for use as a toilet, you'll basically have to teach him one room at a time, gradually expanding his access to the house.

Other dogs who may need extra time to housebreak include young puppies and rescued dogs. The younger the puppy, the less mature his mind is going to be, and the less developed his bladder muscles are, too. A rescued dog who is new to you may have been outside or in a kennel his whole life and then suddenly finds he has a new set of rules he needs to follow. That takes extra time, too. Same thing for a dog who's always been an apartment dweller using pee pads who has to learn to go outside.

Lastly, senior dogs may have the will to follow the rules but not the control they once had. If your senior dog develops a new house-training problem, be sure you check with his veterinarian to rule out a medical issue like a urinary tract infection. If the cause is just the natural deterioration that comes with age, make sure your old dog has more frequent opportunities to go outside to do his business. If he's been housebroken all his life and suddenly can't completely control his bladder or bowels anymore, chances are his accidents in the house are even more stressful for him than they are for you.

The Problem: Indoor Marking

We've all seen it and we all feel the same about it: nobody likes a dog who marks in the house. This nasty habit stains furniture and makes your home smell like a kennel. It's definitely one of the drawbacks of having a male dog. A lot of dog owners don't even realize a dog is marking until the day they notice one area, and then another—and then I get calls from people who've suddenly figured out the dog has been marking in the house for months. It's a discouraging moment when you realize your dog isn't as house-trained as you thought. Fortunately, this is a correctable bad habit. I've created a reliable technique and used it on countless dogs over the years, and 90 percent or more pick it up within the first week. Those are pretty good odds, so let's get started.

A Step-by-Step Plan

You'll need a few tools to deal with this problem, and a couple of them may surprise you:

- A leash
- A flat collar or harness
- A cinder block
- A baby camera
- A UV black light

Don't be intimidated by those last couple of items; any cheap baby camera from a garage sale will do (you can even rig up the webcam on a laptop or phone if you have a way to monitor it). You can pick up a new ultraviolet black light flashlight in the ten- to fifteen-dollar range at any discount hardware store or pet-supply store. Now that you're all geared up, let's break this down.

Step 1. The first thing you have to do is determine where problem areas already exist. If you've just figured out your dog is marking, he may have been hitting the same spots for months. During that time, those areas become, in your dog's mind, part of his territory—places where he should continually reassert his owner-ship. Locating all these areas is the first step in solving the prob-lem. After dark, pull out your black light, turn it on, and shine it around each room in your house. Those glowing areas you couldn't see with the naked eye? They're not the auras of passing ghosts—no such luck. They're most likely urine stains that identify the places where your dog's been tagging your belongings with his signature scent. Not sure whether your dog is really guilty? Consider the location of the stains. Typically, dogs mark on the corners of furniture and fixtures, in spots low enough for them to hit by lifting a leg. Often, there will be matching stains on the floor beneath the "target" where urine has dripped onto the floor. Wiping a suspect location with a dry white rag and finding sticky yellow residue will confirm your suspicions.

Before you can move on to the next step in this process, you'll have to steel your nerves and do a little dirty work. Those spots need to be cleaned—thoroughly enough that the odor comes out of the furniture, carpet, or other area. This may take a couple of passes if your dog's been using a space for a long time. Whatever it takes, this is the root of the problem and must be dealt with before training. As long as an area smells like your dog's scent, his instincts are going to tell him to keep marking it. By cleaning those places, you're taking away the smell and throwing him slightly off his game. Once you've cleaned the areas as best you can, you can begin the real training.

Step 2. Next, set up your monitoring camera. Put it in a room you're sure is totally cleaned of previous markings and let your dog roam free while you watch on the monitor from somewhere out of sight. Markers with really bad habits will likely show their cards in a minute or so, especially when in a room alone. This is often the first thing they do as they pass through a room. Other dogs will take a little longer. Whatever the case, wait for your moment. Once your dog lifts his leg on something, immediately walk into the room and reprimand him with the *NO* command, showing him the area he just marked. Make your reprimand short and sweet because it's the next step that will make all the difference, and you need to get to it immediately. Once you've given the *NO* command, take the leash, attach it to your dog's flat collar or harness, and tie the other end to the corner of what he's just marked. Be sure to tie it with enough slack so your dog can stand up and lie down, but no more than that. It's vital that you measure this correctly for it to be effective. If your dog marks an area that you can't tie the leash to (like the middle of a couch), haul out that cinder block we discussed, place it right next to the marked area, and wrap the leash around it. Now give your dog thirty minutes of supervised time to think about what just happened while he sits next to his handiwork. During this time, you need to ignore him, even if—*especially* if—he starts to cry or bark. If you have to pull out your penny bottle or Shake & Break and give him a *QUIET* command, by all means do it. There is no negotiating during this process. The dog was guilty of the crime, and he's got to do his time. Once your dog has spent the entire thirty minutes in place,

Lulu attached to the table leg she marked. Use only a flat collar or harness, make sure the leash has enough slack for your dog to lie down and stand up, and always supervise your dog during this process.

unclip him. Do not praise, reward, or even speak baby talk to him while you set him free. This is a discipline exercise and must be treated seriously, so the best thing to say is nothing at all. Once your dog has been turned loose, you'll need to thoroughly clean the area he marked to get rid of the scent.

Step 3. Repeat the whole process, starting with you observing your dog on the monitor. Be sure to quickly bust him in the act the next time he makes his mark, then follow through with the same simple, to-the-point consequence. Repeat this process for as long as it takes. Many dogs learn the lesson in just a couple of days. Others might take a week or so. The theory behind this is simple. Dogs instinctively hate being near their own mess, so by making them stand next to it for a period of time, you're utilizing a form of reverse psychology. Basically, you're giving them more of what they've claimed as their own than they've bargained for—turning their positive association into a negative one. It's kind of like the old-school parenting practice of making a teenager who gets caught smoking smoke a whole pack of cigarettes. This consequence isn't as harsh as that one, but it does make a firm and clear point about a completely unacceptable behavior that needs to be dealt with.

Training Tips to Remember

There are a few vital things to point out here.

Be Sure the Leash Has the Right Amount of Slack. The leash should have just enough slack to allow your dog to lie down and stand up, but no more. If you give too much slack, your dog will simply walk to the end of the leash and be far enough away from his mess to avoid learning the lesson. Too little slack and he won't be able to lie down. This is not a corporal punishment—your dog's only discomfort during this training should come from his disdain at having to be so close to his own excrement—not from any physical distress from being tied on a leash that doesn't allow him to move.

Never Connect Your Dog to a Choke or Prong Collar while Doing This Training. A regular flat collar or harness is all that's needed.

Supervise Your Dog During This Process. You can simply be doing chores around the house or reading, but please do not leave the house while your dog is tied up.

Stop Leash Chewing. If you see your dog chewing on the leash during this time-out (and a lot of dogs do), give him a quick, firm *NO*. If he persists, rub the leash with a little lemon to discourage him.

Last, but Not Least, Be Consistent and Patient. Giving up on your dog only reinforces the bad behavior you're targeting. This is the main reason dogs get away with so many bad habits—not because they're bad dogs, but because they're not getting good instruction. Remember that you are the owner and the teacher. So be the best, most consistent teacher possible. The face you show your dog is the face that'll be shown back to you.

One Lucky Dog

It didn't take long for Chance to master his house-training and learn the 7 Common Commands. He was ready to go to his new home with a marketing executive who couldn't wait to be Mom to a new dog and show off her puppy at the office. Christina was a

very special adopter. She'd already rescued one dog from a shelter, and that puppy did not survive a bout of distemper he'd contracted while he was homeless. Christina was devastated but still willing to put her heart on the line and adopt again. I wanted things to be perfect for her and for Chance. While Christina was away on vacation, I had artificial turf installed in the dirt lot outside her office building to create a yard. When she got back from her trip, I was able to give her not just a new dog but also a new lawn! Chance immediately showed her he knew how to *GET BUSY* on command. And just like that, they were ready to start their new life together.

Outtake

When I was in my early twenties, I had a client who asked me to watch his house and his two Great Danes who I'd been training. Both dogs were struggling with house-training, so I figured this was a perfect opportunity to teach them, once and for all. I stood there in the driveway with the dogs by my side and waved good-bye to the client and his wife. Later, they called and made me promise to keep the dogs off the rug in the den. It was a beautiful $10,000 Persian work of art, so of course I vowed to keep it safe.

All week, training went just as I'd planned, and in addition to their other accomplishments, at six days in with one day left, these dogs were basically house-trained. Accidents were now just that: accidental. They knew how to hold their business and they knew what the grass was for. They'd been great students all week.

That last day, I realized there wasn't enough dog food left, and I had to run to the store for more. But that store didn't carry their brand. And neither did the next one, or the one after that. It turns out this was a specialized high-end diet, so I called the owners and asked if a substitute would be okay. They were fine with it, so I grabbed a bag of good-quality food and headed back to the house. The dogs chowed down, then went outside to do their business just like they'd been taught. I headed to bed, giving them the run of the house they'd finally earned through their week of dedicated house-training. I slept great, one of those deep sleeps that makes you feel like you're completely buried in the bed.

When I woke up, I walked both dogs straight to the door to let them out, but they had no interest in going. I tried to convince them but got a pretty firm *No thanks* when they backed away. I left the door ajar and headed to the kitchen to make coffee, and that's when I smelled it. I'll spare you a description. It didn't take long to find the danger zone—and of course it was that exquisite Persian rug.

The scene wasn't just ugly, it was my worst nightmare. Apparently that new off-the-rack food hadn't agreed much with Dane 1 and Dane 2. They hadn't just dropped a nugget or two on this family heirloom, they'd buried it in the evidence of their night of digestive distress. I ran to the kitchen and grabbed every cleaning solution I could find, then started blotting, scrubbing, and rubbing the rug. I was making the slightest bit of progress when I heard the front door open. And there I was, the expert animal trainer, on my hands and knees trying to clean the one and only object I'd been asked to keep out of harm's way.

I'd had a few moments in my life where I've wished I could completely disappear, but that one topped them all. I'll never forget it. I'm pretty sure the well-meaning owners of the Great Danes will never forget it, either. If only I hadn't been so consumed in my own embarrassment, I would have loved to catch a picture of the total astonishment on their faces when they found me. I could have kept it as a reminder that in my line of work, even when it seems like you're doing everything right, sometimes crap happens, and then there's nothing to do but break out the rubber gloves and start cleaning up.

12

DOOR DASHING

When I met Lolita at the shelter, she was scared and lonely. Her family had abandoned her, and you could almost see how she was still trying to puzzle that out—why she was in that cage and where the people she'd loved and trusted had gone. She was so starved for attention that the minute I opened her kennel door, she lunged, planting her whole body against my chest, holding on like a little furry gecko, and stretching up to kiss my face. Even after being dumped by her human family, this dog was still eager to bond and willing to trust someone new. Her optimism was one of the best things she had going for her, and I couldn't help but think *who would give you up?*

The shelter staff called me about Lolita because they knew she already had two strikes against her. First, she was a Chihuahua, a breed heavily represented in almost every big shelter in the United States. Second, she was an older dog, and many potential adopters prefer a puppy. People often look at adult dogs with more scrutiny than puppies, wondering if it was behavior problems that brought them to the shelter in the first place.

Back at the ranch, Lolita quickly proved herself to be a dream to train—focused, cheerful, and eager to please. Her let's-do-this attitude made everything easy with her. Plus, she was always staring me right in the eyes, as if she was trying to hypnotize me. I have to admit it was kind of working—I kept thinking *this dog rocks*. I needed to find a perfect home for her—nothing less would do.

But at the end of a long day in the training yard, Lolita revealed a habit that could seriously narrow her options. I opened the gate, and just like that, she was gone. Don't worry, I don't mean gone, like, forever. I mean she took off like a bat outta hell. Thankfully, the area had a perimeter fence and she couldn't get much farther. Door dashing is a seriously bad habit for any dog, but for a small dog in a rural area well known for its wilder inhabitants—including coyotes, rattlesnakes, and mountain lions—it's a potentially deadly one. And in the city, passing cars would be an even more imminent threat.

I put Lolita's 7 Common Commands training on hold then and there to turn my attention to this dangerous behavior. Fortunately, this was an issue I'd dealt with in many shelter dogs who had passed through the Lucky Dog Ranch, and I was confident I could break Lolita of her risky habit.

The Problem

It's a simple fact that dogs don't believe in "after you" manners when it comes to an open door—you open it, and many of them just barrel on out. In fact, nine times out of ten when I go to dog owners' houses (and in my line of work that happens a lot), the person who answers the door has to hold a dog back to let me in. Without that restraint, the dog would be long gone—sometimes just a few yards and sometimes as far as four legs can run. Dog trainers call this behavior door dashing, and it's one of the main reasons dogs end up lost or, worse, injured or killed. That's not safe or acceptable.

You can take your pick of the dangers that are lurking outside: wild animals, other dogs, traffic, drowning hazards, poisons, sharp objects, and the bogeyman all come to mind. But whatever the biggest dangers are near your home, your dog needs to learn to wait for your invitation to walk through an open door—even when you have the leash in your hand.

Luckily, this practice, which can be a lifesaver, is relatively easy to train. I'm going to give you a reliable technique to help your dog break the habit, plus a few variations for special challenges like strong and willful dogs and dogs who dash out of car doors.

The Approach

The secret to this technique, like so many techniques designed to eliminate troubling behaviors, is in beating your dog at her own game. If you turn the tables and take the fun out of door dashing, she'll stop being entertained and excited about doing it. Once the fun is over, she'll be ready to give it up and turn her attention to a less dangerous pastime.

A Step-by-Step Plan for Door Dashers at Home

First things first. The only tools you'll need to train this technique:

- A twenty-foot leash
- A harness or flat collar

You can also give treats if you'd like, but it's not usually necessary. I almost always give treat rewards for behaviors that are taught, but not always for issues that are solved. For example, when a dog is learning a new command from scratch, she needs a positive reward to be motivated to do it. When I'm curbing a bad behavior, I don't typically reward the dog for not doing things she should not be doing anyway. That's kind of like rewarding your kid for stopping at red lights when she's learning to drive. If you think your dog needs a little extra motivation to pay attention during this training, there's no harm in adding in a few treats. But keep in mind that some dogs are so intelligent they'll quickly learn to do something bad just to be corrected and earn a treat! It's one of the oldest tricks in a smart (and food-motivated) dog's playbook.

Step 1. Attach the long leash to your dog's harness or collar and let it drag behind her. The leash will be there just in case you need to step on it if your dog gets ahead of you during this training. Otherwise, it won't be necessary to use it for a while. Next, walk your dog to the front door.

Step 2. Open the door just an inch or two, then quickly shut it. Most dogs will focus on that opening, some so much that they'll try to run through even a couple-inch gap. Having the door come straight back at them will stop most of them in their tracks. Do not hit your dog in the face with the door—just open it and shut it before she gets close enough to get through. Timing and speed are the keys to making this work. With the door closed, wait for your dog to settle down—to back away or even sit. As soon as she does, repeat the same sequence: open, shut, wait. Focus on timing and speed. This process needs to be repeated over and over. After you do it a few times, your dog is going to back off and sit or lie down. You want her to be at least two feet away before proceeding to the next step. If she doesn't retreat that far, guide her back a couple of feet to position her.

Open the door just an inch or two, then quickly shut it.

Step 3. Open the door again, but this time open it three inches wide—and again, shut it right away. Your dog is likely to still give it a go, and the extra two feet or so between her and the door will ensure she doesn't get over the threshold. As soon as the door is closed, wait for your dog to settle down and back away again. Repeat this maneuver, opening the door five inches before quickly closing it, then waiting for your dog to settle.

With each step, don't open the door any farther until your dog is content to stay still at the current gap. For example, if you're opening the door three inches and your dog is still trying to dive toward it, don't move on to four or six or ten inches until she's calm and patient at three. Most dogs get the message after the first five to ten times of doing this, so by the time you reach a foot, your dasher should be able to watch the door open and close without moving.

Continue to open the door a little wider as your dog progresses. Eventually, you'll be able to open it the whole way and your dog will stay in place. When this happens, praise her good behavior. Be sure to keep praises short and sweet.

Continue to open the door a little wider as your dog progresses.

Step 4. Once your dog has become conditioned to stay in place in the face of a wide-open door, then she's ready for the next phase of this training. It's time to teach the *OKAY* command. This is where you'll teach your dog when it *is* acceptable to cross the threshold. To do this, open the door and wait a few seconds. If your dog tries to run out, back up to Step 3 and work on conditioning a little

**Use the *OKAY* command to signal it's acceptable
to walk across the threshold together.**

longer. When she does stay those few seconds, simply pick up the
leash, say *OKAY*, and walk your dog out the door.

As always, conditioning is key, so practice this maneuver over
and over again until your dog looks to you to pick up the leash,
even when the door is standing open.

Training Tips to Remember

There are a couple of things to point out here.

Be Ready to Stop a Bolter. Your goal is to be able to open a door all the way and have your dog stay put. If she decides to run out during this training (and she probably will at some point), you have two options: either close the door before she gets to it or step on the leash. That's what it's there for.

Another good way to stop a bolting dog is to stomp on the floor or quickly give her an emphatic "Ah, ah!" as she's running out. This stops many dogs in their tracks.

Save the STAY ***Command.*** People often ask if they should use the *STAY* command while training this technique. This is basically a silent command, so it's not necessary to add the *STAY*, but it's okay to do so if you want to. I choose not to tie this training to a specific command because I want the dogs I train to respect the front door as a place they do not pass unless I say so—with or without a *STAY* command. If you train this way, your dog will learn that it's *never* okay to blow through that door frame without your permission. That way, no matter who opens the door or under what circumstances, your dog will stay safe on her side until you give the *OKAY* to go. Taking this one step further, I have a general rule that the dogs I train are never allowed to cross that threshold unless they're on-leash. Period.

Take Baby Steps. Don't move on to adding another inch until your dog has mastered the one you're on. Some dogs will appear to be content with a door that's open eight inches—then suddenly bolt out when it opens to nine. If that happens, simply take your training back a few inches. This is all part of the process of conditioning—one inch at a time. If your dog is having a stubborn moment, take things slow and don't give up. If you show her you are calm and prepared to stick it out, she'll eventually accept that at face value.

Remember: Training is what makes your dog *good*. Conditioning is what makes her *great*. Keep at it if you want to be worry-free when you open that door.

Variations

In my experience, deep down *most* dogs are door dashers, and with so many different kinds of personalities and breeds exhibiting the behavior, chances are there's no single technique that's going to cure them all. So I'll give you a few alternatives and variations to help convince even the most determined, rogue, and difficult students. Most of these methods focus on creating additional physical blocks to help convince your dog that her best option is to do what you want and stop racing through the door.

Create an Auto-Stop. For larger, more powerful dogs with strong wills to match, sometimes the most effective way to get this training under way is to make a clear statement that going through the door is just not an option. To do this, hook your dog up to that long leash before beginning training. When you open the door and your dog starts to charge through, immediately step on the leash to stop her in her tracks. She will not have gained enough speed at that point for the sudden stop to hurt her, but it will reset her idea that the door is available for her to dive through at will. Repeat this technique a few times in ten- to fifteen-minute sessions and your dog will get the idea and start paying attention as you teach the primary technique above. If your dog is stronger than you can handle, tie the leash off to something solid to use it

as an anchor leash and as a fail-safe for the first few practice runs
of this method.

Add a Visual Block. A closing door should be all the block most
dogs need, but if the door you're training at opens the wrong way

**Use a big piece of cardboard or poster board to add extra
evidence that dashing through the door isn't advisable.**

for my technique or if your dog seems to need a little extra evidence that dashing through it isn't advisable, get a big piece of cardboard or poster board and have it ready at the door. When your dog starts charging toward the threshold, slide this prop—which serves as a big stop sign—in front of her at the door frame. It will take your dog by surprise, it will annoy her, and it will stop her long enough for her to reconsider the wisdom of dashing through that door the next time. Be sure your dog's long leash is hooked on when you do this.

Make It a Tactile Experience. When I meet a dog whose mind is clearly focused on *go, go, GO* and nothing else, I add another element to this training to help disrupt the thought process. This simple trick has helped a few of my toughest customers see the error of their ways. Take a couple of three-foot-long sheets of aluminum foil, crumpled a little bit so they'll be noisy when they get stepped on, and lay them on the floor right in front of the door before your session. A few dogs will start getting leery as soon as they see the foil, but most won't think much about it until they step on it. At that point, most dogs really do not like the metallic feeling beneath their feet. When you combine that unpleasantness with the closing door, suddenly you've got their attention. Now you can train away.

Special for Car Dashers. To break your dog of the bad habit of diving out of the car the second the door opens, you can use this variation of the door-dashing technique. *Do not* attempt this training on a busy street, or on any street for that matter. Practice it in a garage, driveway, or empty parking lot, where your dog will be safe if she successfully evades you even one time while you're mastering the technique. Just as above, be sure your dog has a long leash clipped on.

For this method, start with your dog in her customary spot in the car, and open the nearest window enough so she'll be able to hear you talking but won't be tempted to poke her head out. Stand outside the door and open it just an inch or so (just like in the front door technique). As soon as your dog makes a move to jump, quickly shut the door. Repeat this several times until your dog doesn't take the bait of the slightly open door and sits still instead.

Once your dog resists the temptation to jump toward a slightly open door, it's time to move on. Open the door a few inches farther and hold it for three to four seconds, continuing to quickly close it if your dog makes a move to jump. Again, repeat this as many times as it takes for your dog to stay put and not respond as the door opens and shuts.

When your dog reliably sits still with the door partway open, it's time to take the next big step in this process. Open the door the whole way and immediately step in front of your dog, effectively blocking her from exiting with your body. If she tries to jump out, go back to the last training step. But if she stays put, repeat this several times until she seems comfortable with the door open and you standing in front of her. Each time she successfully stays in her seat with the door open, give her a quick praise and reward.

Your next move will be to take one big step back with the door open, repeating as necessary until it's clear your dog isn't going to jump. At that point, take another big step. Remember to return to your dog to praise her when she masters a new distance milestone. Gradually, you can use this technique to work your way back to a few feet away—and farther—from your dog.

At that point, it's time to give her the *OKAY* command, take her leash, and guide her out of your vehicle, just like in Step 4 above.

One Lucky Dog

Lolita needed a lot of love and affection, and I had a family in mind who could use some of the same—a newly divorced dad who was raising three young boys. The family was coming to the end of a difficult time, and they were looking to add a second dog to their household to help them forge their way ahead. To help the boys feel invested in their new pet, I taught them some training techniques they could practice with Lolita—and with their less-trained but loving dog, Rascal.

The most difficult part of my job is always letting a dog go, and I had fallen a little bit in love with Lolita during my time training her. She reminded me a lot of Lulu. To be honest, I wasn't that much of a Chihuahua guy until I rescued Lulu, but since then I've become a fan for life. This breed is a reminder that big personalities come in small packages, and when I took Lolita to meet her new family, their enthusiasm and commitment to training her and making her feel at home put me at ease. Lolita was bringing a new energy and a renewed joy to this family at just the right time, and I had no doubt she was going to find her happy ever after in their home.

INTRODUCING A PET DOOR

Important Note. *If you have a brachycephalic breed, read all the way through to the special section on training them to use a dog door before following any of the steps below!*

I get a lot of calls from people who encounter a surprising problem: they've installed a pet door to allow their dog the freedom to come in and go out as she pleases—and the dog refuses to go through it. For you and me, it might seem silly for a dog to be afraid to pass through that flap, but we can't know just how the dog perceives it. As I explained in a couple of the earlier chapters, most dogs won't plow through a physical barrier— even when they know they can. We can use that to our advantage when we're teaching a command like *STAY*, but it can work against us when we're just trying to make sure our dogs don't get trapped inside (or outside) if we have to be gone all day.

Teaching a dog to trust a pet door is a simple process, but it's one that's easier to accomplish with two instructors than with one, so enlist a friend to help you. If you need to, though, you can manage this alone. This won't take long at all. The only other tools you'll need:

- A six-foot leash
- Some of your dog's favorite treats

Step 1. Clip the leash to your dog's collar, then run the end of it through the dog door to the other side. Now take your helper and go to the outside of the door. Have the helper stand next to the door, holding the pet flap all the way open so your dog can see through the cavity. You should stand a little farther away from the door, holding the end of the leash you had threaded through. Then offer your dog a treat and call her to you. (If you're doing this alone, you'll drop the leash and hold the flap open and the treat.) Most dogs will run right through because they can clearly see where they're going, that you're on the other side, and that you've got something for them. If your dog is a bit reluctant, hold the treat a few inches from her snout and guide her through. The first time is the most difficult. Once she makes it through that initial pass, every time after will be easy. Repeat this same process—with your helper holding the pet door open—a few times in each direction. Don't move on until your dog is running effortlessly through the door.

Encourage your dog through the door with a treat.

Step 2. Next, lower the flap partway, about 50 percent. Your dog should still be able to see through it, but the new opening will be smaller than she is, so she'll have to trust it a little bit. Hold the flap up and call your dog through again. If she's reluctant, open the flap a little more. Since your dog goes through it once, she'll know it's possible. Now you're just adding a new obstacle. Guide your dog again, with the treats closer to her snout if necessary, until she runs through. Repeat in both directions. Once your dog is comfortable with this step, you're going to add a new wrinkle to the process. As your dog passes through the door, ask your helper to very gently touch her on the back with the door's flap. Repeat a few times in each direction.

Lower the flap partway and call her through again.

Step 3. Now it's time to close the deal. Have your helper fold up *just the corner* of the pet door so your dog can see through just a little bit—or hold just the corner up for her yourself. Now she'll have to push through and feel the flap moving to pass. Be sure the helper has a treat in hand right where the flap of the door is open. This will lure the dog to the area and guide her through that small space. Do everything else the same—holding the leash on the other side, calling your dog through, and being ready with a treat. When she pushes through and realizes that the flap moves with her, that's the big moment of clarity you've been waiting for. Once most dogs understand that the door is soft and they can control it, they'll blow right through with no fear at all. Repeat a few more times with the flap slightly open until the dog has built up the knowledge and the courage to push it on her own. Most big dogs have no problem getting this down in a few minutes. Smaller dogs might take a little longer.

With just a corner of the flap raised, the dog will have to push through and feel the flap on her back.

In most cases, once your dog understands that the door is soft and she can control it, she'll fearlessly pass through it.

Special for Brachycephalic Breeds. This method takes a little more creativity for breeds that don't have a long snout to push the flap. Without a snout, the door can push on their bulging eyes and cause a potentially serious hazard. Here's an easy fix to make the training process work. Follow the steps above but have your helper hold the leash this time so your dog doesn't ram the door. With the leash being controlled from the same side of the door as the dog, your helper can set the pace of the learning process so your dog has to *slowly* push the door, forcing her to get a feel for the weight and flexibility of it. This way she can learn to adjust by tipping her head lower or higher to protect her eyes and still open the flap. This learning curve usually happens pretty quickly because these dogs know from experience that their eyeballs can get bumped. The leash just ensures that learning takes place before any injuries can happen. A little extra adjustment from the dog will make the door just as safe a passage for her as for any other dog.

13

CHEWING

When I go to an animal shelter anywhere in the Southwest, there are usually so many Chihuahuas it's overwhelming. Worse yet, too many of any breed in a shelter can make people think that kind of dog doesn't make a good pet. Nothing could be further from the truth when it comes to these dogs with small bodies but big personalities. Instead, there are a lot of factors that play into the high numbers of Chihuahuas who end up abandoned and homeless. One reason is what some shelters call the Paris Hilton Effect or the *Legally Blonde* Effect—basically when millions of people see one of these dogs in the arms of a celebrity, a lot of them want one. But when they get their new dogs home, they figure out that these are living, breathing, thinking beings, not accessories. Also, a lot of people looking for a small commitment mistakenly think they've found it when they get a small dog. But it doesn't work that way. Even the smallest dog needs to be fed, watered, played with, exercised, and trained for any relationship to work. When owners realize a small dog requires as much labor and attention as a big one, sometimes they back out of the deal. By then it's nearly too late for the unwanted dog who ends up in a shelter.

For all these reasons, plus the fact that they can make great pets for almost any dedicated dog owner, I train a *lot* of Chihuahuas. The first time I met Flash, I knew he was a diamond in the rough. He was tiny, only six months old, and completely untrained—but he was also confident, friendly, and trusting. As soon as we started training, he showed me he was a quick study. Unfortunately, he had a hacking cough that the veterinarian diagnosed as kennel cough—a highly contagious condition that can spread like wildfire among unvaccinated dogs at animal shelters. Once I got his diagnosis, Flash had to spend ten days taking antibiotics in quarantine at the ranch before I could really see what he was capable of.

Once he was healthy, Flash loved being let loose for playtime with the other dogs. He held his own with all of them, despite the fact that he was usually the smallest in the yard. I had a great family in mind for this spunky little dog—a couple with an energetic six-year-old boy who could match a puppy's energy and become his playmate. I could imagine the two of them growing up together.

Unfortunately, at the end of his first long day of training, Flash revealed a habit that wasn't going to work in any house with a young child and plenty of toys: he wasn't above helping himself to things that didn't belong to him so he could chew on them. I caught him chomping away at my shoe, then later on the corner of a pillow. Before I could place him in a home, I'd have to teach him to keep his teeth to his own toys and treats.

The Problem

Whether your dog takes the corner off your grandma's heirloom rug, demolishes your remote, chews the leg of your favorite chair, or mauls your kid's beloved stuffed animal, chewing is an unacceptable problem that will only get worse with time. For your dog's safety and the well-being of your stuff, he'll have to learn to resist temptation. There are lots of different reasons dogs chew, and knowing which kind of chewer you're dealing with can help you find a solution.

Puppies. Puppies teethe just like babies do, trying to ease the process and the pain it causes by biting down on anything they can find. It's a stage they all go through. Many veterinarians believe that when puppies are teething, their gums actually itch from the process. Since they can't very well scratch their gums, the next best relief comes from applying counterpressure. Think of what happens when you've got an itch on your foot and can't get to it to scratch it right away. Most of us will try to stomp it out. That's the same thing a puppy is trying to do during those teething months. But for lots of dogs, the chewing doesn't stop there. Many puppies keep on exploring the world with their mouth long after that last adult tooth is firmly in place. That's what gets them into trouble in *our* world, where chomping down on anything that looks or smells interesting is a pretty big taboo.

If you have a young dog with a chewing habit or even an older dog who just never learned any better, it's time to teach him what is and is not okay to chew. The first technique below is all about helping a dog understand that concept.

Adult Dogs. Adult dogs sometimes chew because they're bored or have developed the habit and it feels good to them. The longer a dog has been at it, the harder it's likely to be to bring chewing to a halt. If your dog has a deeply ingrained chewing habit, he'll probably need more than just a few lessons in what he can and can't chew. He'll also need a deterrent. And a dog of any age who's chewing on something potentially dangerous needs that deterrent *stat*.

Separation Anxiety Sufferers. Dogs who are chewing because they're panicked or suffering from separation anxiety have a whole different kind of problem. If you think this may be the case for your dog, Chapter 17 is entirely devoted to this complex problem and offers solution suggestions.

The Approach

The reality is that you're never going to be able to completely stop a dog who needs to chew. Instead, you need to redirect his habit from something that's forbidden to something that's allowed. It's all about steering your dog the right way. Think of it as backseat driving. If you remind the driver to be careful and slow down often enough, you can eventually help instill that habit. Of the many ways to break a dog's chewing habit, this first approach is one of my favorites. If your dog has a more severe habit, keep reading for additional techniques to include or add to this one that's all about trial-and-error learning.

Before You Begin. Most of this book is about training the dog, but once in a while we have to focus on training ourselves. That's definitely the case with chewing, where there are two guidelines I hope you'll follow before you even start teaching your dog.

First, prevention is always the best way to avert a disaster. Before you start anti-chew training, dog-proof your house as much as possible, especially if you're bringing home a new puppy. Puppies can't help being a little (or sometimes a lot) destructive, so preventing them from capitalizing on their first instincts—to explore and to chew—is highly recommended. And no matter how old your dog is, if there are certain items that are big chewing temptations for him, don't leave them lying around.

Second, keep a close eye on your dog when he's roaming free

until he's well past the chewing phase. Too much freedom—especially the unearned kind—is an invitation to your dog to do his worst. If you leave every door in the house open and choose not to supervise, well, that's just irresponsible. Much like you wouldn't let your toddler walk around the house unsupervised, you shouldn't allow your puppy to, either. Use doors and baby gates to place limits on your dog's range of exploration.

A Step-by-Step Plan

For this technique you're going to need:

- Plenty of chew toys. I prefer natural chews (like bully sticks, hooves, etc.) because they are made of materials a dog can easily learn to identify as okay for him to chew; some people prefer stuffed toys or tug and rope toys. Either kind of chew toy will work fine for this training technique.
- A few household items (we'll get to those in a minute).

Step 1. Okay, now let's talk about the dog. Once you've limited how much trouble yours can get into, it's time to focus on teaching him what's okay to chew and what's forbidden. This method uses a simple process of elimination your dog can easily understand.

Start by choosing six objects—four things your dog *is* allowed to chew, and two he *is not* allowed to chew. The objects he's not allowed to chew should be typical things he might find on or near the floor. For example, you might choose a stuffed dog toy, a bully stick, and a rope toy for the chewing-approved options; a remote control, a book, a shoe, or even an unplugged power cord work for the don't-you-dare options. If there's something your dog has been grazing on that's forbidden, include it in this exercise.

Now, set all six objects out on the floor in no particular order, scattering them a foot or so apart and staying nearby to supervise.

Next, you wait. If this is an ongoing problem in your household, before long your dog will approach one of the objects and begin to chew. If he chooses one of the okay-to-chew options, praise him, pet him, and allow him to enjoy it for a minute or two before moving the object away. You want to heavily reinforce the fact that he's chewing something that's allowed. If it's a don't-chew object, reprimand your dog with a sharp (but not angry) *NO* command or a clear, firm, "Ah, ah!" As soon as you clear the don't-chew object out of his mouth, place it back on the ground and go back to waiting. Play this game with your dog for twenty minutes, ending the session on a positive note by praising him for choosing one of his own chew toys. Repeat with multiple sessions each day for a week until your dog starts to get the idea.

Considering okay-to-chew and don't-chew options.

Step 2. Once again, spread all the training objects out on the floor and wait, but this time use different items so your dog can learn which ones are his to touch and chew, and which ones he should leave alone. This time, balance the ratio at three okay-to-chew objects and three don't-chew objects. Praise and pet your dog when he goes for the things he can chew. Verbally reprimand him and pull him away when he chooses the things that aren't allowed. This is an exercise you should repeat a few times each day, spending fifteen minutes on each session. Through this simple process of elimination, most dogs learn very quickly which chews lead to corrections and which ones lead to rewards. It's a much more effective training method than just yelling at your dog when you happen to catch him chewing the wrong thing. That kind of broad correction can confuse him, making him wonder just what he did wrong. But a week or two of this process will have your dog figuring out the distinction between what's acceptable to chew and what's not.

Training Tips to Remember

As always, the training is in the details, so let's discuss a few points.

Take Away Temptation. The last thing any puppy or new-to-you dog needs is too many ways to make a mistake. Until your dog gains an understanding of what is and isn't okay to chew, don't give him more options than he can handle. Keep your shoes and socks, your kids' toys, and other likely chewing targets out of sight. The easiest way to do this is to establish a dog-safe area in your home and confine his free time to that space. As he matures and learns the rules, you'll be able to expand this area to include more (or all) of your home. Start small, and as your dog shows he understands what is and is not okay, give him access to one more area at a time. Only a dog with proven good behavior should have free range.

Remember How Your Dog Learns. Dogs are trial-and-error learners just like we are. If you send them clear signals about which behavior is acceptable and which is not, they learn from their mistakes and try to follow the rules as they understand them. You can take an extra step to help your dog keep all this straight by eventually gathering all his chew toys in one place and rewarding him for choosing things from that spot. Many dogs come to love the idea of their own toy basket or box almost as much as kids do.

Keep Corrections Quick and Calm. When you reprimand your dog, it's important to use the right tone and volume. I never recommend yelling unless it's to save a life. A slightly raised, stern voice is all you need. In addition, never spend too much time on a reprimand. A second or two is all that's needed, then quickly redirect your dog to an acceptable alternative. If you've ever seen how a mother dog or any other older dog handles an overzealous puppy, you know what I'm talking about. The mom only needs to give a quick, firm grunt or growl to get her point across when she's had enough nonsense—and she is the master of getting compliance from her little troublemakers. Spending too much time on a reprimand only leads to confusion—and in the long run, it can lead to your dog shutting down on you.

Most dogs pick this up quickly, but if you work this technique with your dog for a week and don't see positive progress, try one of the alternative methods below. There are a lot of ways to solve this problem, and there's definitely one that will work for you.

Alternative for Dogs Who Can't Stop Chewing That One Irresistible Thing. This method of combating inappropriate chewing works best if your dog has one or two specific objects he can't seem to leave alone. The underlying theory behind this technique is simple: after a while, too much of a good thing starts to negate its appeal. A favorite food is a perfect example. Let's say you love pizza (and who doesn't?). Now imagine how you'd feel if you had to eat pizza for breakfast, lunch, and dinner every day for a month. By the end of that month, I'm willing to bet you'd be in the market for a new favorite food. You might even get so tired of it that you stop eating pizza altogether.

So let's apply the same logic to a chewing dog. Let's say your dog is irresistibly drawn to your shoes. It probably doesn't take too much imagination to summon up that image—I meet a *lot* of dogs who are fascinated with anything that smells like their owners' feet. It's kind of a cute behavior in a puppy, but it's something that can turn into a big problem if your dog keeps it up. To break this habit, take the shoe your dog wants so badly and tie it to his collar. Make sure it's a flat collar, not a choke chain or pinch. If it's a martingale, be sure to loosen it or hook it on so it won't cinch up. This means tying it around the part without the ring. You'll have to supervise this activity to make sure your dog doesn't trip or get hung up anywhere. I've used this technique many times, so here's a summation of how it typically plays out:

- **Hour One.** Your dog's first hour of close bonding with that shoe is usually pretty magical. For a while, he'll be thinking something along the lines of *This is great! I love this thing, and now it's MINE!*

- **Hour Two.** By this point, most dogs are starting to get a little bored of their new appendage.

- **Hour Three.** By now, many dogs are ready to move on to something else. But they can't. The shoe (or other object) is still there, like their own personal albatross.

- **Hour Four.** Four hours in (if not sooner), most dogs are completely over the shoe. At this point, you can take it off your dog's collar and put it back on your foot. Chances are he'll be more than ready to move past it and get on to something else. Be sure to offer an alternative approved chew or toy as a replacement and to praise your dog when he takes it.

That's all there is to it, but remember to keep an eye on your dog during this exercise. If he's the rare animal who decides to try to actually *eat* the shoe during that time, then you'll have to move on to another alternative training method.

Only use a flat collar or loosened martingale and always supervise your dog when using this technique to break him of chewing an irresistible but inappropriate chew toy.

Alternative for Dogs with a Taste for Danger. A couple of years back, I had a rescued black-and-white spaniel mix who loved nothing more than sitting on my lap and watching TV after his training was done for the day. His name was Lucky, and he was going to make a great pet for some laid-back family who wanted a mellow, affectionate pet to love. Things were looking great for Lucky's future right up until I caught him doing something that could spell big trouble: he'd crawled around the television and was gnawing away on the tangle of wires behind it. Lucky was in fact very lucky—he could have been electrocuted, but he walked away unscathed. While some dogs like to chew leather or socks or stuffed toys, others develop a taste for potentially deadly chew "toys," and that has to be dealt with immediately. I kicked into high gear to break Lucky of his habit using a technique called negative scent association to make it happen.

Some people use products designed just for this purpose, including bitter-tasting anti-chew sprays available in pet stores. These can work, but at the ranch I usually just turn to something I have in the fridge: lemon. It's cheap, I can use it anywhere, and I know it won't do any harm if I put it in or on the dog's mouth to teach him an important lesson.

To use this technique at home, simply slice a lemon into small wedges and keep it handy while you wait for your dog to start chewing on the problem object. You can move this step along by bringing your dog near the object and showing it to him. When he puts it in his mouth, give him a firm *NO* and squeeze a little bit of that lemon directly in his mouth. He won't like it, but it will *not* hurt him. Now offer the object to your dog again. Most won't take it the second time, but if yours does, repeat the *NO* and give a second squeeze of the lemon. Don't yell at your dog while you're doing this; you want to deter him, not scare him.

Next, rub a lemon wedge on the object (and around it if possible). In doing so, you'll create a heavily scented zone that will help your dog remember the next time he passes by that he had a bad experience there and should keep his distance. The negative scent association of the lemon in his mouth and the smell of it on the wires or other no-chew object should do the trick. This is a lifesaving tactic, so a little tough love here isn't against the rules.

The *Other* Puppy Chewing Problem: Nipping

You can't blame puppies for being full of bad habits—after all, they're brand-new to the world and don't know the rules. One of their most annoying behaviors is nipping. Like chewing, this habit arises from a combination of a puppy exploring the world with his mouth and teething at the same time. Those baby teeth are sharp, and nipping can turn into biting, so it's critical to get this issue under control sooner than later. I've seen far too many adult dogs who have this problem because the issue wasn't dealt with at the puppy stage. In fact, dogs who don't learn to stop nipping as puppies can grow up to be large dogs capable of exerting hundreds of pounds of pressure—with no malicious intent. They don't understand that their jaws have gotten stronger.

I knew someone a few years ago who had a Lab with a nipping problem that was never solved. The dog was two years old and weighed nearly ninety pounds—so the nip was more like a bite. He nipped at a neighbor's kid and broke the skin. After that, animal control was called to investigate. No charges were filed, and the dog was able to remain with his family, but that event was just a huge wake-up call for them.

Luckily, I have a quick-and-easy technique to solve this problem for good so you don't end up in a situation like that, so let's get started.

Step 1. Choose a natural chew or chew toy your dog really likes and will want. Don't have it on you, but keep it near enough for you to grab but out of reach of your dog. Most puppies are pretty predictable about nipping at playtime. If yours is one of these, start playing with him. It may seem strange to go looking to get bit, but bear with me because this technique is all about timing and it's easiest to do if you can be prepared to respond. Play with your dog, getting your hands close to his snout, and he'll likely nip at you.

Step 2. When the bite happens, you're going to grab your puppy's collar with one hand and insert the thumb of your other hand into his mouth in a move I call the remote control hold. You're going to hold your dog's bottom jaw exactly like you'd hold a remote control for a TV. Your thumb will be inside his mouth on his tongue while your other four fingers are on the bottom of his jaw. Don't squeeze; just hold on to the collar so your puppy can't back away. Now you've turned the tables on him and made his annoying habit annoying for him. As you're holding on, give your dog a *NO* command and maintain your grip. Many puppies will struggle, but hang on until your dog settles down. Use the collar—not the jaw—to control him if he struggles. Once he's calm, wait another five seconds and release. Do not praise.

Step 3. As soon as you release your dog, give him the chew. This will divert his mouthing to something more appropriate. Reinforce the idea that the chew is an acceptable target by petting him as he chews on it. After a few minutes of reward time, take the chew and put it back out of sight, then begin playing again. If your dog nips at you again, repeat the process. Most dogs pick this up after two or three times, quickly learning the difference between reprimand and reward. Some might take a little more practice, but almost all of them choose the reward once they figure out they have a choice.

Training Tips to Remember

Don't Squeeze. Be sure you don't squeeze your puppy's mouth as you're training this. You're just holding on with minimal pressure and holding his collar with your other hand. You want to make this annoying for your dog, but it should never hurt him.

Hold Out for a Full Five Seconds. It's important that your puppy shows he is calm while still in the remote control hold for about five seconds before you release him. This teaches him that remaining calm will get him what he wants. If you let him go when he's still struggling, all he'll learn is to fight his way out of the situation—and that's a bad habit you definitely don't want to instill.

Hang On to That Collar. Keep a firm grip on your dog's collar while you use this technique. Most dogs will try to back away as you're doing this, and holding the collar ensures that doesn't happen and keeps you in control.

Fair Warning. As a general rule, this technique works great on medium and large dogs. It's not as useful on dogs who weigh less than fifteen pounds.

One Lucky Dog

Once he learned that he was only allowed to chew his own toys, Flash was ready to move on to his next lesson—and it was a big one. The young boy in his new family was so excited about getting a dog—and Flash was such a quick learner—I wanted to find a way to start their relationship off with something fun and exciting for both of them. On an early visit with the family, I'd had an idea about how to make that happen. AJ loved to ride his bike, and Flash loved to exercise, so I took a little extra time to teach this dog how to run alongside a bicycle before he went to meet his new family.

Flash figured it out right away, and AJ couldn't believe his luck when I told him his new dog could explore the neighborhood with him if he followed the safety rules I gave him. The two of them

bonded almost instantly, cementing another great friendship between a kid and his dog. I couldn't imagine a better forever home
for Flash. It was an ironic but happy turn of events for a dog who
may well have ended up in a shelter in the first place because he
just wanted to *be a dog* and not just a furry, four-legged accessory for somebody's handbag. Oh, and for the record, Flash hasn't
chewed up one thing since he joined his new family!

Outtake

When I was in my early twenties, my grandmother asked me to
watch her house and dog while she was away. Amber, her two-year-
old dalmatian, was probably one of the worst-trained dogs in history. On her best day, you were lucky if she'd *SIT* for you. She also
barked too much, was barely housebroken, and chewed everything
in sight. I knew she was a handful, so I was well prepared for the
weekend ahead. But, you know, I still had to get the mail.

I didn't think my walk to the mailbox would give Amber enough
time to find trouble, but I was wrong. When I came back inside,
the house was eerily quiet. I knew she was in there somewhere and
that the silence was a bad sign. I walked through every room looking for her. Nothing. I retraced my steps. Back in the living room,
I couldn't see her, but I could hear loud chewing. I tiptoed toward
the sound and ended up right outside the pantry. As I slowly pulled
the door open, I just hoped I wouldn't find Amber chowing down
on anything toxic.

The good news was she was "only" eating dog food. The bad
news was that she'd chewed a hole through the bottom of a pre-
viously unopened forty-pound bag of it and put her entire head
inside. It appeared she'd already eaten about half.

I shouted, "Amber! *Bad* girl!"

She startled and tried to run away, but her head was so far into the bag that she was stuck. Rather than sit tight and wait for me to free her, Amber took off running, bag and all. Luckily, the bag served as a makeshift helmet so she didn't feel it much as she ran into the walls and the furniture. At that point, I wasn't even worried anymore about all the food she'd eaten. I just wanted to get the bag off her head before she hurt herself. She was in full panic mode and needed help.

When I finally managed to corner her and remove her feed bag/helmet/blindfold, Amber stared up at me covered in kibble dust, looking confused but satisfied. She wasn't sure what had just happened, but she'd eaten like a queen—easily a week's allotment of food in one sitting. I'm pretty sure she felt the hardship of being trapped inside the bag was worth it.

14

BARKING

Daisy was a ten-month-old terrier-poodle mix who was abandoned by her family. When I met her at the shelter, my first impression was that this dog was so small and scared it was hard to imagine how she'd survived on her own at all. There was nothing intimidating about her—not the little Mohawk she had going on with her fur; not the mad-scientist-looking eyebrows that lifted hopefully when I approached; and definitely not the earnest are-you-my-friend look she was giving me as I opened up the metal door to her kennel. When I picked her up, Daisy hung like a rag doll in my arms. It was as if no one had ever held her before.

Back at the ranch, a day with the pack seemed to do her a world of good. By the time I took her to the training yard on her third day, she'd transformed from an extremely cautious puppy to an enthusiastic student and an impressive athlete. This dog was able to leap on and off even my highest training pedestal like an all-pro jumper.

When we started working on her 7 Common Commands, Daisy was practically consumed with a wobbly, pent-up energy that made it tough to get or hold her attention. With the help of the Double Leash Lock-Off and some extra good treats, though, I was able to gain control and get her to focus. After that, Daisy took to training like a duck to water, breezing through her commands and moving on to more advanced challenges in just a couple of days. It might have been in her genes—poodles tend to be exceptionally smart and terriers are usually highly trainable—but whatever the reason, this dog was shaping up to be an obedience star. I could hardly wait to tell the family I had picked out for her—a great mom who was about to get married and her young daughter, who was hoping her new family unit would include not just a loving stepfather but also a dog.

I met with the family to tell them about Daisy and was pretty sure I'd made a good match. But when I got back to the ranch and went to check on her, what I found stopped me in my tracks. I could hear Daisy barking long before I got to her—a squeaky bark, steady like a broken record: *arf, arf, arf.*

I replayed the previous days in my mind and realized this was part of a bigger pattern. Daisy barked when she saw the mailman, barked when a squirrel ran across the top of the fence, barked when a leaf fell from a nearby tree, and barked, barked, *barked* when she played with the rest of the pack. It hit me then that Daisy's barking might have been the reason she ended up in the shelter in the first place. Now she was barking incessantly while she waited for me to get home. I stood outside and listened—hoping maybe she had some good reason for making such a fuss and would settle down on her own.

No such luck. Now I was faced with a big problem. Nobody likes to have a dog who barks all the time, but there are some situations where this behavior is a deal breaker. Daisy's new family lived in an apartment complex—and there is no worse mismatch than a barking dog for a family with neighbors just on the other side of their windows and walls. I felt a pang of regret for having already told the family about Daisy. If I couldn't cure this barking problem,

I'd have to call the deal off—and disappoint an eager six-year-old in the process. I can't tell you how much I wanted to avoid having that conversation.

I needed to solve Daisy's barking problem once and for all.

The Problem

Lions roar. Birds sing. Dogs bark. It's only natural. This is probably one of the things early humans liked about dogs because a barking companion kept intruders at bay. But problem barking is something else—something most of us instantly recognize, despite some owners who choose to tune it out. The reality is that we as a culture have advanced and moved on, but the dog still has instincts from thousands of years ago. There are lots of different motivations for dogs to bark, from boredom to protection to trying to get a little attention. Dogs coming from shelters often develop a barking problem simply because they've spent weeks (if not longer) at the epicenter of a bark zone. Since all the other dogs are doing it, many otherwise quiet animals join in—and soon it becomes completely normal to them.

Whatever the root cause, barking can easily begin as a small issue and then manifest into a big problem—sometimes right under your nose. Sometimes owners even inadvertently contribute to its worsening by giving their dogs treats to shut them up. It works, but do you see the problem? In the dog's mind, that's a reward *for barking*—a reason to keep it up!

Barking is an especially important behavior issue to take seriously because it's one of the most common reasons animal control or even the police are called about dogs. This can lead to warnings from the authorities or landlords, or strained relationships with neighbors. Ultimately, it can even lead to evictions. And you can guess where the dogs of evicted tenants often end up—right back at the animal shelter. Over time, this can become a life-or-death issue for a dog, so I always recommend dealing with barking issues as soon as possible.

The Approach

One of the most important things to remember when you tackle this problem is that barking is a natural instinct in any dog's DNA. There is simply no way to teach your dog to never bark again; that would be like asking a human to never speak. There are, however, ways to teach a dog to *stop* barking on command, and that's how you can get this problem behavior under control.

As with any training goal, there are lots of different ways to accomplish the objective. There are two main techniques I want to share with you here. I've used each of them successfully on hundreds of dogs, but I can't be sure which will work best for yours. Every dog is a unique, intelligent animal, and what motivates one to change a problem behavior may not be the best solution for another. That's why I always like to have options right from the start.

A Step-by-Step Plan

Technique 1

This is an effective, direct way to teach a dog to be quiet on your command, and it's all about perfect timing. The only tool you'll need in this process is—yep, you guessed it—a penny bottle or a Shake & Break.

Step 1. Making sure you're set up and ready is the key to this technique. Your bottle must be in hand. Next, you'll have to get your dog to bark. Usually the easiest way to make that happen is by ringing the doorbell or knocking on the door. With your bottle at the ready, reach your hand out (or enlist a helper) to ring the bell. Bad barkers will start yapping right away. As your dog starts to bark, *firmly* say the word QUIET, immediately shake your noisy training tool vigorously, and then say QUIET again. The sound will momentarily startle your dog and stop the barking. Some dogs will even back up a few feet at the new and unpleasant sound. That short startle is the secret to this technique.

Here's why it works: When a dog goes into a full-steam barking frenzy, all five senses slowly fade away. The barking is the first step in an instinctive protective response. The more fired up your dog gets, the more that tunnel vision takes effect—so much so that unless you yell at the top of your lungs, your dog probably won't even hear you. Unless you jump right into her line of sight, she probably won't see you. Let me explain it another way: Imagine you're watching TV at home and someone is sitting beside you, talking. If we're honest, I think we've all had that moment when we know that person is talking, but we're so focused on our show that we aren't hearing the words. We just hear the sound, *blah, blah, blah, hoopity, hoopity, blah, blah* . . . It's only natural that your ears focus on one thing at a time. But if the talking person catches your attention and you start listening to him or her, then the noise of the television becomes the *blah, blah, blah* in the background. This is exactly what happens when a dog is completely focused on a perceived intruder or other barking motivation. That's her TV show. Does she hear you while she's thinking about it? Barely, if at all. You need to create a distraction to recapture her attention. And that distraction is your penny bottle or Shake & Break. They make such distinctive sounds that when your dog hears them—especially for the first time (or the first time in a long time)—they cut right through and snap your dog back into reality for just a few seconds. This is where your timing comes into play. Saying the word QUIET right as your dog startles is how you teach her the command.

Eventually, your dog will need to understand the verbal command *without* the jarring noise. The order of things here is key in making that happen. Be sure to keep it consistent: ring the bell, your dog starts barking, give the QUIET command, firmly shake the bottle, and say QUIET one more time.

When you say the command the first time, you're subtly embedding it in your dog's brain. She may not even hear you before you shake the bottle at first, but there's a method to the madness, so bear with me. After you shake the bottle, you'll quickly give the command again. This time your dog will hear you—and associate QUIET with that noise she doesn't like.

Step 2. Practice this technique with your dog a few times a day every day for a week. Each day, shake the bottle a little less loudly and give more emphasis to the command—both before and after the shake. The shake of the bottle and the command will slowly but surely become inversely proportionate. As that happens, your dog will begin to focus on your voice along with, and then more than, the bottle. This is why you used the QUIET command all along—to condition your dog to respond to that word, whether she hears the sound of rattling metal or not. At first, what your dog hears is *blah* (SHAKE, SHAKE, SHAKE), QUIET. As the week progresses, though, she will reach a moment of clarity and know that *blah* was actually you giving the QUIET command. Once you reach the point where your dog stops barking upon hearing that first QUIET, your penny bottle or Shake & Break can be officially retired . . . for this technique.

Training Tips to Remember

When You Say* QUIET, *Say It Firmly. This is a disciplinary command. You're not asking your dog to keep quiet; you're telling her to do so. This is a place where your role as a benevolent leader or parent comes in. Use your best mother- or father-knows-best voice to convey your definitive, confident authority.

Be Focused on Your Timing. The command must be given and the penny bottle or Shake & Break shaken *right after* the barking starts. Waiting too long will get no results because the dog won't make the connection. Timing is a very important factor in the technique.

I've only encountered a small percentage of dogs over the years for whom this technique did not work, so set your goals not only to get the timing right and to practice consistently but also to not give up. Don't lose to your dog's will on this—your friends, family, and neighbors will all thank you once you've succeeded.

For the minority of dogs who don't respond to Technique 1, I have another technique that utilizes a different kind of training. It's a bit more complicated, but when you've finished, your dog will have learned not just one new skill but two.

Technique 2

This one is very advanced, so proceed only if you're ready for a challenge! It's kind of ironic, but over years of trial and error, I've found that one of the best ways to get a dog to be quiet on command is to teach her to bark on command first. This is a technique I learned while training dogs for television and commercials—especially in situations where the director wanted a dog who could bark on cue.

Most people think I'm crazy when I mention this approach, but when it's properly executed, it works like a charm.

All you'll need to get started:

- A leash
- A bag of treats

Make sure your dog is good and hungry for this training, because it's going to be real work for her. You can even train this technique at mealtime and feed your dog her whole meal as you work.

Step 1. Attach the leash to your dog's collar and hold the far end in your hand. This will give you control by keeping your dog in a steady position while you work. If you have a second person to help you hold the leash, that's even better. Now you're going to teach your dog to *SPEAK* on command. This isn't too difficult with excessive barkers. All you need to know is what triggers yours, and you can teach her in a matter of minutes. A knock or doorbell is a common trigger. If that's what cues your dog to bark, crack open your door just enough to reach the bell or knock, then do it. Your dog will instantly start barking—no surprise there. As she barks, stand between her and the door and give the command *SPEAK*, along with a corresponding hand signal. Choose a distinctive hand signal, like waving your pointer finger left and right in the air or maybe moving your hands like a puppet speaking. While she's still barking, give your dog a treat, but don't offer any praise.

Repeat this process several times over multiple short training sessions. This will lock in the *SPEAK* command and help your dog remember what it's all about. When you're finished, you will have given her structure for her bad habit—and in doing so you will have changed her game to your game. Keep practicing till your dog is speaking on command with a verbal command and hand signal only (no doorbell needed). Once she's mastered this new trick, it's time to add the next and most important step.

Step 2. Once your dog will *SPEAK* on command, give the signal and wait for her to bark. As soon as she starts, give her a new command: *QUIET*. Be sure to say it firmly—don't yell—but say it like you mean business. If your dog keeps barking, wait her out. She doesn't know what you're talking about yet. When she stops barking, wait a couple of seconds, then give her a treat. It's very important to wait those couple of seconds because this will teach your dog that she's being paid to be quiet *not* to bark. Every session, try to add a second or two of silence before you give your dog the reward. Within a week, you should be up to ten to fifteen seconds of silence, just for the asking. You'll want to give this process lots of repetition before you move on. It's important that it's firmly lodged in your dog's memory bank.

The more you practice this technique, the better your dog will get at it. Soon she'll be so good that she'll be ready to be tested when someone actually rings the doorbell. Remember that you're not teaching your dog to *not* bark; you're teaching her to *stop* barking when you say *QUIET*. Practice the *QUIET* command with planned doorbell rings, keeping in mind that this will be challenging for your dog. Don't spend more than ten to fifteen minutes in a single training session, and take long breaks in between sessions so your dog can process what she's learned. Some dogs take longer to consistently respond to this technique, but that's no surprise because barking is often a deeply ingrained habit. Remember, patience always wins the training game.

Training Tips to Remember

First things first. Why is this technique so effective? Because by teaching your dog to bark on command, you turn her bad habit into a trick. When we teach our dogs tricks, we're teaching them focus. And when they're focused, they watch, listen, and learn. So they hear you when you say *QUIET*, as opposed to when they're in a barking frenzy and not hearing a thing. Over the week, your dog will learn the meaning of *QUIET* and become conditioned to the word.

The Method Works Best for Obedient Dogs. If you're going to train this technique, keep in mind that having an obedient dog makes the process much easier. This isn't a starter skill, so if you're coming into it with a dog who hasn't learned the 7 Common Commands (or most of them) yet, start small with a couple of simpler commands before tackling this one.

Don't Overdo It. This is a challenging command. A few short sessions spread out over the day is ideal. Overtraining is never a good strategy.

Don't Shout. Remember that since it's the *QUIET* command you're teaching, you don't want to have to yell to make it happen. In general, it's never a good idea to get into the game of having to raise your voice when you ask your dog to do something. This is often the most difficult part for people because they want instant silence when they train this command, and it seems like yelling might be the way to get it. Instead, in the first few sessions, expect that it might take your dog twenty seconds or longer to quiet down. If you wait her out, that twenty seconds will turn into two seconds in just a few days. Keep a steady head and take your time.

Tools You Can Use

I'm a technique junkie, so I like to solve problems through training. However, if you need a quick fix to help until you get results, there are a couple of tools that can make a difference.

Citronella Collar. A citronella collar sprays citronella in your dog's face when she barks. The pros of this simple collar are that it's fast and effective on a decent percentage of dogs. It's easy for you to use, and it won't harm your dog. The cons are that it can be too bulky for practical use on small dogs, it requires some maintenance from you (batteries, refilling the citronella), and if you don't get the settings right, it can't possibly distinguish between barking you deem to be acceptable (like a *woof* of hello to a neighbor) and the barking that's trouble.

Ultrasonic Collar. An ultrasonic collar works on a similar principle to the citronella collar, and has many of the same pros and cons. A couple of things worth noting, though: because the collar emits a high-pitched sound only your dog can hear, it's not a great option for a home with more than one dog or a dog who spends a lot of time around other dogs in general. Punishing an innocent-bystander dog with an unpleasant sound is kind of a rotten thing to do, and I wouldn't recommend it.

Ultrasonic Remote. Unlike the collar, this is a remote control you hold in your hand. Most come with at least two settings—a positive sound and a negative sound. You can reinforce the positive sound by occasionally rewarding your dog at the same time you use it. The negative sound is extremely high-pitched and off-putting to most dogs. The advantages of this are that you have more control—you can utilize the remote when you want to deter your dog's barking. That's also the bad news, though, because if it isn't consistently used in conjunction with problem barking, your dog may have a hard time figuring out why on earth she sometimes hears that terrible noise.

Consult with a professional trainer if you're having a hard time deciding whether to use these tools.

Reality Check

As I stressed in Chapter 1, understanding your dog's breed is an important part of training. There are some breeds and groups that are known not only for barking but also bred for it. So if you have, for example, a beagle, don't be surprised if any technique takes a while for her to grasp. And know there's a small chance she won't grasp it at all. Scent hounds are barkers, period. This is not breaking news. It's in their DNA to bark loudly and excessively, and every scent hound owner should know this. If you educate yourself on your breed, you'll not only have a better understanding of why your dog behaves the way she does but also know whether you should be prepared for a long-term training program rather than one that requires only a few days' work.

One Lucky Dog

Thankfully, Daisy was almost as quick in her response to training to stop her barking as she'd been to her 7 Common Commands. In order to make absolutely sure she could be quiet, I left her alone for a long stretch at the ranch—all the while listening outside with a baby monitor for any barks. Daisy passed the test with flying colors.

She passed a few other obstacles, too—pretty much everything on the agility course I put together for her. I had hoped going this extra mile in her training would give Daisy an outlet for her excess energy, and watching her tackle agility was like seeing her find her calling. This dog was born to jump, and the hurdles focused all her energy and excitement into the joy of being able to do it.

In the end, Daisy was able to go to the family I'd picked out for her, and as I watched them put her through her agility paces at the playground, I was positive she'd found the right forever home. To this day, I still get e-mails from her family telling me about how she's the best in her agility class.

15

DIGGING AND ESCAPING FROM THE YARD

Years ago, I trained a three-year-old schipperke named Ernie for his owners. The big problem with this dog was specific to the backyard—a problem I couldn't miss as soon as I walked outside. At first glance, it appeared that this piece of property in Bel Air was afflicted with one heck of a gopher problem. There were holes everywhere—it looked like the mangled golf course from *Caddyshack*. But there was no gopher tunneling around underneath this family's house. The guilty party was Ernie, who'd started digging holes as a puppy and had been allowed to keep at it right up until the day I arrived.

Like any behavior problem, this dog's cute puppy pastime had turned into a big problem—so much so that by the time the family called me, only Ernie was really able to use the yard. For everyone else, it was a minefield. In his three years of digging, this dog had gotten seriously hooked. There was no way to know whether he was convinced his digging was important work or whether it just made him happy, but it was clear he had no intention of stopping.

The schipperke is one of those breeds that might look like a lap-dog but was never meant to be one. These dogs were designed to be independent, industrious workers. Ernie was pretty typical of the breed: intelligent, willful, and very strong despite his small size. Since his habit was deeply ingrained, training him to stop digging could have been a big challenge. But over the years I've found a method for deterring this behavior that's practically foolproof. The approach is more of a trick than a technique, and it works because it engages the dog's own instincts against his bad habit.

The Problem: The Hole Digger

For dogs like Ernie, destruction is an art. Chewing and digging are projects that bring them back again and again to invest a little more time and a little more labor. You've probably seen this kind of

If a dog who was bred to work doesn't have a job,
he'll make one up—often to the detriment of your yard.

artful destruction in your own dog at some point: the chewed-up cushion that isn't quite "right" until the stuffing is strewn everywhere, the favorite toy he licks and pulls at until it *nearly* falls apart but doesn't, the hole in the yard that keeps calling him back to make it a little deeper or wider around. When dogs commit to this kind of destruction, they're not just burning off pent-up energy; they're creating a tangible memento of it. Many will return to the same project to work again and again.

We can't know what's going on in a dog's mind while he's digging a hole, but it's a safe guess that for some, the feel of the dirt under their paws, the satisfaction of the growing pile of it behind them, the possibility of finding some treasure buried deep in the ground—it's all a strangely intoxicating experience. For others, of course, it's just a means to an end—a way out. In this chapter, we'll talk about both diggers and escape artists. Together these two behaviors add up to an absence of backyard manners. Luckily, they can both be managed so you can reclaim your outdoor space.

The Approach

Sometimes the culprit in backyard digging is just a puppy being a puppy. Sometimes, like in Ernie's case, it's a grown dog who's little puppy problem was ignored until it became a big adult-dog issue. Like I've said many times before, small problems become big problems—if you let them manifest. I've seen this issue in both big and small dogs. Many of the little ones, like Ernie, are breeds that were designed to hunt and chase small game or vermin, so they're practically born itching to get their feet down in the dirt. That might have been the reason behind Ernie's habit, or it could have been driven by plain old boredom. He was an exception in one way though—I've never seen such an impressive moonscape designed by such a small dog. His yard was a field of craters. Typically the dogs who cause that much damage are bigger, breeds like Labs, huskies, Samoyeds, and chow chows.

One thing almost all diggers have in common (besides their shared bad habit) is that they're high-energy breeds. It's a good rule of thumb that if you've got a dog who was bred to work all day and you don't give him a job to do, he'll make one up. To keep a bored dog out of trouble, consider offering him more toys, more stimulation, more exercise—or all of the above. We'll talk more about this a little later in the chapter.

The go-to solution for most dog owners dealing with digging is a simple one: fill in the holes and hope the dog doesn't dig them up again. Unfortunately, this answer to the problem doesn't teach the dog anything—except maybe that the ground crew keeps messing with his excavation plans, forcing him to start over. There is a better way. My technique is one of the oldest tricks in the book, hasn't changed in decades, and not only stops most digging dogs in their tracks but cures them of this bad habit forever.

A Step-by-Step Plan

The only tools you'll need to combat your dog's digging:

- A shovel
- A pair of scissors
- Pet waste bags

Your other "supplies" are already in the yard—because, believe it or not, the best way to stop dogs' digging habits is by using their own poop against them. A lot of people laugh or look at me like I'm crazy when I say this but then come back to thank me after it works. Let's break this down.

Since dog poop is the magic weapon in the fight against the destruction of your yard, you're going to need a little stockpile of it for this to work. So when you scoop, find a place to save it—preferably using individual bags stored someplace cool and dry. How much you need just depends on how many and how big the holes in your yard have become. Once you've read through the steps below, you should be able to come up with a good quantity estimate.

Step 1. Locate every hole your dog has dug. As I mentioned above, those holes are your dog's art projects, so he likely makes a habit of constantly returning to them to make them deeper or wider or better in some other way. Once you've found them all, plug your nose, whip out your scissors, cut the tops off the bags, and put a piece of dog poop in each and every hole. Be sure to put it at the bottom.

Step 2. Use your shovel to cover over each hole (and the surprise you put in them) with an inch or two of dirt. This will camouflage the booby trap. If you skip this step, your dog will get wise to this game very quickly and just start a new hole instead of coming back to the old ones—and that won't help solve the problem at all.

Step 3. Let your dog out in the yard, pour yourself a lemonade, and sit back and watch the magic happen. Given a little time, most dogs will begin digging at one of their established holes, not knowing what's underneath that fresh dirt you added. When your dog does this, he'll hit the poop with the tip of his paw—and stop right there. Dogs hate the sight, smell, and taste of their own poop. Once your dog gets a little on him, he'll try to hold it away from him, wipe it off on the grass, and generally put some space between him and where he found it. From there, he may explore another one of his holes, which will also be booby-trapped.

It takes a number of tries for most dogs to grasp that something bad has happened to *all* their digging projects. Fortunately, the

AN UNNATURAL HABIT

Like most creatures, dogs naturally want to steer clear of their own poop. This aversion to their excrement is what makes it possible to successfully crate train and housebreak them. Sometimes, though, I hear from owners who are alarmed to discover their dogs—usually puppies—aren't just interested in their own waste, they're eating it. This is a pretty common short-term behavior in puppies—and a more unusual one in adults. The reason is simple: the only time it's normal and healthy for a dog to eat poop is when a mother dog is working hard to keep her den clean for a litter of puppies. Mother Nature temporarily turns off a momma dog's aversion so she can keep her little ones safe. She will consume their poop until they start to eat solid food—at which point she'll start expecting them to relieve themselves somewhere else. This behavior gives us two reasons why some puppies pick up this bad, but usually temporary, habit. First, they've seen Mom do it, and they are wired to copy her actions. Second, puppies explore *everything* in their environments with their mouths, including the icky stuff that really should not be tasted.

Unless your puppy is suffering from some kind of nutritional deficiency, he'll likely outgrow this habit. The most important thing you can do to make sure he gets past it is simple: keep your puppy's space, indoors and out, clear of poop. As soon as he goes, make it disappear. As long as he's not looking around and seeing it as either a mess that needs to be cleaned up or a mystery to be explored, he won't put it in his mouth. And if he doesn't get into a bad habit of consuming it when he's young, the natural aversion to his own waste will kick in as he matures—and this problem will resolve itself.

poop does all the work. Some dogs will return a couple of times to a hole to make sure. Others will get smart to the situation and start new holes. This is normal and expected, and when it happens, you simply need to repeat the same process. Put dog droppings at the bottom of the new hole, cover them with dirt, and leave it alone. At its most basic level, this approach—like so many behavioral fixes—is just a matter of transforming your dog's game into your game. It's your turn to make the rules and decide what happens next, but because of the way this process is designed, your dog has to figure those rules out for himself. If you've ever known (or been) the kind of person who has to learn every lesson the hard way, you already know that personal experience is the ultimate teacher—and that holds true for dogs, too.

Once trial and error convinces your dog that every time he digs a hole it ends up having an unpleasant surprise at the bottom, he'll give it up. Most dogs—about 90 percent of the ones I've worked with—decide this habit isn't worth the aggravation after just a few days of consistently finding their artwork's been tainted. Once your dog gets it, you'll just need to keep an eye out for any new holes in case he needs a quick reminder of why digging is no longer his favorite sport.

Step 4. I almost forgot to add one important footnote: be sure to check your dog's paws before letting him back into the house!

The Problem: The Escape Artist

There are certain breeds, including huskies, malamutes, border collies, and many terriers and scent hounds, that have a hard-earned reputation as escape artists. Most of the time, I see this behavior problem in high-energy working breeds. Some of them start digging to cool off or get comfortable, and then somehow figure out they can use their labor to get outside the fence to freedom. Others dig for the sole purpose of escaping. If your dog has this problem and curbing his digging with the method above isn't enough to keep him from trying to tunnel out, you're going to have to escape-proof your yard. Please don't chain your dog to combat this problem—no dog deserves that kind of life. Instead, enlist the help of a couple of friends and spend one afternoon beefing up your yard's perimeter so your dog can still enjoy the great outdoors without getting into trouble.

The Approach

Like the digging solution above, this method isn't about training; it's basically a construction project. But since we're fighting instinct here and your dog's safety is at stake, I'm all for taking the simplest solution. I usually think of the huskies I've known as I'm explaining this kind of animal-proofing. Over the years, they've been the most impressive escape artists I've met. It's no surprise, since the husky is one of the world's oldest breeds, which means they were bred not from other breeds that had been through centuries of genetic refinement but from wolves. As a result, many of them still maintain a pretty compelling wild side. So if you can create a yard that can keep a husky in, almost any other dog will stay put, too.

A Step-by-Step Plan

To escape-proof your yard, you'll need:

- A shovel or a hoe
- Concrete blocks, large stones, or rocks to span the length of the fence panel that contains your gate

Be sure you have enough blocks, stones, or rocks so that when you lay them end to end they're as long as the fence panel you want to dog-proof. Rocks are simpler and cheaper than concrete, but if you use them, make sure each one is softball-size or bigger. If your escape artist is a small dog, you can use less bulky stones, but be sure to choose ones that your dog will not be able to move. Rule of thumb: the bigger the dog, the bigger the stones need to be.

Step 1. Take a lap around the yard to assess the places your dog has escaped from. Most dogs do this near the gate. If that's the case with your dog, start there. Confine your dog inside and then dig a small trench—several inches deep—under the section of fence that has the gate. Extend it a foot or so past each end of the gate frame (for example, if your gate is four feet wide, your trench should be six feet wide). Now place the concrete blocks or stones in your trench and cover it back over with dirt.

Step 2. Now that the hard work is done, you can let your dog out, and let the blocks or stones do their job. Dirt is an easy medium for a dog to work in—but concrete is not. As soon as your dog hits a stone or block, he'll stop digging in that place and move on. Chances are he'll try a little to the left and a little to the right of his usual digging area, looking for an easier route—and that's why you built your trench wider than your gate. For many dogs, a couple of days of trying to figure this out will be all it takes to break them of their digging-to-freedom habit. Those who are more persistent, though, may move to another section of fence—and that will mean another day of shovels and blocks for you.

Even though this method is labor-intensive for the couple of hours it takes to place the concrete or stones, once it's finished, it works like a charm to keep escape-artist dogs safely in their own yards.

Getting to the Root of the Problem

One important thing to remember about both of the processes I've described in this chapter is that preventing your dog from digging only solves the problem he's creating. It doesn't address the reason he's doing it. The underlying issue in almost all cases of digging is that the dog is bored and actively looking for something to do about it. If you don't help your dog find an acceptable outlet for that energy, he'll find some other way to express it—and that method could be another kind of "artwork" that damages your home or property.

Instead of waiting for the dog to make the next move, introduce something new into his schedule to engage his body and mind at the same time you deter his digging habit. Take a walk at a different time or to a different place. Pick up a new retrieval or tug toy and play together. Sign up for an obedience class. Visit a dog park. Fill a food-puzzle toy with treats and let your dog work on it throughout the day. Any activity that engages your dog's intellect and lets him burn off excess energy will be a win-win for both of you.

If all else fails, consider getting your dog a friend from a shelter. In some cases, more dogs mean fewer behavior problems!

One Lucky Dog

Ernie was a smart dog—so smart that once he discovered all the holes he'd worked so hard on in his yard were tainted—he decided to take up a new habit. His owners helped him out with an "upgraded" walk schedule that provided him with more exercise every day. I'm happy to report that he's never dug another hole

since his first week experiencing this classic technique. Not coincidentally, no one in his family has twisted an ankle in the yard since then, either.

16

MEALTIME MISCHIEF

Tweety was a Maltese mix with a respiratory infection and a severe case of malnourishment. When the shelter reached out to me about her, they weren't sure if this little dog was going to make it. Four years old and weighing in at just five pounds, she was only at about half of her healthy weight. When I petted her, she was all ribs and hip bones—with no fat and hardly any muscle on her small frame.

When I first brought her back to the ranch, this tiny, fragile girl was nowhere near ready to start training. She was just a ghost of the dog I thought she could become, but before I could even think about assessing her, I needed to nurse her back to health. The veterinarian put her on a specialized high-calorie diet, along with an antibiotic. But after failing to thrive in her previous life, Tweety was cautious about everything, and I had to coax her to eat, a little at a time. I even pretended to eat a few bites of her food myself to get her interested. Through it all, this dog was as sweet as she could be, leaning into me, kissing my face, and always looking at me as though—despite whatever she'd been through before we met—she totally trusted me.

It was about two weeks after Tweety came home with me that she turned a corner. Suddenly she wasn't just this sad little lump of a dog. She started moving more quickly and confidently, and she showed me her silly side, racing around the training barn and then up to me for a quick head butt before taking off to do it again. She also gained two pounds. That meant she was ready for a red training collar and healthy enough to meet the pack of dogs at the ranch. Tweety loved them and they loved her. When she was playing with the pack, she never stopped wagging her tail for a second.

With her confidence back, it wasn't long before Tweety showed me that food—the thing that had been so scarce when she'd been living on the streets—was at the center of her one real behavior issue. After scrounging for so long and then regaining her health, she couldn't get enough to eat. And she didn't just want *her* food; she also wanted mine. I had a great family picked out for this dog, but it was a big family with young kids, and I needed to be sure Tweety could respect their boundaries at mealtimes and let them eat in peace.

The Problem

Tweety's issues of begging and trying to steal food were just a couple of the many behavior problems I encounter all the time in dogs who've never learned any mealtime manners. This is extremely common in shelter dogs, partly because many of them have never been properly socialized or trained, and partly because many of them know what it's like to go hungry and understandably get in the habit of doing whatever's necessary to secure their next meal.

These problems can all be managed and corrected with a little patient, consistent training. Trust me—I've had a *lot* of practice dealing with them over the years. Sometimes it seems like every dog I've ever allowed into my kitchen or onto my couch has taken its best shot at stealing or sharing my meals.

Let's break this down by behavior so I can give you tried-and-true solutions to combat begging, stealing, counter surfing, and that classic canine crime: garbage raiding. Keep in mind as you read that while these solutions are behavior specific, helping your dog brush up on her *NO* and *OFF* commands will give you two additional—and effective—tools in dealing with any mealtime misbehavior.

Solving the Begging Problem

If I had a dollar for every time I've sat down to enjoy a meal only to feel (and smell) the hot, stinky breath of a dog who's trying to horn in on my food, I'd probably be a billionaire. Some of those dogs even got close enough to steal from my plate. It's an occupational hazard I've learned to tolerate in dogs who are new to me. But that's not the way meals are supposed to be, so whenever I discover this is a problem, I teach the dog to respect my space when I eat.

The first rule of dealing with any begging or thieving dog is *do not give in*. If you want to make this behavior stop, you'll have to steel yourself against those big puppy eyes that are trying to convince you she is *so hungry* she can't stand it. If you give in and feed her while you're eating, you can expect to see an encore performance of the starving dog routine at your next meal, and the one after that—basically forever. So tell your dog *NO*, never feed her from your plate or the table, and get on with your meal. If I can manage to resist sharing food from my plate with a dog like Tweety—who actually *was* starving before I nurtured her back to health—then I'm confident you can resist giving in to your dog, too.

The first rule when dealing with begging: do not give in.

The next step in ending this behavior is creating a little extra distance between your plate and your dog. Mealtime can make man's best friend want to get *really* close to us, and that just doesn't work when we're trying to eat. The simple technique I use to make this point requires nothing more than a penny bottle or a Shake & Break and some consistent use.

Decide where you want your imaginary do-not-cross line to be. Some people want their dogs to stay a few feet away from the table, some just don't want dogs *on* them while they eat, and some don't care much where the dog is so long as she's not whining and begging at their every bite. How much personal space you need is totally up to you, but your dog will learn to respect your boundaries more quickly if you're consistent about it. So if the rule is no dogs on the couch while Mom's eating, enforce that every time. If it's no begging, enforce that.

Now all you have to do is prepare your meal, sit down in your usual spot, and plan to stay there. Have your bottle ready and set it on the table or right beside you. When your dog gets too close or starts to whine, tell her *NO*, shake the bottle, and say *NO* again.

Remain sitting and calm during this process, because if you have to get up to reposition your dog each time she gets too close, she won't learn how this whole mealtime thing is supposed to work.

Have your penny bottle or Shake & Break ready.
When your dog gets too close or starts to beg, tell her *NO*,
shake the bottle, and say *NO* again.

That's really all it takes. Repeat this same process during a few meals in a row, always keeping your rules consistent. After a few days of corrections and no rewards for begging or encroaching on your food, your dog will figure out that begging doesn't pay.

Solving Counter Surfing

Most of us know at least one dog who's found a way to use height or ingenuity to grab food off the countertop. This behavior is one of the most common reasons owners call me for help. This one is actually a bit tricky to fix because most dogs learn very quickly to be perfect angels when their owners are near—but the minute they're alone, they go surfin'!The solution to this problem starts with a trick every great parent knows—having eyes in the back of your head. Actually, a little secret surveillance is the tool you'll use to get this done, but your dog won't know the difference between a hidden camera and your ability to see all things at all times.

You'll need eyes in the back of your head, courtesy of a hidden camera, to stop counter surfing.

Let's break down the process. You'll need a couple of tools for this technique:

- Your trusty penny bottle or Shake & Break
- A baby camera or other video monitor
- Bait

You only need monitoring equipment good enough to let you see what your dog's up to—so an inexpensive used monitor from a garage sale is as good as a new one for our purposes. You can even set up streaming video on your phone, tablet, or laptop as long as you're able to monitor it from the next room.

For the bait, I'd recommend something tempting but pet safe like sliced roast beef or chicken—good stuff your dog is going to want badly enough to pull out all the stops to get it.

When the trap is set, watch your viewing monitor with
your noisy training tool in hand. Get ready to move quickly
once your dog's paws hit the counter.

Step 1. Place your camera in a location with a view of the counter-top. I recommend choosing a bird's-eye view of the room instead of a close, tight view. This will allow you to see what your dog is up to *before* she makes her move, so you can act in a timely manner to catch her mid-theft.

Next, place some of that bait on the countertop. Don't place it right on the edge; set it far enough back so your dog will have to work a little to grab it. You want her to get caught red-handed (with her paws on the counter) when you're making the correction. She'll learn the lesson faster if she's busted in the moment.

Now that your trap is set, grab your viewing monitor and your penny bottle or Shake & Break and leave the room. Be sure to stay close enough to be able to quickly return, but not so close your dog knows you're right outside the door. She may be too smart to fall for an obvious setup. Watch that monitor and wait. Habitual

counter surfers will most likely make their move in the first minute or two, but some dogs may take longer. Whatever the case,
wait out your dog.

Step 2. When your dog approaches the counter, get ready to move.
The moment you see her place her paws on it, quickly walk into the
kitchen, vigorously shake the bottle, and give the *NO* command.
As soon as your dog gets down, walk out of the room and go back
to waiting mode again. When your dog jumps up again, repeat this
process. I find that most dogs quit after the first couple of times
they experience this, but that doesn't mean the issue is solved. It
means you've won the first round. Tomorrow is another day . . .

Since dogs learn by trial and error, they're always testing to
see what they can get away with. Figuring out they can't feast
on deli meat today doesn't mean they won't try again, especially
because counter surfing is an easy gamble that's probably paid big
dividends in the past. The key to making this work is to convince
your dog that grabbing food off the counter actually triggers the
dreaded noise—and there's a good chance you'll have to repeat
the technique a few times a day for a week to convince her. Each
session should only take ten minutes or so, and each time you
should focus on pulling off enough of a surprise to startle your
dog. Over the few days this conditioning takes, your dog will
learn not to jump on the counters—and undoubtedly get to wondering how the heck you know what she's up to when you're not
even there.

Training Tips to Remember

Mix It Up to Convince Your Dog She's Alone. Some dogs
need extra convincing that they're alone before they'll fall for
this technique—especially after you've done it a time or two. For

starters, be sure to keep completely still and quiet when you're in the next room waiting for the jump. Next, change where you wait so your dog doesn't decide that surfing only has to be postponed if you're in one particular room or chair. Lastly, don't hesitate to get a little creative as you test this technique over a few days. Say good-bye. Put on your shoes. Slam a door. When I'm training tough cases, I often grab my keys and pretend to walk out the front door. I've even gone as far as having someone else sit in my truck and drive it down the block—that usually convinces even the smartest dog that it's time to belly up to the buffet.

Set the Game Up So You Win. Keep in mind that if your dog happens to actually grab the food while you're training this technique, that's not a reason to get angry with her. Remember, you set the game up, so set it up so you can win. If your dog beats you in a round, set it up better the next time. The key is to set the food far enough back that your dog has to work for a few seconds to get it, struggling to get her mouth around the prize. Those seconds are vital to ensuring you catch her in the act. If your dog is really superfast, you can put a leash on her for the first round so you can quickly correct without a struggle.

Don't Leave Food Unattended. Try not to leave food unattended on the counter unless you're training this technique—it's an invitation for your dog to get into trouble and potentially ingest something that could make her sick. I really can't stress this enough. Expecting an animal to ignore perfectly good food on countertops day in and day out is a lot to ask. It goes against every instinct. The technique here is for teaching your dog to steer clear of food occasionally left on the counter. But if you make a habit of leaving steak bones or cold cuts at the counter's edge, well, that's basically like dropping a hundred-dollar bill on a city sidewalk and expecting no one will take it. It's a *lot* of temptation—far more than the average dog who breathes and eats can withstand. All I'm saying is be reasonable and realistic.

Keep Chews and Toys in the Kitchen. Be sure to have some attractive chews and toys in and around the kitchen that your dog is allowed to gnaw on and play with. Providing an alternative to counter surfing will help ease the hardship of having her surfing days come to an end.

Solving Garbage Raiding

Sawyer was a young Lab I rescued from a shelter, and he was going to make a great pet for a family one day. But Labs are notoriously adventurous eaters—over the years I've had people tell me theirs have eaten everything from batteries to diapers to lightbulbs, rocks, and socks. These are dogs with no *full* sensor whatsoever, and that makes them frequent offenders when it comes to raiding the kitchen trash. Sawyer was no exception.

While I was reading on the couch one day, he sat down beside me and started working over a banana peel—which could only have come from the garbage can. A little bit of fruit is no big deal, but there was no telling what Sawyer might get into next. Another trip to the trash might bring him in contact with something poisonous, sharp, or otherwise dangerous.

Over the years, I've had a front-row seat to witness the consequences of a number of dogs eating dangerous things out of trash cans, and it's not pretty. This is why the lesson I designed to teach dogs to stay out of the trash is a little more bitter than most of my techniques.

I always tell my clients with this problem: when life gives you lemons, teach your dog to stay out of the trash can. For this technique, all you'll need is a little patience and a couple of fresh, sliced lemons.

Step 1. Take your dog to the scene of the crime as soon as you notice she's been dumpster diving. Show her that great spot where she found her last treasure and see if she goes looking for another one. You can even speed things along by showing her something you know she'll find interesting in the can. I know this sounds like entrapment, but it's better for your dog to learn this lesson sooner than later. In Sawyer's case, I brought him and the banana peel to the trash can, threw it in, and he went right for it again.

Remember that this is not the time to punish your dog for taking whatever she stole five, fifteen, or fifty-five minutes ago—in her mind, that's ancient history. Do this either while your dog is in the trash or within a minute after.

Step 2. If your dog goes for the bait, use that opportunity to correct her in the moment. Have your lemon wedge ready, tell your dog *NO*, and then quickly squeeze a little lemon into her mouth. In Sawyer's case, the moment he jammed his snout in the trash can to retrieve "his" banana peel was the perfect moment to correct him. If your dog goes for the object again, give her another shot of lemon. Most dogs won't want to get a mouthful of lemon juice twice.

If your dog isn't interested in taking the bait from the trash when you lead her to it, then you'll have to wait for her in order to get this process started. To do that, you can stay close by, or you can set up a monitor as was outlined to combat counter surfing earlier in this chapter.

Once your dog has been caught and given a shot of lemon for getting into the trash, take the rest of your lemon wedges and rub them all over the can. I like rubbing the rind on it because it tends to be a little more pungent and less sticky. Doing so will leave a strong scent your dog will associate with a bad taste in her mouth, and chances are she'll leave it alone. Dogs explore the world through their noses, so if your dog comes across the harsh scent of lemon in the future, she'll remember this lesson.

One Lucky Dog

By the time I was finished rehabilitating and training Tweety, she'd gained five pounds and mastered the 7 Common Commands. She was ready to go to her forever home. Tweety had been with me for several weeks, and we'd developed a close relationship. I had been her nurse, her trainer, and her family at a critical time in her life. Whenever I get that close to a dog, I worry a little bit that bonding with a new family might be difficult.

The family Tweety was about to join needed and deserved a dog who would be completely committed to loving them. They'd been through the loss of a loved one and were finding their way to a new normal in the wake of that tragedy. They hoped Tweety would bring a new energy and joy to their household, and that she'd give the children a new sense of purpose and responsibility.

When I brought Tweety to their home, the family welcomed her with open arms. I hoped she would embrace them, too. As I worked with the oldest daughter, Leilani, to help her become the primary handler, she put Tweety through all her commands. They both did a great job. And then I showed her the one extra command I'd taught Tweety during our time together. Since she was going to be a lapdog in her new home, I taught her *GET UP THERE* as a way to tell her it was okay to climb on someone's lap.

With the family sitting in a circle in their living room, Leilani guided her new dog from person to person, telling Tweety *GET UP THERE* as she moved around the room. Tweety moved from one lap to the next, happy to obey and meet the family. That little lap-sitting ceremony cemented it for me: I knew that this dog who'd been barely surviving when we first met had finally arrived in the place she belonged. She'd found her forever home.

17

SEPARATION ANXIETY
(A 7-DAY START)

When I first met Grover, his story was a mystery, but he was clearly in trouble. At just two years old, he was already a boomerang shelter dog. The facility that was holding him was a typical city shelter—cold and stark, with concrete walls and floors, bars on the doors, and no heat or air conditioning. The volunteers who kept the place running were doing everything they could, but with hundreds of animals on-site and few resources, the best most dogs could hope for was a few minutes a day out of their cells. I walked in to a deafening storm of barks, growls, and cries from every dog in sight—a sound that's as unnerving the thousandth time it's heard as it is on the first. As I made my way through the aisles, passing dozens of big, imposing dogs who looked like they could hold their own on the streets, I spotted Grover hunkered down against the noise, staring at the floor. The little poodle mix was pure underdog—small, defenseless, and scared.

Grover met me right up front at his kennel, as if he knew I'd been on the way to rescue him, and it was about time. He sat quietly while I opened the door and hopped on my lap as soon as I sat beside him. It was easy to see how he'd become a pro at getting adopted. What wasn't clear was why this charming little guy was getting so much practice.

I needed to figure out why people kept falling for Grover and then changing their minds, because every return trip to the shelter made it less likely he'd find a forever home. In all likelihood, with his track record I was about to give him his last chance.

In his assessment, Grover showed mastery of a few basic commands. He was able to *SIT*, get *DOWN*, *HEEL*, and *COME* on my first request—pretty impressive. Getting him to *STAY* was another story. Grover couldn't handle being more than five feet from me—and even then, his response was lackluster at best.

His first night at the ranch, Grover cuddled next to me on the couch and then slept like a baby through the night. No whining, no chewing, no marking, no accidents. But in the morning, I went outside to grab a leash from my truck, and the calm demeanor I was just starting to get used to disintegrated.

The second I closed the door, Grover started screaming—and I mean *screaming*—like he was wounded or under attack. I ran back inside, thinking he'd hurt himself. Grover met me at the door, wagging his tail as if I'd been gone a hundred years. I scooped him up and put him on the couch to check him for injuries. I pulled on his legs and poked around his body to see if he had some tender spot I'd missed before, but he was fine.

I went out again to grab that leash, and the screaming started as soon as I closed the door. From there I went into test mode. I had a hunch about what was going on, but I needed to be sure. I walked outside and simply stood behind the door. On the other side, Grover went ballistic. The second I peeked my head back inside, he quieted down and wagged his tail. I repeated this process a few times, always with the same results.

After that, I had a pretty good idea what the mystery of Grover was all about. He hadn't been attacked, but he might as well have seen a ghost. This dog was suffering from separation anxiety. And he had it bad.

Grover's was a classic case of a dog who'd become a product of his environment, whose life experiences had profoundly altered his personality. A life spent in and out of shelters, combined with an innate craving for companionship, had left him terrified of being abandoned. In just seconds spent alone, the specter of his deepest fears rose up and threw him into total, desperate panic. Grover's fate had come to be defined by a cruel catch-22: his fear of abandonment was causing him to be left behind again and again. Each time he came back to the shelter, his separation anxiety got worse, and his odds of being adopted into a loving home decreased.

If Grover continued on this path, he'd never find a home. I had a prospective owner in mind for him—one who worked from home, no less, but she lived in an upscale apartment complex, and unless I could cure Grover of this problem, he'd end up evicted by her HOA after just a small sample of the banshee-like antics he was showing me at the ranch.

Grover couldn't afford one more rejection. As I walked toward the door to go get that leash, I could see him gearing up for panic mode—whining, panting, and starting to shake.

This dog and I had a lot of work to do.

The Problem

It can be difficult to appreciate how traumatic separation anxiety is for a dog when you're the person who comes home to a wrecked room, a torn sofa, a soiled floor, and complaints from the neighbors about the awful racket that's been coming from your house. It's easy to feel, in that moment, like you're the victim in this situation, or even that you're dealing with a "bad" dog. If you have a dog with separation anxiety, I'm guessing you know exactly what I mean.

The thing is, though, dogs suffering from separation anxiety don't wreak havoc or bark themselves into a stupor when they're alone as a way to pass the time; they do it because they're overwhelmed by feelings of fear, panic, and grief. Being alone can be incredibly stressful for some pack animals, and it can be a cruel reminder of a troubled past for those with abandonment issues. The dog knows you've gone away, and he's terrified you'll never come back. That's separation anxiety in a nutshell.

Some dogs are much more susceptible than others to this condition, and Grover was the perfect candidate for a bad case: a sensitive personality who'd suffered a lifetime of neglect. He was loyal. He didn't like change. He had an active mind. He'd been abandoned before. All these components of his personality and experience, combined with his deep-seated fear of being alone, made him just the kind of dog to suffer a genuine, overwhelming sense of heartbreak each time the door closed and he was left behind. His case also highlights the reason training for separation anxiety is tricky—it means battling both nature and nurture.

If I had to guess, I'd lay odds that one of Grover's old families kept him as a neglected outside dog. Some dogs are bred for independent, outdoor work and might be able to handle an environment like that—at least for a while. But poodles are definitely not that kind of dog. They're a sensitive breed that needs attention and affection, and when they don't get it, they start fighting for it. It's in their nature to crave human contact and to build close relationships with their families. Grover probably got none of this at a young age—and then he was abandoned altogether. In the fallout, he turned his intelligent mind to coming up with creative, expressive ways of trying to prevent it from happening again; things like not letting the new owner out of his sight and screaming bloody murder every time I walked out the door.

There's really no way to overestimate how serious this problem can be. I've known dogs who've had such extreme cases that they've ended up wounded and in need of veterinary care. One terrier pawed at a door for so long some of his nails came loose and his feet began to bleed. Even then, he kept at it, thinking his actions would somehow let him out or bring his owner in. In another case, a shepherd mix chewed at the side of his crate until the metal came apart, damaging his mouth and teeth.

A dog afflicted with separation anxiety rides a devastating emotional roller coaster every single time he's left alone.

What would make a dog behave this way, to harm himself or your belongings, or to bark and whine for hours? Think about it like this: In the mind of a dog with separation anxiety, the minute you walk out the door is the minute you are *leaving* him. He believes from the moment you depart that you are gone—not for an hour or an afternoon, but forever. He thinks about what he can do about it, and really, what has he got? He barks, or whines, or tears into the curtains, the door, or a pair of your shoes. Destruction is often an animal's way of acting out or melting down. When you're gone, your dog is like some poor, sensitive, trusting kid who's getting his heart broken for the first time, and so he keeps calling and texting and trying to reach out—and getting no answer. The lump in his throat gets bigger and bigger and his composure falls apart, opening him up to acting erratically.

A dog afflicted with separation anxiety gets on that devastatingly emotional roller coaster every single time you leave.

This is a behavior millions of dogs and their owners struggle with, and it's one that can have serious consequences. In addition to the obvious issue of property damage, dogs who bark or whine incessantly when left alone can trigger hostility from neighbors or even calls to animal control—which can in turn lead to owners who give up on their pets. For the dogs who wind up in a shelter, actually being abandoned is the realization of their worst fears—and it will make it that much harder for them to overcome their issues if they ever get adopted again.

Cause and Effect

There is no single hard-and-fast cause of separation anxiety. It's a condition that impacts dogs across all breeds and ages and personal histories. Some dogs seem to be born to it, exhibiting an innately clingy nature and fear of being alone even as puppies. Others come by it as a result of life experiences—moving from home to home, being abandoned, being left too long on their own, or having a bad experience while alone. That leaves you coping with the fallout from someone else's irresponsibility, picking up the pieces of their neglect.

Because you may be dealing with a personality trait that's deeply ingrained in a dog's DNA or firmly rooted in his psychological past—or both—separation anxiety is one of the most difficult problems to tackle and train.

A Layered Approach

To deal with the unique and complex challenges of separation anxiety, I've devised a tactic I call a layered approach, a term I coined to describe a combination of different tactics and methods to achieve a behavior goal. This is a completely different process from teaching basic obedience. In obedience, I always have a plan A, plan B, plan C (and sometimes more). I know what I'm going to do, and I know at what junctures a dog is likely to resist and how I'll respond.

Treating separation anxiety, on the other hand, is a process of trial and error, and it's often one in which the best solution turns out to be neither plan A nor plan B, but an approach that incorporates elements of A, B, C, and more. The secret to making this work is figuring out which layers, in what combination, have an impact on your unique dog.

Before we delve into training specifics, take a moment to think about the gravity of the task at hand. The only way you're going to get results in a dog with an anxiety disorder is by training your dog in a spirit of calm, patience, and reassurance. The face you show your dog is the face your dog will show back to you. You need to present steady confidence for this to work.

Too often, I encounter dog owners who are so frustrated by a dog's separation anxiety they start to lose it at the very first sign. The thing is, you won't get anywhere by shouting *QUIET* or by laying into your dog for chewing your shoe or having a house-soiling accident during the breakdown he had while you were out. Trust me when I say he already feels bad enough. At the outset of this process, the only thing that makes your dog feel better is your return, and if that's marred by anger and punishment, he may start living with anxiety all the time instead of just when he's alone.

Your Dog's Individual Plan

Because we're taking a layered approach to this intervention, you may not need to take all the steps—each of them can be effective on its own, or you may want to pick and choose combinations. Be aware at the outset that this kind of training takes some time. It's possible to make great strides in seven days of anti-anxiety training, but only if you can make time to monitor your dog and respond appropriately. Don't be surprised or disappointed, though, if it takes longer.

Technique 1

A Lesson in Object Permanence. We're going to teach your dog that when you leave, you always come back. The best way to tackle this training is with the help of a baby monitor (an inexpensive used one is fine) and a ready supply of treats your dog loves. Position the monitor's camera in an area that has a good vantage point of a portion of your home. You want to be able to keep eyes on your dog at all times, so set up the camera with a broad view and close doors or otherwise block areas that would be out of sight. Put your dog's bed in this area.

Next, with the treats in your pocket, the monitor in hand, and patience on your mind, walk out the door. Go far enough away that your dog can't see you, but stay close enough to get back to the door in a hurry. From here on out, it's a stakeout. You're going to observe the monitor and wait for the right moment.

Like Grover, most dogs who are afflicted with severe separation anxiety will instantly go into panic mode when you leave: crying, pacing, scratching at the door, or exhibiting whatever other behavior has cued you into the problem. You are going to have to wait it out. It might take a minute, or it might take fifteen minutes or more. Whatever the case, you're going to watch and wait for a break in your dog's panic. Even the worst-afflicted dogs have moments of silence, so hang in there.

When you see the moment of stillness you're waiting for, count to ten and start moving those treats from your pocket to your hand. When you get to ten, hustle back inside, praise your dog calmly, and offer a treat. Make the whole interaction short and sweet, fifteen to thirty seconds should be good because you're still in the middle of a training exercise and have to get back to work. Remember, this whole technique is all about teaching and rewarding *calm*.

From there, we repeat the process. Walk out the door and out of sight, keep your eyes on the monitor and be ready to hurry back to calmly reward the next ten seconds of silence. You're going to do this over and over, but with each passing session, add a little more time. At first, this will only be a few extra seconds. As your dog starts to figure out that silence earns rewards, you'll help him work from seconds to minutes and longer.

This type of exercise is called memory association training, and the goal is simply to start replacing your dog's existing negative association of being alone with new, positive experiences. I needed to teach Grover that he could count on a happy reunion with me every time I left him alone. I wanted to change his focus from my departure to my return.

It's a lengthy battle, but the results are worth the fight.

Grover's anxiety was extreme, but he's a smart little guy. It took him all of about ten minutes to figure out I'd only come back if he was quiet. As that first session went on, I built his silent moments from just a few seconds to about two minutes. Eventually, though, we hit a plateau.

Hitting a plateau is totally normal and expected, no matter what—or who—you're teaching. You're dealing with an emotional being, and emotional beings have all kinds of limits based on endurance, tolerance, and personal sensitivities. It's almost inevitable in training that after a period of building and progressing, you're due to hit a wall. At that point, it's time to end the session, reassess your plan, and get ready for the next step in the process.

In this case, that meant incorporating another facet into the layered approach of Grover's training.

Technique 2

Appeal to Your Dog's Dominant Sense. For this step, you'll need a T-shirt that you've worn for at least a day. That way it'll smell like you. This is an old technique I learned when I was a teenager training wild animals. Many animals explore the world through their noses—which is a little hard for you and me, with our comparatively weak sense of smell, to understand. I may not be able to detect all the complexities of smell an animal can, but I've seen firsthand how important those smells can be.

When I was growing up, we had a grizzly bear who could be a little temperamental with new people, so we had to take great pains to make sure he could safely go out on jobs. Of all the techniques that might have made this possible, there was only one that worked amazingly and consistently. Whenever we booked a movie or commercial for Brutus, we'd have everyone who would be on the set wear a shirt for a day and give it to us. We'd then pin all those shirts up in the bear's pen for a couple of weeks so he could get used to the scents. We'd feed him, play with him, and give him an overall positive experience in the presence of his laundry line of tees. Come shoot day, we could safely bring our temperamental bear on the set, because as far as he was concerned, he already knew everyone there. He was familiar with every scent, and we had our green light to safely get to work.

If you've ever wondered why your dog sleeps on your dirty laundry or eats your underwear (or shoes) while you're away, this is the reason. He's trying to remain close to you despite your absence, and he's using his strongest sense to make that happen. In order to capitalize on this instinctive draw toward the scent, I apply a technique called positive scent association in training. I use it on a lot of the dogs I rescue and train on *Lucky Dog*, especially as a means of introducing them to their new families before they ever set foot in their forever homes.

Something as simple as a familiar smell can drastically lower a dog's anxiety, giving him comfort when he's alone. So as you start your next phase of training, get your T-shirt ready. If you have a small dog, put the shirt on his bed in view of your monitor camera. If you have a big dog, you can put the shirt on the bed, or, if it'll fit and he'll tolerate it, you can put it right on the dog. This is the next layer of your anti-anxiety program.

With the extra layer of comfort your scent provides in place, try Technique 1 again to see how your dog does.

Technique 3

Let Your Dog Hear You. In addition to bringing positive scent association to your dog's alone time, you can also soothe his sense of hearing. Some people just leave a television or radio on to combat the silence, but we're pulling out all the stops here, so let's take that one step further. Make a recording of your own voice, speaking in a calm, positive tone for your dog to listen to. For Grover, I recorded an essay about the remarkable intelligence of poodles. Use your computer, a CD player, an iPod, or a tape recorder to play that recording on a loop. That way the sound of your voice, just like your scent, can be a comfort in your absence.

Once again, repeat that first technique. Work as long as you're seeing steady progress, but don't push too hard, and always stop when (or better yet, before) your dog starts backsliding. Remember that this is a wildly advanced endeavor—one that's trying to counteract your dog's most deep-seated fears, so your daily goal should be a little improvement, not a miraculous cure.

Rome wasn't built in a day. This is going to take at least seven, and possibly a few more. Of the seven behaviors we're correcting in this part of the book, separation anxiety is the one most likely to require extra time to be successful.

Technique 4

Tools You Can Use. This step is all about giving your dog a feeling of security when you're not home. There are a number of products designed to accomplish this goal, but two of them worth considering are an anti-anxiety shirt (or a similarly designed compression garment) and a plush toy designed to mimic the presence of a littermate.

The anti-anxiety vest or shirt works on the premise of swaddling, just like you might do to soothe an infant. You wrap your dog snugly in the shirt and secure it with Velcro. Although this method doesn't work for every dog, I've seen enough who are soothed by it to believe it's worth a try.

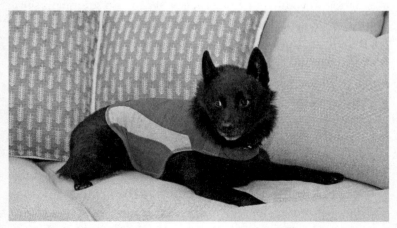

An anti-anxiety vest may help soothe your dog.

The plush dog is a toy designed to come home with a new puppy. It looks like a stuffed dog, has a warming pack inside it, and has a "heartbeat" your dog can hear and feel.

To increase the odds that either of these tools helps your dog, try putting them under your pillow for a night so they pick up your scent before offering them to your dog. Again, with this new layer in place, work on your dog's timed intervals, stretching them into the several minutes range.

Technique 5

Provide Treats and Toys for Test Days. As you make gradual progress with your dog's calm-time training, the day will come when you're ready to take a step back and see how he does without you for an hour or more. On that day, you can add another layer to your dog's coping arsenal by providing him with something to keep him busy. Food puzzles, chew toys (for dogs who aren't in the habit of swallowing them whole), and interactive toys that can be filled with small treats are all good tools to keep your dog occupied while you're away. Bully sticks are great for this because they take hours to get through. Whatever object you use to fill this bill, save it till the day of your departure so it's new and interesting, introducing it to your dog just before you go.

Out-of-the-Box Alternatives

In addition to training-based measures you can use to combat separation anxiety, there are a couple of other possibilities you might consider if your dog isn't improving with steady work. These are serious steps, but each offers a type of solution not available through training alone. Remember that these options are all layers you can add to the ones you've already put into play.

A Second Dog. It may sound counterintuitive to suggest a second pet when the one you have is extremely needy, but a companion dog is sometimes a solution to the anxieties that plague a pet who hates to be alone. I'd recommend finding a local rescue group that offers trials prior to any adoption so you can see how the two dogs get along. This way you're not committed if it's a bad match.

Medication. There are very few dogs I'd recommend anti-anxiety medication for because the medicine doesn't solve the problem; it simply masks it for as long as it lasts. But it is a last resort measure worth considering if your dog's anxiety is so bad he's at risk of injuring himself. In that case, ask the veterinarian if there's a medication available that might help relax your dog's nerves so you can ease him into training. Any use of anti-anxiety meds should be paired with training. You want to solve the problem, and the only way to truly do that is by working with your dog.

Following the same line of thinking without getting into prescription meds, you might also consider incorporating a veterinarian-recommended calming supplement or even a calming spray to help make your dog more at ease so you can focus on training.

Professional Help. You'll rarely hear me saying a behavior issue requires the hands-on help of a professional dog trainer, but separation anxiety is a complicated issue, and there are times when a professional consultation can be useful. As you explore the options in my layered plan—whether you try one of these methods or all of them—keep in mind that this is one of the toughest challenges in dog training, and it's okay to ask for help if you need it.

Separation anxiety is a complicated issue, so maybe we won't get your dog to the point of being completely Zen in his alone time, but we can help him achieve a calmer—and less destructive—demeanor.

One Lucky Dog

In the end, Grover was able to overcome his separation anxiety to the point where he could go to his forever home with a Southern California antiques dealer. Re-homing a dog I just taught to deal with separation anxiety posed some unique challenges, since the last thing I wanted to do was make Grover feel abandoned again. I knew he was going to have a wonderful relationship with his new owner, but he had to learn that for himself before I could leave him. When Grover went to his new home, I went with him, and kept coming back over several days, spending a little less time on each occasion until he seemed fully bonded to his new owner.

These days, Grover and Laurie spend most of their time together—in her apartment, at client meetings, out for walks. It's a lifestyle that suits Grover perfectly. But when he has to be alone, the dog who once had me convinced he'd suffered some grievous injury as I walked out the door has learned an important lesson: if he just waits patiently, the person he loves most in this world always comes home. To this day, I get e-mails from Laurie saying how much her life has changed with Grover. He's completely settled in his new home, finally secure in a family he can count on.

Outtake

When I was living in New York City, I was working with a terrier who had terrible separation anxiety. I had him at my place in the East Village for about two weeks of intensive training. Even though I was committed to helping this dog overcome his problem, there were times when I had to leave him in my apartment to meet other obligations—and he didn't like it.

The neighbors didn't like it, either. Each time I went out, I'd come home to find notes taped to my door telling me my dog was too loud or to please get him under control. Every day, the terrier and I were making slow progress, but as I've been saying, this is an issue that takes time. About a week in, I went out for a couple of hours and returned to find a note that ironically summed up the whole situation—but the owners' situation, not mine. Scrawled in big, bold letters with multiple exclamation points to make it clear this neighbor had had enough were just four words: GET A DOG TRAINER!

18

AGGRESSION
(*NOT* A 7-DAY PROJECT!)

Before we delve into the specifics of canine aggression, I'd like to tell you about a pivotal moment in my experience with dogs who have this problem. Years ago, when I was a young animal trainer and had worked with a few thousand fewer dogs than I have today, I took on a client with a difficult 120-pound shepherd-chow mix—let's call him Odin. The family told me Odin had gotten aggressive with a couple of people coming into their house—a dangerous situation with such a big, powerful dog. I needed to test his reactions for myself to be able to work with him, so I asked the owners to put two leashes on him—one from his collar and one from a harness—and be ready to pull him back. Then I put on a bite sleeve—a protective arm cover trainers wear when teaching bite work or working with aggressive dogs. I walked through their front door and took a few steps toward the dog, leading with my covered arm.

It only took a few seconds to realize that the reports of Odin's aggressive nature had not been exaggerated. In fact, as often happens when owners talk about their dogs' aggressive behavior, it had been downplayed—a lot. Odin lit up, grabbing me with enough force to nearly rip my arm out of its socket. The leashes made no difference, and if I hadn't been wearing the bite sleeve, that quick, brutal attack would have maimed my arm for life. Even two people holding him couldn't stop his horsepower as he lunged forward. Even with the protection of the sleeve, I was black-and-blue for a month after that meet and greet. This dog meant business.

Even though that first interaction sent up a huge red flag about this dog's temperament, I was a young, optimistic trainer, still holding on to the belief that training could change almost anything about almost any dog—even when DNA was a likely factor. I was determined to turn Odin into the trustworthy, good-natured animal his family wanted him to be. I spent the next two months working with him, socializing him to different situations that might set him off, raising his tolerance for people coming into his territory, and rewarding him for staying calm. When I was sure he was a changed animal, I told the family he was ready for his next big test.

I put on a hat and glasses, pulled on a bite sleeve (just in case) and covered it with a jacket, then walked into the house and right over to the dog's bed. Odin didn't move. I sat down on the floor next to him; he looked away. I turned to the owners and started talking about their problem being solved. I was focused on the family and not paying any attention to the dog or his body language—and was totally unprepared when Odin snapped, lunging at me with ferocious strength. I only had a split second to react—just long enough to give him the arm with the bite sleeve instead of a more vulnerable target.

I've had a lot of close calls with big animals in my career, but in that moment I nearly had my face rearranged. It probably should have put me off aggressive dogs for life, but what it really did was make me wonder how many dogs I'd walked away from in the past, saying, "Problem solved," when it really wasn't. After that, I trained hundreds more aggressive dogs, obsessed with answering the age-old question *of whether* aggression can be eliminated. The short answer is *no*. But there's more to it than that. I'm probably the last person to give up on a dog who can be trained to be a good companion, so the powerful lesson I learned that day with Odin— and have seen proven true more times than I can keep track of since—is this: instead of focusing on *solving* canine aggression, dog owners need to focus on *managing* it. In many cases, it is possible to get this problem under control—but you can never erase it from a dog's DNA. Aggression is never cured; it's just in remission.

Does this mean that there's no hope for your dog if he has aggressive tendencies? Absolutely not. It means that as an owner you need to acknowledge that while some dogs are aggressive for specific temporary reasons, others just *are* aggressive, born with a trait embedded deep in their genetic material that isn't going away. We've all heard the expression it's all in how you raise the dog. But that's just not true if the behavior is part of a dog's biological makeup; DNA matters just as much as environment. What is true is that as a good dog owner, once you accept that your dog may always harbor an aggressive streak, you can learn how to recognize his warning signs and how to defuse a situation before it escalates into something where a life is in peril. We'll talk about how to do both of those things in this chapter.

A dog with managed aggression can still be a great pet, but not every aggressive dog is suitable for every family. Before I realized that Lulu was destined to be my dog, I had to rule out homes with kids and homes with other dogs for her—she was just too aggressive to be a good fit for either. Deep down, she still has that same streak in her today. It starts with her low tolerance for the unpredictable—so if she sees a toddler careening toward her or a big, dopey, loose cannon of a puppy coming her way, she feels threatened and gets ready for a fight. She was hurt in the past, and she's not about to let it happen again. That's *fear aggression,* which we'll talk more about in a minute.

But I know my dog's triggers and I know her signs. So when I see a likely target for her aggression or notice her getting tense or ready for a fight, I bring her attention back to me and change the dynamic before things get out of hand. I basically put water on the fire while the flame is still small.

In a nutshell, that's what being a good owner of an aggressive dog is all about.

The Problem

For dog trainers and owners alike, aggression is a huge gray area. No two aggressive dogs are alike because what triggers one dog might be completely different from what triggers the next. The ways aggression is activated and the ways it's exhibited are almost as unique as the dogs themselves. For this reason, I'm always reluctant to give advice on this topic over the Internet or on television, and I'm stepping out of my comfort zone to even write about it here. That said, I don't think it would be right to write a dog-training book that ignores this make-or-break behavior problem.

Before we dig into this topic, I want to make it clear that aggressiveness is not a behavior issue to be taken lightly. I firmly believe that most dog owners are more than capable of teaching the commands and handling the other behavior issues in this book with little more than the instructions I've provided and a positive, patient attitude. However, when it comes to aggression, I recommend you trust your instincts if you feel your problem is more than you can handle. There are times when consulting a professional trainer is the right thing to do, and this is one of them. I hope you find the information in this chapter helpful, but I want to be sure you know it is in no way a substitute for a meeting with an experienced training professional.

A Dog's Dark Side

I've never been the kind of trainer to claim I have all the answers, and there's no area where this is truer than when it comes to aggression. I make it a point to be honest with my clients, always telling them that I can't take the aggression out of their dogs. What I can do is teach the owner how to spot the signs of an escalating situation and how to defuse it before it's too late. Anyone can have an aggressive dog, but what sets good owners apart is that they know exactly how to handle a potential outburst.

Before we dig into the specifics of aggression and how to recognize and prepare for it, let's acknowledge that in extreme circumstances, any dog can reveal a dark side. When he's threatened or cornered, a dog's instinct kicks in and his mind and body go into fight-or-flight mode. His senses narrow, focusing on whatever it takes to ensure survival, and everything else falls away. That's why dogs don't seem to even hear us when they're in fight mode. They're only hearing, seeing, feeling, smelling, and tasting the struggle ahead. In the moment, nothing else matters to them.

This is courtesy of millions of years of evolution in which wild dogs had to protect their dens and fight for females, food, or land. The wild can be a very unforgiving place, and the domestic dog as we know it today is just one step out of that wilderness. We see a fuzzy little lapdog sitting on a couch and quickly forget that his recent ancestors were hunters, fighting for survival day in and day out. Trust me when I tell you your dog in many ways is still that animal; you've just taken away the reasons for him to fight.

People experience the same kind of adrenaline-driven responses, sometimes in miraculous ways. A 120-pound nineteen-year-old woman from Virginia lifted a truck off her father after it slipped off a jack and pinned him to the garage floor. She couldn't explain it afterward except to say she'd experienced a "crazy strength." I'm sure you've read about other examples of that crazy strength. Parents save their children. People save themselves. And sometimes people hurt each other, fueled by the very same fight-or-flight drive. It happens because in survival mode all energy in the body is committed to the fight. The same thing happens when a dog feels he needs to fight for his life.

So if your dog gets cornered or stepped on or attacked, and reacts aggressively one time, that doesn't mean you have an aggressive dog. It just means you have a living, breathing dog with an instinct for self-preservation. Problem aggression is something else. It's what happens when dogs display this kind of instinct and behaviors repeatedly and in ways that are not acceptable.

Two Categories of Aggression

Aggression can usually be classified into one of two main categories: defensive and offensive. A dog being bullied by another dog or involved in play fighting that gets too ruff (pun intended) and feels the need to fight to get out of the situation is displaying defensive aggression. A dog who goes to the dog park and charges up to another dog snarling and snapping is displaying offensive aggression. There are also subcategories of each area.

I want to point out that whether it's defensive or offensive, aggression rarely starts or stops all at once. For decades, a three-color scale has been the standard to describe dog aggression escalation: yellow, orange, and red. Aggression at the yellow level is still in a safe but on-alert zone. Orange is crossing over into a danger zone. And red is the zone in which there's nothing left to do but break up a fight. Your goal should be never to let your dog's aggression get past yellow.

Let's talk about how that's done.

Defensive Aggression

A dog who feels the need to defend himself and lash out is exhibiting defensive aggression. This kind of aggression is typically reactive, responding to some outside threat stimulus (or something the dog perceives that way). There are a few main varieties that I frequently see:

Fear Aggression. This kind of aggression is common in timid dogs who find themselves feeling cornered. Many small dogs, like Lulu, have fear aggression. There's no single reason for a dog to have fear aggression. Sometimes it's a personality trait an animal is born with; sometimes it stems from a lack of socialization or is a response to past abuse. Either way, this type of aggression is often directed toward strangers.

In most cases, dogs with fear aggression give you plenty of time to deal with their issues before anyone gets bitten. That's because a dog with fear aggression will typically back away and try to evade the threat before finally committing to a confrontation. It takes a lot of provocation to make a dog with fear aggression snap, though some can get into the yellow zone pretty quickly. Any dog who backs away while showing his teeth is basically announcing, *Get away or I'll bite.* As this is happening, the dog is in the yellow zone and the situation is still escalating. But once the dog backs up as far as possible and is snapping or growling, he's reached the orange zone. At this point, it's up to you to defuse the situation—by either removing the threat or getting the dog under control. With such clear warnings coming from the dog, fear aggression should never go red. There's plenty of time to deal with it before that happens if you're paying attention to your dog's signals.

If fear aggression is an inborn personality trait in your dog, there's not a lot you can do about it *except* take the very important step of being prepared to respond if you see your dog in the yellow or orange zones. Better yet, figure out what kinds of perceived threats provoke your dog and steer clear of them.

However, if a lack of socialization is a factor in your dog's defensive aggression, then you may be able to improve things by cautiously, positively socializing him to different situations so he learns they're not a danger to him. A dog with this kind of aggression can benefit from calm, gradual exposure to strangers, crowds, other dogs, and so on. I'd recommend socializing him with calm dogs who you know aren't reactive fear biters—dogs who can be peaceful around your dog and not back him into a corner. If you see progress when you try socialization, keep it up. But if your dog continues to be fearful and lash out, don't force it. Instead, focus on reading his body language and keeping him away from his triggers. Over time, a dog who stays out of the orange or red zones may actually become less fearful—and ultimately less aggressive— because his fears are not being realized.

Bottom line: never allow a dog with fear aggression to get cornered. Cornered animals feel the need to fight for their lives. If you take control of situations where you see this possibility, you can prevent the next bite or fight.

Possessive Aggression. Many dogs are born with a possessive streak. It's easy to spot, even in puppies. If you watch a group of littermates play with their toys, you'll see the occasional fight break out, usually instigated by a dog who just doesn't want to share. As dogs with this trait get older, some get more possessive and learn that fighting gets them what they want. It's all fun and games when you're dealing with puppies, but in adult dogs, this behavior is definitely not cute.

In puppies, this type of aggression is often responsive to training, though there's no such thing as an aggression fix that's 100
percent. If you're dealing with a possessive puppy, your dog has
not had time yet to get familiar with the feeling of wanting to have
or keep something at any cost. To discourage a young dog's possessive aggression, simply take away the object (food, bowl, toys)
he covets for a few seconds at the first sign of possessiveness. Then
return it. Repeat this process over and over, increasing the time
you take the item away a little more with each repetition. Eventually you can build up to minutes and then to hours. If your dog
shows any aggression at all, just stay steady with this routine. If
you do it gradually, a puppy will learn that there's nothing to get
angry about because the object of his desire always comes back.
This method conditions a puppy's immature mind to ease up long
before it reaches aggression mode.

Possessive aggression can be more difficult to deal with in an
adult dog because his mature brain knows what full-blown aggression feels like and may have made a habit of it. A dog who's had
years of experience getting into possessive battles already knows
what it's like and probably knows how many of those battles he's
won and how many he's lost. Typically, the more often a dog has
been successful with possessive aggressive behavior, the harder
that dog is willing to fight to keep it up. If this is the case with your
dog, proceed with caution if you're going to try to desensitize him
by taking things away and returning them. If your dog is not too
set in his ways, it can still work. But if the problem is more serious,
a better remedy may be to take the elimination route.

My grandfather used to tell me that I shouldn't take a pill to get
rid of a headache; I should get rid of the reason for the headache. If
your adult dog has objects that trigger his possessive streak, eliminate that headache by simply getting rid of those objects. Many
dogs are ball possessive but are fine with other toys. If the culprit
is the ball, take it away. If the problem is an object you can't get rid
of like food or a bowl, start feeding your dog in a different location

every day. This will throw him off his game and undermine his possessive streak.

You can also use your trusty penny bottle or Shake & Break to help with this issue. If your dog displays possessiveness over an object you need to eliminate, shake the bottle before taking it. This will potentially take your dog's mind out of aggression mode. At that moment you can start the process of trying to get him over it.

Bottom line: use caution when dealing with this kind of aggression. Confrontation is never the answer. It's not worth pushing things to that level because a dog's bite can get him a one-way ticket to a shelter, possibly to be euthanized. If you need help, don't hesitate to consult with a trainer who specializes in this area.

Fence Fighting. This behavior is so common that many people don't even consider it a form of aggression. This is a territorial behavior in which a dog becomes more and more aggressive as he nears a fence. At point-blank range, dogs can easily get to the red zone, fighting as hard as they can with only the fence between them. People who have dogs who fence fight can attest that it's extremely difficult to get their dogs' attention sufficiently to stop this behavior.

This kind of fighting is driven by a dog's territorial instincts. Wild dogs mark their territory as a warning to other animals—a way of saying *no trespassing* to any creature that gets too close. Your dog has likely marked your property in the same way, tapping into that ancient instinct. So when other animals come along, a lot of dogs feel threatened and decide they need to defend what's theirs.

This is one of the less dangerous kinds of aggression, mainly because the presence of a fence prevents direct contact and injuries. It can still be unnerving, though, and it gives your dog practice at acting aggressively—something no dog needs to work on.

There are tools that can help discourage this behavior. One deterrent I recommend is the citronella collar. This quick, effective, and humane tool gives your dog a quick spray under his face every time he barks. I've seen this work for a lot of dogs over the years, though definitely not all of them. An alternative is the ultrasonic collar. It works like the citronella collar, but instead of spraying the dog, it emits a high-pitched sound that he'll dislike. Dogs who are receptive to it learn quickly not to bark with this on. Many of these collars are programmable to allow different levels of barking before they're activated. At the higher settings, a simple *woof* won't be enough for your dog to get a correction, but a big confrontation along the fence line definitely will.

Both of these training collars are tools that do the work for you when you're not around to correct your dog, but neither is a substitute for training. When you're working with your dog directly, I have a simple tool and technique that solves this problem a good percentage of the time. And that tool, my friends, is the penny bottle. When your dog starts barking at the fence, walk toward him, give a firm *NO* or *QUIET*, then briskly shake the penny bottle for a few seconds and follow that up by repeating the command again. This works on most dogs because the unexpected sound cuts through their hyper-focused attention. For tough cases, this is an ideal scenario to use the Shake & Break, which makes an even more disruptive sound than that of the penny bottle. Timed correctly, this technique should work to deter most fence-fighting dogs in only a week or so. You just have to put the work in.

Bottom line: you're combating instinct here, so know that while this problem can be dealt with, it will still lurk somewhere within your dog. Think of any progress you make with tools and techniques as putting your dog's fence-fighting tendency into remission. You'll need to stay vigilantly on top of it to keep it there.

Pain-Induced Aggression. Pain-induced aggression can be tricky to diagnose and treat, and it's a common issue with senior dogs, expectant dogs, or dogs with some sort of injury. Pain-induced aggression occurs when a dog is hurting and acts aggressively to protect himself. This type of aggression is something that can crop up even in a dog who's always had a gentle, mellow temperament. It's easy to understand how this happens if you think about how you feel when you have an injury. If you have a broken bone or a fresh cut or stitches, you instinctively go to great lengths to protect your wounds from getting bumped or touched. And if it happens anyway? You might recoil or cry out or get angry. You might even act aggressively if someone bumps you hard enough, even if it's an accident.

Just like us, dogs have an instinct to protect themselves from pain. But unlike us, dogs are not usually inclined to share the details of how they're feeling or to warn us to keep our distance when they're hurting. Another instinct is in play for most dogs—one that tells them to avoid appearing weak. So if your old or possibly injured dog suddenly starts acting aggressively, you might want to schedule a visit with his veterinarian before taking any steps to combat that behavior with training.

Although pain-induced aggression is really just a form of self-preservation, you still need to proceed with caution if your dog is exhibiting it. A dog who's guarding is a short hop away from aggression and can easily race through the yellow and orange zones to red if he senses he's in danger.

This is a condition that can usually be dealt with. You can't solve pain-induced aggression with technique, but you can take measures to make your dog feel safe and prevent any incidents.

If your dog is recovering from surgery or an injury, crate him or keep him isolated until he's mostly healed. Doing so will not only keep your family, neighbors, and other pets safe but also allow your dog to heal as quickly as possible. The time right after an injury or surgery is a common window for an aggressive act, so short-term isolation is an easy way to avoid a serious problem.

If your dog is a senior and he's getting grumpier with age as he deals with aches and pains, that's a different story. Cases like that call for bigger, possibly longer-term lifestyle adjustments. Dogs in the final stages of their lives deserve to feel loved and secure, and we have to do our best to protect them. What that entails depends on the individual dog. For some, it means you'll have to proceed with caution when strangers or other dogs approach. For some it may mean creating a safe space—a place your dog can go that everyone in the family respects as his own personal do-not-disturb area.

This is a phase in which it's up to you to make decisions that ensure your dog is protected and all other parties are safe. Don't hesitate to let anyone who gets too close know that your dog's gotten a little testy in his old age and needs his space. This is a time when your dog will be relying on you to be the leader who can be trusted to keep him (and those around him) safe.

Bottom line: this kind of aggression is reactive, so if you can pinpoint your dog's pain, you can avoid cueing it. If you can't pinpoint the problem, it can be difficult to know when a dog might react aggressively. Avoid unnecessary contact with any injured dog, and take extra care to make sure your achy older dog is able to avoid unwanted contact without having to fight.

Offensive Aggression

A dog who instigates aggression is exhibiting offensive aggression. If your dog goes after other dogs or people without being provoked, or if he sometimes seems to be looking for a confrontation, chances are this is the kind of aggression you're dealing with. Like defensive aggression, it can take a number of different forms.

Leash Aggression. Leash aggression is one of the most common forms of canine aggression. It's defined by a situation where a dog is aggressive on-leash but perfectly fine when off. This Dr. Jekyll/Mr. Hyde behavior can be confusing for pet owners. In fact, over the years many people have told me their dogs were aggressive—

and then the assessments showed those dogs were only leash aggressive. Since some of those dogs had rarely been outdoors without a leash, nobody knew their problems were isolated. Sometimes when I take these dogs to a dog park and let them go, they're not just calm, they're also friendly and excited, playing with every dog in sight.

Why does this happen? Simple answer: a lot of dogs are conditioned to behave this way. It usually starts when a well-meaning owner pulls a leashed puppy away from every dog who comes near. The best thing you can do to socialize a puppy is allow him to approach every dog he sees (every friendly dog). This gives him the knowledge that there is nothing to protect or get upset about when he sees another dog. But if you pull the same puppy away from every strange dog he sees, he'll eventually begin to assume there's a reason for it and he needs to protect himself—and you—when he's on a leash. Even worse, your dog learns that starting a fight with a strange dog is almost always a win because you pull him to safety before things get serious every time he starts something.

Basically, this behavior is a lot like that of a school bully: He's always tough with his friends around, but when you take the other guys out of the picture, he's just another vulnerable kid. The same thing is happening with a leash-aggressive dog. You're the group of friends your dog knows will back him up if needed. That leash is connected to you, and you'll pull him away like you've done hundreds of times in the past if things get heated, so he lunges and snaps at everything that gets close—a four-legged bully counting on his crew (you) to back him up.

This is generally a problem that can be fixed. One way to go about it is by redirecting your dog's attention toward you with food or a toy—showing him the reward *before* he begins to go into fighting mode. Remember, you want to keep your dog in that yellow zone, so you need to anticipate his behavior before it reaches orange. This only works if your dog has a strong prey drive or food drive, so it's not a fix for every dog.

My favorite technique to deal with this problem once again involves that miraculous tool, the penny bottle—or the even more attention-getting Shake & Break. In this case, when your dog zeroes in on another dog and starts pulling, give him a firm *NO* followed by a swift and vigorous shake of the bottle, and followed by another *NO*. With enough practice, this technique conditions your dog to the *NO* in the context of fighting on-leash. This works on a large percentage of dogs because it refocuses their senses away from the potential fight and back to you.

Bottom line: although you can't make your dog like other dogs when you walk by, you can definitely control him in the moment. Managing this aggressive bad habit makes you a good dog owner— and it may ultimately prevent the kind of fight that gets too out of hand to stop with just another tug of the leash.

Unsocialized Aggression. This is a very common type of aggression and one of the main reasons dogfights break out. What it boils down to is that a dog with aggressive tendencies who has not learned that his world is a safe, nonthreatening place spends a lot of his time looking for a fight. Unsocialized dogs who exhibit this kind of behavior can be very dangerous, but if the root of the problem is a lack of socialization, than this type of aggression can sometimes be solved or improved through socializing the dog. How do you know if your dog's aggression comes from a lack of socialization? Look at the circumstances that set him off. If your dog has a sweet disposition but is prone to aggression when confronted with something unfamiliar, a lack of experience and understanding of his environment may be a factor.

The good news is if your dog's aggression has more to do with socialization than with his genetic tendencies, you may be able to get his behavior under control. The bad news is you're likely to need the input of a trainer with a depth of knowledge and experience in this area to help you determine if your dog's aggression is rooted in a lack of socialization or not. I do not condone any plan for socializing a dog known to be aggressive around other dogs, kids, or other people unless an expert trainer is involved. Otherwise, it's just too much of a risk to take.

Genetic-Based Aggression. Unfortunately, many people are under the impression that if you socialize any dog at a young age, that dog will grow up to be a friendly, well-adjusted dog. I wish it were that simple, but it's not. The fact is there's a firm limit to how much say or control you have over how your dog turns out as an adult. Many dogs are born with aggression issues that stem from their breeding. I talked extensively about the role of breed in temperament and behavior in Chapter 1, and this may be the most difficult fact of genetics for dog owners to accept. If your dog comes from a long line (or even a short one) of fighters bred for aggression, there's a chance he will be aggressive as well. I often tell clients not to blame the breed. Blame the breeder. Genetically driven behaviors aren't any dog's fault; they're wired into the animal's DNA. The fact is there are some breeds out there that were originally bred for fighting sports. Although these sports have been banned, the personality traits that made the dogs so good at what they were bred for over hundreds of years remain.

If your dog has been offensively aggressive in both familiar and unknown situations all his life (or as long as you've had him), then all the socializing in the world may not cure his problem. If this is the case with your dog, the only thing that will really make a difference is being a strong handler who knows how to make the dog behave in the moment. Just as you can teach a dog to stop the instinctive behavior of barking on command, it is possible to interrupt a dog's aggression cycle in its early phases, even though it's likely not possible to erase his inclination to fight.

The following steps are only suggestions and should *not* be considered a guaranteed fix for any dog with aggression issues.

Know Your Dog's Warning Signs. The first step in becoming
the handler who can manage your aggressive dog is learning his
warning signs so you can defuse any potentially dangerous situations before they escalate. One of the most beautiful things about
dogs is that they don't lie. Their body language tells us exactly
what they're thinking. Consider any of these body language cues
a tip-off that your dog needs to be contained or redirected ASAP.
They're all yellow-zone warnings that can quickly give way to
orange- or red-level aggression:

- When your dog's hackles—the hairs along his backbone
  from his neck to his tail—go up. People often joke that this
  is their dog's Mohawk, but this is a warning sign that needs
  to be taken seriously.
- When your dog stiffens his body.
- When your dog gives a low growl.
- When your dog curls his lip.
- When your dog gets big—with his chest out and head up
  high.
- When your dog is holding his tail all the way up in the air
  and stiff. This is a cautionary sign that's frequently misread.
  It does *not* indicate a friendly wag; it's a warning.

If your dog shows you any of these signs, it's his way of telling
you, loud and clear, to intervene now, before it's too late. From
there, the body language only gets more obvious and more difficult to deal with. By the time a dog starts showing his teeth, he's
crossing into the orange zone. Once he's moving toward a fight,
he's in the red, and your options to keep things from getting out
of control are nearly gone.

Keep Your Distance. Many genetically aggressive dogs feel
threatened by every dog they see. It's not possible for you to physically remove someone else's dog from a potentially tough situa-

tion, but you can remove your own dog from it. If you can't get away completely, create some space. The farther away you are from that other dog, the lower your dog's aggression level will be. Look at it like an algorithm; the closer your dog gets to any other dog (or other target of his aggression), the greater the danger. The strike zone is within the length of the leash, and you should take pains to keep every possible target out of that point-blank range.

Bottom line: consult with a professional trainer who specializes in anti-aggression. An experienced trainer needs to make the call as to how much training and what techniques are safe to use with your dog. You may be able to learn to be the handler your aggressive dog needs—someone who knows all his triggers and is able to make the right decision at the moment it's needed to maintain control. But for the safety of your dog and everyone around him, you'll need professional guidance to get there.

The Last Word

More than anything, being a good owner to a dog with an aggressive streak is about being prepared and being careful. Most of the time, your aggressive dog may be a loving pet, but you can never lose sight that at his worst, he may be a danger—and you would be accountable. The biggest mistake I see people make is investing way too much emotion and reasoning behind their dogs' aggression— in essence, making excuses for their dogs. This causes them to be fuzzy or even blinded to the fact their dog can inflict serious damage to an animal or a person. The fact is that just like people, dogs have bad days. On a bad day, one dog might retreat to the corner and give you the stink eye. Another might be pushed as far as a growl. But if your dog is capable of reaching the point of lashing out or biting, that possibility needs to be taken seriously—not just until you train it out of him, but for the rest of his life.

CONCLUSION:
7 LAST LESSONS

In the house where I grew up, there were always all kinds of animals around. Somewhere I have a picture of me sitting in the crook of my mother's arm. In her other arm she's cradling a baby tiger. That's what our lives were like. Even our family dog, a German shepherd named Zeke, was in on the tiger act. He helped raise them from cubs, and when they became adults, they'd still look at him and respect him like he was their big brother (even though they'd long surpassed his size). That made it easier for him to help teach them to sit on their pedestals and mind their manners for my dad, who was one of the top tiger trainers in the world.

The point is, for as long as I've been able to walk and talk, I've been an animal trainer. I actually got my first paying job when I was just six or seven. I wanted to earn a little pocket money, so I put up flyers on the telephone poles near where we lived. They had the catchy pitch: "Dog Trainer Availabel" (spelling was not one of my early talents) with our phone number scrawled at the bottom. When I got my first call, I hopped on my bike and hustled to the address the man had provided. You should have seen his face when he opened the door and found me—a waist-high boy carrying a dog leash. Knowing I had a small window to make an impression, I said, "*Hello*, sir," and barged right in, straight to the golden retriever who was running toward the door. I snapped the leash on her and launched into teaching her a *DOWN* and a *STAY* while the man stared openmouthed, not sure whether to laugh or clap or kick me out.

Once the dog had a general idea of the technique, I turned to the owner and gave him a quick lesson in how to get the same results and a lecture on how important it was to do it every day. Then in my squeaky little voice I said, "That'll be five dollars, please. Just call me if you need me again." The guy was quick to pay. He'd gone from confused to impressed to just plain happy my services were only going to cost him five bucks.

By even the most conservative math, I've worked with between eight thousand and ten thousand dogs since then. Along the way, I learned from other trainers who approached their animals with every philosophy and method under the sun. Some of them showed me what to do, and others—sometimes inadvertently—showed me what *not* to do. You might say I've learned from the best and also from the worst. But I always learned something, whether it was a technique I still use in my arsenal, a rule to follow, or a method to avoid. The goal is always to learn and make myself a better trainer.

I think I could write a thousand pages about training dogs and still have a little more to say, but I hope this book is a good start. To wrap things up, I've put together a list of seven final Lucky Dog lessons. I hope you'll keep them in mind as you embark on training your own dog.

1. Seven Days Is a Great Start. Since I've been working on this book, there's one question I hear all the time: Is it really possible to train a dog in just a week?

Yes. It is. I'm positive because I train between five and seven dogs each week myself. Most of the shelter dogs who end up on *Lucky Dog* are with me for just seven days to get their basic training—and we *almost* always get it done.

But that *almost* is important, because lots of dogs for lots of reasons need extra time. If your dog is very young, very old, unsocialized, traumatized, a little on the slow side, or too smart for his own good, it may take you a little longer to teach him his 7 Common Commands and curb his behavior problems. A rule to remember is it can be done. In the long run, spending two weeks or even three to teach your dog these basic lessons is a time investment that will pay you back in years of peaceful companionship. It's a great trade-off.

2. Breed Matters. From the time I was a little kid, I learned to respect the power of breed. Our German shepherd Zeke (actually, there were three Zekes over the course of my young life) was an amazing natural herding dog. I could spend a year trying to teach a dachshund or a bloodhound to do that same job and never get near the level the Zekes were born with.

That's no dig against the dachshund or the bloodhound. Each of them has his own gifts. Every dog breed does. Before you lift a finger to train your dog, learn about his breed so you know where his talents and shortcomings may lie. That information will help you set realistic training goals and teach to your dog's strengths.

3. Training Is Not Dominating. I first learned this lesson in my years of training animals who could literally eat me if they wanted to. There is no good way, for example, to force a five-hundred-pound tiger to lie down when you say so. He has to want it, too. Over the years, I've continued to live by this philosophy in training animals of all sizes because I believe that the most effective training happens when an animal does what I ask willingly.

Training your dog isn't about bending him to your will. It's about using your role as the leader in your family—along with all the tricks and techniques you have at your disposal—to get your dog to *choose* to do what you want.

4. *You're the Teacher; Play the Part.* Training any dog has its highs and lows. You're going to have great days and days where you feel like you've taken two steps back. Much like we all have bad days, so does your dog. I hope I've shared enough stories of my own mistakes and learning experiences in these pages to make that clear. Sometimes the producers of *Lucky Dog* have a laugh at my expense by keeping a scorecard as I try to teach a particularly difficult student the 7 Common Commands. Maybe you've seen one with tallies like *Rover: 5, Brandon: 0*. The thing is, even the dogs who totally blow me away in those early rounds eventually master each and every command.

Training is a marathon, not a sprint, so if it all goes south, take a break, remind yourself that you *love* this dog, and then start again. Try to enjoy the process, bond with your dog, and see the humor in your occasional failings. Remember that the face you show your dog is the face that will be shown back to you. Be confident, glad to be there, and kind. Be assertive and even strict when you have to. Most of all, be consistent; as long as you stick to it, the training will happen.

5. *Let Your Dog Know What He's Doing Right.* You can help your dog understand what you want him to learn by letting him know whenever he's doing things right. That means having treats at the ready and timing rewards just right: at the moment your dog figures out what you want. If you're having a hard time capturing the exact moment, use a clicker. Or do what a lot of my clients tell me they do: copy the way I encourage my dogs during training with an intensifying, "good, Good, GOOD," as they figure out how to follow a command. Using this kind of verbal encouragement is kind of like helping your dog play the Hot and Cold game most of us played as kids while he tries to learn something new. At first, whoever is "it" is wandering around blindly, trying to find the hidden object. But when your friend gets close, you start guiding with your voice, saying, "warmer, getting very warm, hot, HOT!" You can guide your dog the same way, giving him a verbal nudge to keep doing something right. The sound of your voice will encourage him to keep trying and figuring it out. After all, your voice is one of your most powerful tools in training.

6. Training Is a Daily Diet. I know you've heard me say you need to train daily—but it's the key to everything. You can't just train a dog and let that be it. If you don't keep it up, no matter how great a job you do in that first week, your dog will eventually regress. Think about it this way: Teaching your dog something new plants a seed. But just planting it doesn't make it take root. You'll need to take care of it and water it every day. Take ten minutes, three times a day for a week to set your dog up with a new command or behavior modification. After that initial training period, you can follow up once a week, and later once a month, forever. And keep this in mind: use it or lose it. If you don't use the commands you teach your dog, he'll forget them over time.

7. Any Dog Can Be a Lucky Dog. I got my first celebrity dog-training client on a music video shoot. I came in with my Doberman and rottie and worked them all day. They were tough-looking dogs who were sweet. At the end of the day, the rapper who was making the video made a beeline for me. He wanted my number. He had a couple of tough-looking dogs at home who were not so sweet; they were out of control and getting kind of mean. Could I come to his house, he asked, and teach his dogs to be more like mine?

And I did. Over the years, I've seen more dogs than I can count who seemed like lost causes become well-trained pets. Whether your dog is hyper, hard of hearing, headstrong—whatever the challenge is—he can be trained. If you put in the effort, I promise you'll see results. But it only works if you work it.

Last Word

You may have heard me say it on *Lucky Dog*, but I think it bears repeating. My mission is to make sure these amazing animals find a purpose, a family, and a place to call home.

If we all share in that mission, as a team we can save thousands of lives—maybe even more. This year alone, nearly four million dogs will go into animal shelters, and more than a quarter of those dogs will never come out. Those dogs are living, emotional, intelligent beings who deserve better. They're dogs like Bruno, the dancing terrier mix; Skye, the dignified, sensitive white shepherd; Ari, the Malinois mix who just needed to learn a little self-control; and Tweety, the Maltese mix who came to me on the brink of starvation. And, of course, Lulu—the Chihuahua who was terrified to let anyone get close enough to love her. People had given up on every one of those dogs; and every one of them was saved and became a well-trained, loving, cherished family pet.

If there's one thing I've learned over the years about people, it's that dog lovers stick together. We share a common bond. When I first started rescuing shelter dogs to rehabilitate and train them, other animal lovers came out of the shadows to help me place them in forever homes. With almost no publicity, we were able to create a vast social media network that helped my rescues start new lives in loving families. From there, a major network series was born—all from a little idea I had when I was flat broke, living on a friend's couch, just hoping for an opportunity in life. Sometimes I think I have a lot in common with the dogs I rescue.

If each of us contributes in some small way—by rescuing a dog, fostering a dog, volunteering to help train a dog, or donating to feed and house one a little while longer—we can save the next Bruno or Skye or Lulu who comes along.

One dog at a time.

Ruff,

Brandon

ACKNOWLEDGMENTS

Before I go I'd like to say a few things:

When I started writing these chapters, I was intimidated because I'd never written a book before. But as the days went by, it became easier and easier. By the last few weeks, I couldn't wait to write more. I've learned a lot about myself through this process because putting it all down brought me back to rescuing and training each of the dogs in the book.

It also brought me back to learning animal training technique and reminded me how grateful I am to the people who taught me. I owe everything to them because they took the time to show me the correct way to train. I especially want to thank Mike Herstik for showing me so many incredible and practical techniques that I continue to use daily; Boone Narr for being an inspirational movie animal trainer when I was a kid and just learning; Gunther Gebel-Williams for teaching my family how to train large animals when they were kids in Europe; and my uncle Brian for teaching me how to train large predators when I was a teenager.

Thanks also to Dave Morgan, Roy Barudin, and the entire Litton

Entertainment team for discovering me a few years ago and putting their faith in me; CBS Daytime for allowing us to air such a great series; and Petmate for its support and the great products it provides the dogs at the ranch.

This book wouldn't have become a reality without the wisdom and guidance of my publishing team: agent Jeff Kleinman of Folio Literary Management, who believed in my book before there was a single page to read; editor Julia Pastore at HarperOne, who took a giant risk on this first-time author and never wavered in her support; collaborator Jana Murphy, who combed through my drafts, notes, blogs, and *Lucky Dog* episodes to help me shape an ocean of material into an organized book; photographer Craig Mathew, who perfectly captured the pack and me training at Lucky Dog Ranch; my publicist Suzanne Wickham and marketer Kim Dayman, who worked tirelessly to make sure the book would reach dog lovers everywhere; and the entire HarperOne team for their enthusiastic support.

A special thank-you to our canine cover models: Wacha, Goldie, Chester, and Chico.

On a personal note, I want to thank my mother for lifting me up during the darkest periods of my life and my sister for giving me direction when I was a lost soul. Last but not least, thank you to my little girl Lulu for showing me the meaning of true love. I'm forever in debt to you all.

If I forgot anyone, please forgive me—you know what an airhead I can be sometimes. Now, if you'll excuse me, I'm gonna go take a nap for a month.

ABOUT THE AUTHOR

Brandon McMillan is a professional animal trainer and behaviorist who has spent his entire life learning about and working with all types of animals from household pets to the wildest and most untamed beasts.

Born into a family of animal entertainers, McMillan jokes that he's been picking up animal poop for as long as he can remember. Even though his one-of-a-kind upbringing may not have always been glamorous, it gave him the skills to become an accomplished trainer at an early age. It also helped foster the attachment and empathy he feels for animals great and small. McMillan uses his unique skill set every day in his career as a Los Angeles–based animal trainer for film and television. As a result of his on-set accomplishments, he's also frequently hired by Hollywood's A-list celebrities to transform their out-of-control pooches into well-mannered dogs. His extensive client list includes Ellen DeGeneres, Rod Stewart, James Caan, Wolfgang Puck, Don Cheadle, Snoop Dogg, Eddie Murphy, Ronda Rousey, and many others.

Although McMillan has a diverse background in working with

all kinds of animals, his greatest personal and professional commitment is to rescuing and training shelter dogs. Long before *Lucky Dog* became a staple of CBS Saturday-morning programming and introduced his philosophy and methods to the world, McMillan was already regularly, quietly saving dogs from shelters' death rows, then turning them into well-trained pets, service animals, and sometimes even movie stars. He takes every opportunity to remind his fellow dog lovers that over a million dogs are euthanized every year in the United States because they can't find homes. With that devastating statistic always in mind, Brandon McMillan has made it his mission to reduce shelter populations, one dog at a time. He hopes his efforts will inspire others to do the same.

INDEX